Wishing
ou the

woody .

Staff party at the Bluebird restaurant, on the
King's Road, with a young Fred Sirieix.

Confessions of a
Waiter

The good, the bad and the
downright outrageous side
of the hotel industry

David Woodward

First published in 2023 in Great Britain by
David Woodward
In partnership with whitefox publishing

Copyright © David Woodward, 2023

www.wearewhitefox.com
david.h.woodward@hotmail.com

ISBN 978-1-915635-51-8

Also available as an eBook
ISBN 978-1-915635-52-5

This book is a work of non-fiction based on the
experiences and recollections of the author. In some
cases the names of people and other identifying
details have been changed to protect the privacy of
others. All of the events in this book are true to the
best of the author's memory. The views expressed
in this book are solely those of the author.

Designed and typeset by Euan Monaghan
Cover design by Eric Wilder
Project management by whitefox

This book is dedicated to my beloved son, Jack. It was my aim to show him that life might not be easy, but with a great deal of hard work and treating people the way you would like to be treated yourself, you can go a long way.

I would also like to thank my mum, whose constant support has made me the person I am today. We have shared each other's trials and tribulations, but always with a smile on our faces. You have not only inspired my story, but have touched the lives of so many people.

CONTENTS

Introduction.. 1

PART ONE

1. 2020 – Had it all been worth it? 5
2. My entrée into hospitality.. 20
3. 2005 – Meeting Ewa 29
4. 2014 – Keats Cottage, Shanklin 38
5. 2015 – Opening for business... 45
6. Putting the ghosts to rest at Keats Cottage 56

PART TWO

7. 1990 – Switzerland, where it all began 65
8. Learning the right path – a high-end apprenticeship 78
9. Swiss tipping culture... 92
10. Settling into the Kulm Hotel...................................... 102
11. Back to Switzerland with a new plan of action............. 111
12. Good-time Charlie and falling in love for the first time 118
13. The Lipp Brasserie, Zurich... 129
14. Girls, girls, girls 138
15. Hotel School, Switzerland... 148

PART THREE

16. 2019 – Life and death 155
17. My mum exercises her charms 167
18. Gotti lands 181

PART FOUR

19. 1990–1998 – The other halves 193
20. 2015 – *Four in a Bed*, social media
    and the dreaded reviews 202
21. My first experience with the super-rich 228
22. 1990–2005 – The many vices and pitfalls
    of catering – the demon drink 235
23. Detoxing, Swiss-style 248
24. 1997–2000 – The Bluebird Restaurant,
    King's Road, London 253
25. 2005–2020 – The essence of service 268
26. The rich and famous 306
27. Friendships, owners and those who left an impression ... 319

PART FIVE

28. 2022 – The finale – what will life have in store? 339

Acknowledgements 361

Confessions of a Waiter – nothing is off the table. David Woodward takes readers on a hilarious journey where everything goes to extremes. Where melon balls have to be the same shape and size for six hundred diners. He takes us through the ups and downs, the vices and pitfalls in the life of catering. Every single bite of the story is a delicious titbit. From falling asleep at a strip club to discovering colonic irrigation. He sees his nurse donned in an outfit like she is about to explore Chernobyl. From Gleneagles to Switzerland, from red bow tie waiters to hobnobbing with the rich and famous. Every tale of love and loss in this raw honest account is infused with a brilliant sense of humour. Like a velvety wine, it slips the hours away very nicely.

Hilarious, poignant, and brilliant! This toned my abs from belly laughing. I loved every minute!

—Liz Lawler, author of *Don't Wake Up*

All the chapters in this book relate to different periods in my life, the ups and downs, the pitfalls, but with the main thread being my catering background. It is my journey through life.

My aim was for this book to be for people aspiring to grab life's opportunities. I wanted people who work within the industry to relate to the anecdotes, but also for the thousands of guests I have served to see some of the lighter aspects in themselves. I have always been told by my guests that I can tell a story and that I should put my story in writing.

Although there are funny, relatable stories, my wish is for those both in and out of the industry to relate to the person who outwardly seems so optimistic and who inwardly is flapping away to achieve a dream. From the outside, it is an industry that appears glamorous, with celebrities, TV and aspects that appeal to people, but from the inside it can be a huge struggle to deal with an ever more demanding public.

It is not simply a book about owning and working in a bed and breakfast (B&B) on the Isle of Wight. Nor about entering the industry. Instead, it is one person's raw account of what life brings, with an emphasis on catering. I think people in the industry will relate to the book, but I also see my guests as the main target audience. There will be parts where they will see me in themselves!

I would like to see my book in hotel bedrooms, read by guests and staff alike. In general, it has always been chefs who are the focus, not the server, and this is something I wanted to change.

Part One

CHAPTER 1

2020 – Had it all been worth it?

Despite the chill air, I reclined in a deck chair on my patio and sipped a rather delightful I Muri from Italy. Life seemed somewhat surreal. Although now November and with no end to this dreaded Covid-19 virus in sight, I marvelled at how the planet had decided to reset itself, in much the same way I knew that my life needed to change.

Cherry blossom was yet again in full bloom, a phenomenon I hadn't encountered before, neither on the mainland nor since opening my B&B on the Isle of Wight, so it seemed as though nature was attempting to give us a second chance to right our many wrongs. I only hoped that, like the pink and red roses that were once again emerging, despite the increasing chill, I too would receive a second chance and perhaps finally sell the B&B, which had fast become a millstone around my neck.

The scene before me put me in mind of the words of David Attenborough, who had reminded us that the natural world would survive even if the human world were to continue its path of self-destruction. I only hoped

I would have a final chance to achieve a legacy and that my son, Jack, would have a world worth living in.

Despite these somewhat sobering thoughts, I counted myself lucky to have survived the current lockdowns pretty much unscathed. I even had the knowledge that I was going to enjoy Christmas with my dear boy Jack – my first ever, even though he had just turned eight. I'd missed the first six of his Christmases on the island owing to work and now events had taken another twist as my wife, Ewa, had returned to live and work in Bath, taking our son with her. Selling the B&B would, I hoped, enable me to see more of him.

Sitting in the now fading light, I inhaled yet another Hamlet cigar and watched the smoke rise above my rooftop. This wasn't exactly the scene I had envisaged all those years previously when I had started out on my B&B business adventure. Somehow, I thought this new life would be akin to the film *A Good Year*, where Russell Crowe lounges by the pool, basking in the summer heat while overlooking his precious vineyards. But perhaps this little haven was as close as my dreams were going to take me?

By now, the velvety wine was slipping down nicely. A few melancholic thoughts still niggled at the back of my mind, but I was starting to relax and was already contemplating the second bottle. This would usually involve reminiscing about the good old days and dreaming about a better future.

Let's face it, it could have been so much worse. I could now have been sitting in a high-rise flat in London, wishing desperately for some outside space and some air to breathe. So really, I had nothing to complain about.

Being a Sagittarian, one of my more positive traits was a tendency to see the glass half full, rather than half empty.

The problem was, I always tended to give off an air of happiness and confidence, and although I wasn't someone who wanted to be part of the mental health problem that seemed to have gripped the world, it's fair to say that the inner demons were beginning to gnaw away at my facade. I was starting to wonder if the dream of owning my own business, all those years ago, had now turned into some grotesque horror story. My major concern was that the B&B had now been on the market for the best part of two years and a series of potential buyers had turned out to be time wasters or they seemed just to want to extract a free stay from me.

My mum, meanwhile, sat opposite me, laughing at yet another joke. These were usually at my expense. It always made me smile how we still laughed at the same things and still took comfort from each other's company. She was lighting up yet another cigarette and, although full of her usual fun, she looked pale and tired in the chill air. Considering she hailed from Switzerland, it always amazed me how she would always feel the cold. She was recounting a recent conversation with her neurologist – she had suffered a bleed to the brain the previous year. Apparently, he'd had the audacity to berate her for her continued smoking.

If he had only known her better, he would have realised that although my mother had a cabinet full of herbal remedies, books full of healthy eating tips and a cure for just about every ailment, never once would she attribute any illness to her forty-a-day habit.

It therefore came as no surprise to me when she stopped the poor neurologist in his tracks with the put-down, 'I've given up drinking, haven't had sex for years, so what fun is left for me other than smoking?'

I guess there wasn't much more the poor man could say and to be honest it wouldn't have been worth his effort either. But as I looked over at the perpetual rock in my life, I was worried that behind the smile and the bravado, a little light was starting to fade. And, after helping me for the last seven years to achieve *my* dream, perhaps her own dream of finding her forever home in the sun wasn't happening anytime soon.

With the second bottle now taking effect as we chatted amicably about future plans, part of my mind drifted to the ups and downs of the last couple of years.

The year had on the whole worked out pretty well, despite the impending doom. After a while, I had decided the best course of action was to ignore all the news, as there seemed to be little in the way of positivity. After the shock of the initial lockdown and a few anxious nights considering whether we would survive financially, somehow events conspired to turn in my favour.

Luckily for me, my regular B&B clientele had agreed to let me hold on to their deposits and I, in turn, had allowed them to have flexibility with their dates following a lifting in travel restrictions. I couldn't understand the travel companies' refusal to give back the money from booked holidays. How would this really benefit anyone in the long run? My understanding guests, coupled with the help of the government grant, had allowed me to enjoy three wonderful months with my son, Jack.

While others were understandably feeling isolated and depressed by their current predicament, which was the way I had felt the previous year when I had been alone in the B&B, I instead felt liberated and couldn't wait to embark on daily adventures of cooking, gardening and home schooling.

Many others have since mentioned this 'reset button', and for me it couldn't have come at a better time, both mentally and physically. My son and I took delight in enjoying the near-deserted beaches and even plucked up the courage to check out the waters of the English Channel in early May.

It was perhaps in those three months that I was able to enjoy the island in a way my customers did on their vacations. Without being constantly consumed with the increasing demands of the B&B, I finally felt as though I was *living the dream* and could take in the stunning scenery and the abundant wildlife that, like me, was at last flourishing.

Even the B&B seemed to take on a different persona. We were able to amble from room to room and fill the place with constant laughter, rather than my usual state of anxiety, trying to keep Jack from disturbing the guests. With Ewa working in solitude from one of the rooms, Jack and I were able to embark on daily adventures without fear of being told off. I often thought, when would we have the chance again to enjoy everything that the island had to offer, so I naturally embraced every second and put the troubles of the world behind me.

•

But with the first lockdown coming to an end, I bid a teary farewell to Ewa and Jack at Shanklin station and with it came the realisation that I was about to embark on yet another season on my own. Ewa would continue with her work from Bath and Jack would be itching to get back to his friends in school.

Somehow, I felt lost, although my mum was still around. I wasn't afraid of the hard work, the seven-day weeks or even the increasing demands of the expectant public. It was the fact that although I was constantly surrounded by people, I felt like I was in some sort of cage. Unable to get out. And this in turn made me feel lonely.

Inwardly, it always made me smile when guests asked in all sincerity, 'So what do you do with all your free time after breakfast?' I think they must have presumed that a magic fairy cleaned up their breakfast, reset the restaurant, waved a duster around the room, checked in the guests who had lost their way, and after all this put on a smile at eleven o'clock in the evening when someone had forgotten their key or wanted one last drink once the bars had closed. Or even at the last second decided they needed an early ferry, and *would you mind awfully if we have a six o'clock in the morning breakfast.*

But of course, this was something I never mentioned. For me, this was the job I had signed up for and it was up to me that every single guest went away with a smile on their face.

After we had reopened, the first couple of weeks turned out to be rather eventful. Firstly, one guest decided to put half the contents of their vanity bag down the toilet and in so doing managed to flood the kitchen.

Not a great start for my mum and I, as we manfully shovelled out shit while pretending to all and sundry that nothing was amiss. Secondly, the council – in all their wisdom – had decided not to resurface the road during lockdown, when no one was on the island. But, hey, why not dig it up in the middle of the night – when all the hotels had finally managed to reopen? Although their drilling and the constant beeping from their reversing lights had ensured that I was somewhat bleary-eyed cooking breakfast – after just two hours' sleep – to my amazement, not a single guest complained. That said, it might have had something to do with my proactive management in trying to avert any impending disaster: I had come up with the plan to get all my guests suitably intoxicated before bed!

•

In the next few weeks, relative calm prevailed and what surprised me most was the way the public seemed to embrace the end of lockdown.

As July kicked in, it soon became apparent that, having been locked away for so long and in many cases unable to travel abroad, all and sundry had decided to descend on the sunny shores of the Isle of Wight. It wasn't just the regulars on their annual pilgrimage but vast swaths of tourists who had either never visited before or had some vague recollection of a visit from thirty years previously.

The sheer numbers that descended on previously deserted beaches amazed me. Our once guarded population now enjoyed the island as though the dreaded virus had somehow vanished into the welcoming sea. This said, it was heart-warming to have a sense of normality as I took in the sight of vast queues gathering outside restaurants and children eagerly lapping up yet another ice cream, while expectant dogs looked on, eagerly hoping for some mishap and a cone toppling in their direction.

All around me there were grandparents indulging in fish and chips by the sea. This was mostly due to the new restrictions, which meant they had been unable to get into the restaurants. Or, as was more often the case, because they had decided two-hour queuing wasn't worth the effort.

Everyone seemed to be satisfied by the merest of pleasures that had been denied during lockdown. Even the attractions were bursting to capacity and families seemed not to mind waiting in large queues just for the joy of paying exorbitant fees for a mere round of mini golf. Once deserted driving ranges at my local golf club at Westridge now had cars waiting to get into the overflow car park, never used in my recollection.

However, some things were more shocking than surprising. For example, thinking that at least half the population now had to rely on food handouts – such was the speculation sparked by the media – I didn't think I would have any trouble getting help in my little B&B. On reopening, I had received a deluge of phone calls asking for work, but when the interviews were pencilled in, no one actually had the good grace to turn up. So, I guess the country wasn't on the brink of poverty after all.

I had initially thought it was just a case of bad luck, but it soon became apparent that I wasn't alone. Several harassed B&B owners had the same problem. Over the last few years, and particularly in rural areas, we had relied on either more mature adults or adolescents to fill the voids in catering. I often wondered – after the virus and our withdrawal from the European Union (EU) – where our next budding hoteliers and restaurateurs were going to come from.

The other noticeable fact was that hundreds of apartments were being snapped up on the island by people desperate for any kind of outdoor space and by many people who now craved a total change of lifestyle. More amazing to me was the number of guests with no background in catering who thought being the next Felicity Kendal from *The Good Life* and trying their hand at a B&B might be more suitable than their high-flying city careers. Not unheard of, I guess, but I did have to smile at one particular guest who had noticed my business was for sale. He worked in finance and declared he would much prefer a less stressed lifestyle, '... like your own'. The only problem being, 'I'm not very good at getting up in the mornings.' I suppose he has subsequently had second thoughts!

•

As the weeks wore on and yet more closures and redundancies were highlighted on the news, we were thankful to be still open.

Just before lockdown was lifted, Ewa and I had decided to highlight our garden on every social media site at our disposal. With the garden now in full bloom, we were offering an outdoor dining space that could only be accessed by those guests staying in the apartment that was part of the B&B. This little oasis of tranquillity turned out to be exactly what our discerning clientele were looking for. It was almost like having your own self-catering cottage, with the bonus of having both a service and breakfast included.

As soon as we were able to reopen to bookings, reservations went through the roof. Not with the usual two-night stays, but with guests looking to stay one to two weeks. Unbelievably, sixty nights were sold in forty-eight hours.

In addition to the bookings soaring, what I really noticed was the shift in people's attitude. I have always believed that service is everything and that one good turn begets another, but what I really noticed was that all the little extras, which I believe are the essence of good hospitality, were now appreciated as never before.

The basics of a good breakfast, comfy bed, powerful shower and a spotless establishment are a given, but if you asked a guest what they really enjoyed, it would undoubtedly be all those small touches that go the extra mile. This is why I have prided myself in making a difference to the *guest experience*. This might be offering a guest a complimentary drink on arrival or volunteering to dry the clothes of some sodden walker or remembering their likes or dislikes from a previous stay. I can guarantee these acts will be the overriding memory for the guest and the deciding factor in why they book again.

However, during this time, what astounded me most was the wave of appreciation. Maybe it was the relief of finally getting out or the gratitude for receiving a genuine service. Let's face it, by this time I was constantly at my wits' end whenever I heard the words – or should I say excuse – 'I'm sorry, sir, we can't do that because of Covid'. It seemed to be the stock response of anyone I encountered. So, nothing had prepared me for the avalanche of envelopes containing notes, the heartfelt thank-you cards, the chocolates, the cases of wine and other assorted goodies that seemed to be coming my way, each and every week. I guess it did pay to be nice!

What I also became aware of was that the whole pandemic seemed to have brought out either the very best of human kindness or the worst in despicable behaviour. Luckily, in my own little haven I only witnessed the former, and perhaps my ideal of 'what goes around comes around' had never been truer than in those difficult months.

•

There are two instances over that balmy summer that will live with me. Firstly, noticing that there was a rare vacancy in the apartment, I had decided to upgrade one of the regulars who had booked in with me. While I offered them a drink on the patio, they noticed that I had been unable to tend the garden. I had been so busy, without a moment's respite between guests, and it was starting to look somewhat overgrown. Not quite the picture of calm I had intended. The next day, to my amazement, they armed themselves with gardening gloves, shears and even my strimmer and set about rectifying what was no longer a quick fix. After a well-earned beer, I tried to remind them that they were in fact on holiday and really shouldn't be doing this. The only reply was, 'Well, you are always good to us and anyway we would only be bored, so we are glad to help.'

The second surprise came from a couple who had stayed a week with me. We had hit it off from the word go. As they were checking out and loading up their car, they passed by the open door of the apartment, only to see me, somewhat flustered, trying to rehang the television. Unfortunately, the previous guest had taken the idea of being at one with nature a little too far and decided to dismantle the TV from the wall. When the couple passed by, I was somewhat perspiring, and a few choice words were being muttered. Much to my astonishment, the couple, seeing my predicament, decided to ring the ferry company and delay their departure to help me rehang the television. They ultimately helped save the day.

As I have mentioned, these acts of kindness have stayed with me, and it's for these reasons that I've loved the industry I've dedicated my life to.

If all was well with the world inside my little haven, the same could not have been said outside of my own four walls. The news was rife with examples of food being hoarded by overanxious buyers, domestic violence on the increase, fights in seaside resorts.

It was then that I started to worry that the world might not be on the same page when it came to the reset button I was so eagerly trying to embrace. When I read that the Swiss were now protesting, I knew the world was in trouble. I mean, the nearest to civil discord the Swiss usually get is a neighbourly argument over whether a cuckoo clock should be permitted to chime later than ten o'clock in the evening!

•

Closer to home, it wasn't long before the beaches were once again strewn with litter, and drunken louts in shorts revealing sunburnt buttocks congregated in large numbers outside bars and restaurants with absolutely no respect for social distancing. At the other end of the spectrum, matters – in my mind, at least – had started to become somewhat farcical. Even a trip to the local super-market would bring on palpitations, as I had lost count of the number of times I was sneered at for not keeping my distance. The weekly shop had now turned into an assault course and over time I started to go earlier and earlier to avoid the road rage descending in the aisles.

It wasn't just the public who seemed to have lost all manner of sense, but even those individuals who you believed you could count on. I questioned why it was impossible for Mum – who eighteen months earlier had suffered with that bleed on the brain – to see a doctor. Up until that week, she had not even received a follow-up call from her consultant.

In my case, not altogether happy with discussing my ailments over a phone call, I had managed to gain access to the hallowed turf, otherwise known as my GP's (general practitioner's) surgery. My eardrum was a little enlarged and causing me no end of pain. I was somewhat shocked when, after five minutes of poking and prodding, the GP asked me if I was overly sexually active or took drugs and would I like an HIV test? I looked on incredulously and wondered if perhaps things worked a little differently on the Isle of Wight. I mean, for goodness' sake, I'd only gone in with earache. Well, in answer to his question, I replied that although I wished I *were* overly active in the bedroom department, and that perhaps after this consultation I *should* consider drugs, I really didn't think his assessment had anything to do with the state of my ear.

It turned out I had an abscess in my mouth and the inflammation had spread to my ear and the dentist was only too happy to remove the offending tooth – although not before mentioning that my bill would contain a surcharge of £30, to cover his extra expenses for PPE. I might be a little slow on the uptake, but surely a dentist's had to be pristine, all the time?

Regarding GPs' surgeries and my GP's somewhat alternative bedside manner, I recalled a rather animated discussion with one of my regular restaurant guests. She had gone to the clinic a few months prior to Covid, with some mild ailment. This lady was well into her seventies and more akin to a demure housewife than Patsy from *Ab Fab*, so she – like me – was probably a little shocked when said GP asked if she was on drugs. Not quite sure what to say, she had innocently replied, 'Well, I may take two aspirins if the pain gets particularly bad.'

It seemed it wasn't just the medical profession that had taken leave of their senses. Just before lockdown, my mum had decided to put her house on the market.

It turned out to be the ideal time, as everyone seemed to want to buy on the island. The estate agents weren't altogether ready for the deluge of requests to view, and most were still on furlough when all the *foreigners from London* decided to descend on the island. Of course, the overstretched estate agents blamed Covid for just about everything. The situation became so fraught that viewings were only allowed once you had shown proof of funding in advance.

•

But now – sitting alone, as Mum had the sense to call it a night – I contemplated yet another lockdown. The light was fading and although I was wrapped up against the autumnal night in an assortment of scarves, gloves and a hat, my glass was slowly freezing against my hands. My mind drifted and – as was the case after one too many glasses of wine – I looked back with a sense of nostalgia and wondered whether the price of being my own boss had all been worth it.

My entrée into hospitality

My adventure into the world of catering had started at the age of seventeen. Life was an exciting place and I had taken in every word from an enthusiastic careers adviser who had been invited to our grammar school to tempt us into our chosen career paths. Bright-eyed and bushy-tailed, I listened intently to what seemed like a fairy-tale lifestyle: mingling with the rich and famous and taking in the sights of the world.

Hospitality certainly hadn't been my first choice. I had been studying A levels in Latin, English literature and history and, with a reasonable set of grades on the cards, it seemed only sensible that I would follow my father into law.

I would never describe myself as naturally bright, but I had managed to attain ten O levels through a mixture of hard work and perseverance. Whereas my peers had excelled at O levels, with little or no effort, I seemed to come into my own at A level. At that time, Latin was certainly not many people's choice, but I excelled at the subject, mostly due to the harsh apprenticeship I endured at prep school.

Even now I have vivid memories of my hunchbacked headmaster – called Pease-Watkin – who was ever ready to beat or cane the very *best* out of us. Even the ensemble of teachers with pleasing names, such as Major Bamfield or Major Tisdale – teachers who were not exactly politically correct when it came to *punishing* errant children – would cower in the presence of Pease-Watkin's diminutive figure.

Such was the fear that the headmaster would induce that I have seen children literally pee themselves at the sight of this man walking into a room. No lie!

I remember one occasion when there was a total furore as a child inadvertently managed to put a cricket ball straight through the changing-room window. The boy was not forthcoming in owning up, so the headmaster decided to herd the whole school into a circle on the playing fields. He then told the person responsible to come forward. Of course, the boy wasn't overly keen, so the headmaster proceeded to cane the nearest twenty boys and was quite prepared to go through the whole school if need be. After an eventful twenty minutes of a swishing cane, the boy couldn't stand it anymore and came forward to accept his punishment. Luckily, I wasn't one of the twenty, so I breathed a sigh of relief.

This brutal regime did not hold fond memories for me, but to give the school its due, the standards were excellent, albeit gained in a quite harrowing manner. So, on joining my grammar school, I surprisingly found I had a significant head start, especially in the ancient language of Latin. My former headmaster was dismayed that I had joined a grammar school – he deemed such a school far inferior to the usual routes of Eton, Harrow or Down-side, attended by previous generations of my family.

•

Maybe the seven o'clock in the morning starts, the dips in a swimming pool still frozen with ice, the endless reciting of *amo, amas, amat* coupled with the joyful flog-gings had all been for a higher purpose, but it certainly wouldn't be a route that I would want my son, Jack, to endure. Even sport became more enjoyable once I knew it wasn't normal to be berated at half-time for having clean knees, or to have a cricket ball smacked at you from two metres with the word *butterfingers* directed at you for every drop made.

•

Years later, I met with some of my old prep school classmates. I vividly remembered their tweed jackets and knee-length shorts – mandatory all year round, re-gardless of the weather. One, whose parents lived just a few doors down from us in Oswestry, was a teary-eyed boarder who had once tried to escape the tyranny in the boot of my mum's car. To my shock, he declared, 'Those days were the best of my life.' God help him, I thought, but to be honest I wasn't entirely surprised. The head-master had managed to maintain his position for many years with the support of so many parents who – along with many generations before them – believed that such a regime was character-building. This one, previously tearful, child was no doubt sending his own children down the same path.

I had left this gathering wanting to shake the living daylights out of them but realised that it wouldn't have achieved much. Their public-school days had probably been much the same, if not worse. As I bid them farewell, it was obvious that I had nothing in common with my former *friends*. Boys I had always thought of as being larger than life, but who in truth were now bereft of any personality whatsoever. All I could think later was how lucky I had been that my mother had left my father. In so doing, she had ensured that I wouldn't have to follow the previous generations of my family to their school of choice, Downside.

Keen to dispose of me at the earliest opportunity, my father and stepmother had regaled me with stories of fags looking after your every need and how it was wonderful to be sent away to board. But years later, I read that the esteemed Downside had been rife with sexual abuse for many years and that my after-rugby shower might have involved more than I bargained for. I counted myself as having had a lucky escape, even though Rachel, my stepmother, who had been determined to rid herself of her *difficult* stepson, had extolled the virtues of board-ing school and had reminded me that it had done her no harm. To which I replied, 'Apart from making you a first-class bitch.' Needless to say, we never had a close relationship.

It was probably due to my relationship – or lack of one – with my father that steered me away from law. Journalism had piqued my interest, but the thought of a glamorous career in hospitality seemed like a step in the right direction.

After the initial interview with the careers adviser, I received a letter of acceptance for a week's apprenticeship at the five-star Crieff Hotel in Scotland. It was here that my love affair with the industry started. In the summer of '87, I made the gruelling trip from Shrewsbury up to the stunning countryside surrounding Gleneagles and was deposited in the middle of nowhere next to the dual carriageway, alongside the beautiful golf course – which I have since been lucky enough to play.

The week passed by in a whirl of activity, without me pausing for breath – or much sleep, for that matter. I was taken aback by the sheer opulence of the building, the liveried uniforms, the magnificent ballroom – where elegant diners tucked into local delicacies. I marvelled at the smells and tastes of haggis, truffle risotto, lobster bisque, beef Wellington. At the time, all of these were pretty much alien to me.

I soon began to appreciate the attention to detail, and the discipline displayed in front of the guests, while enjoying the camaraderie that took place behind the scenes. But if I thought it was all going to be glamour and glitz, I was soon to be put firmly in my place. Nowhere more so than in the bowels of the kitchen. On the second day, I was introduced to a gruff Scotsman, who turned out to be the head chef. I didn't understand a word he said to me, so strong was his accent, and I think he must have thought he was dealing with some halfwit, as he had to repeat his commands continually, much to the amusement of the rest of the brigade.

He finally managed to explain to me that my job was to prepare the melon ball starter for the evening's service. How hard could that be? I thought. Until I saw the mountain of melons in front of me and the tell-tale sight of the other chefs smirking at me. But I put on a brave face and asked, 'Chef, how many do I need to do?'

Obviously thinking his initial assessment of me was correct, he mustered his first smile and replied, 'Well, all of them, of course. We have six hundred diners, so five thousand melon balls should cover it. And by the way, every melon ball needs to be identical in size and shape.'

Some eight hours later, and after a little berating for my tardiness, I finished my task. Albeit with fingers so numb, they could barely move. After a somewhat exhausting but rewarding day, it seemed my efforts had been deemed worthy enough and I was now allowed to join the inner sanctum of a chefs' night out. This is where my initiation to the world of hospitality really began.

•

Even at the age of seventeen I liked a beer or two, being used to our underage drinking den close to the school gates. But after a night with my newfound friends, events became somewhat hazy. My only real recollection of the night was waking up in some random nightclub's toilet, having totally passed out. This wouldn't have been so bad, but as I woke up and clambered unsteadily out of the cubicle, I realised that the place was in total darkness, and everyone had gone home.

I had failed to notice a poor oblivious cleaner, who naturally presumed the worst and let out a piercing scream. This had the desired effect of sobering me up. I now had to convince her pretty quickly that I wasn't some sort of serial killer. Thankfully, she realised that I posed little threat and pointed me in the general direction of the hotel, which she assured me was only a ten-minute walk.

Still struggling to put one foot in front of the other, I had hoped to hail a cab, but alas I was clean out of luck. So, with my head down and eyes on the pavement, I staggered unsteadily back to the hotel. Either the instructions hadn't been clear, or my sense of direction had deserted me, but the ten-minute walk took well over two hours. I eventually tumbled into bed well past four o'clock in the morning. At seven o'clock, I crawled into the kitchen to a hearty round of applause from my newfound friends, who obviously didn't think I would make it in.

Happy to have passed my second initiation, I approached Chef with somewhat bleary eyes and enquired as to my day's task. He in turn smiled and said, 'You'll be pleased to know, no melon balls. Today it's tomato crowns and lemon wedges – enough for six hundred.'

He turned and left me with the overflowing boxes in front of me.

•

The week continued in a flurry of activities, ranging from helping with marketing, to working in reception, to teaching guests' kids tennis. The elegance of the hotel, the interaction with the guests, the camaraderie of the employees all led me to believe that this was the right path for me. So, on returning to my studies, I took on a part-time position at my uncle Bill's hotel, the Wynnstay in Oswestry, helping in the bar and restaurant under the tutelage of the remarkable Antonio.

I continued to enjoy my learning curve, but it also led to one of the other temptations of catering, one that nearly caused my promising career to stall before it even began. Namely, *the ladies.* One Christmas, just before I left for university, I had been teamed up with a local girl, Imogen, and it was our job to run the function bar over Christmas along with my friend Lee from school. Needless to say, Imogen and I – as I later found out was the norm in catering – hit it off immediately and passions started to simmer.

After a particularly busy New Year's Eve, I had begged the assistant manager, Richard, to let Imogen and I stay at the hotel. This wasn't permitted, but he reluctantly allowed us to stay, with the warning that we had to have left by five o'clock in the morning. The somewhat prudish head housekeeper was on duty and would certainly not be impressed by any youthful indiscretions.

Of course, we both overslept and were woken by the irate housekeeper storming into my room. I was subsequently hauled in front of the manager, Mr Dyson, who berated me for my behaviour – or lack of. He reminded me 'that there was a hard way and an easy way to make it in the industry'. The next time I veered in the wrong direction would be my last at the Wynnstay.

To make matters worse, and still full of reckless

abandon, I made my next error by sneaking Imogen into my mother's house. My mother – being no fool – had realised what I was up to. For the second time in two nights, I had an irate figure storming into my room and telling me in no uncertain terms to get that 'hussy' out of her house.

Several minutes later – with Imogen making a hasty retreat – I sauntered down the stairs in a white dressing down, like Noel Coward, with the largest smirk on my face. Perhaps totally misreading my mother's reaction, I received a rather large slap to the face. I have to say it was fully deserved. But rather than learning my lesson, I continued down the path of self-destruction and booked Imogen and me into the local Travelodge for a night, to continue where we had left off. I would like to say I learned my lesson but that probably didn't happen for at least another fifteen years!

CHAPTER 3

2005 – Meeting Ewa

Ewa and I had met back in 2005, when I had taken up the position of general manager at the Kings Hotel in the picturesque Cotswold village of Chipping Campden. I can still remember arriving on my first day and noticing this attractive girl, with captivating eyes, tousled brown hair and an infectious smile, weaving her very own brand of magic behind the bar. On that very first day, I knew instantly that I had lost a small part of my heart; but I was immediately brought back to reality, for two reasons: firstly, water had decided to pour through the ceiling from one of the upstairs bathrooms and was now dripping on both me and Mike, the owner, and secondly, I had to remind myself that I was already married.

So, when Mike left our meeting with the words 'Enjoy your first day', any thoughts were put to one side by my first problem – the water still dripping through the ceiling.

For several weeks, my days were taken up with relentless hours, a busy bar and restaurant and a demanding owner. I soon found out that Mike was a self-made millionaire and not much older than me. He could be both charming and ruthless in equal measure. It became clear that to him seven-day weeks were the norm, holidays were for wimps and if the hotel wasn't making money, then someone had to go.

Wanting to impress, I knew that to keep up with Mike's constant expectations, I had to come up with a strategy, fast. I checked out the competition. Cotswold House, under the masterful eye of Ian Taylor, whom I would come to know better from my days in Bath, was way ahead of the competition. His rooms were opulent, he had a Michelin-starred restaurant and, even at exorbitant prices, he was continually full. If there was any ray of hope, across the road he had another hotel, The Noel Arms, which I judged to be more like us in terms of what Ian was trying to achieve, but more importantly it was a hotel I could actually compete with.

After a mere week, it soon became obvious that the Kings was staffed with either hard-working Eastern Europeans or a whole host of local girls who – coming from rich mummies and daddies – decided when they would grace me with their presence and turn up for work. The problem was that many of the parents used the bar, but it became apparent that I could never take the Kings forward if it continued to be run like this. So, I quickly moved the time wasters on – much to the annoyance of their parents – and employed in their place several extrovert Aussies and an affable assistant, named Richard, who I had managed to prise away from the Dormy House Hotel in Broadway.

In addition, I had persuaded a talented young chef named Elleray, who had worked with me at the AA

3-rosette Close Hotel, to join me as head chef at the Kings. We devised a strategy of creating a menu that wouldn't compete directly against Cotswold House but would be sufficiently *trendy* to tempt both the locals and the residents of the Cotswolds to a somewhat more relaxed atmosphere. However, we wouldn't compromise on standards. So instead of the usual fare of fish and chips, we might put on battered lobster and chips. We soon increased trade and now had a bustling bar and busy restaurant. Mike turned out to be suitably impressed and I was treated to Michelin-starred dinners and healthy bonuses. Throughout all of this, with her ever smiling demeanour and willingness to learn, Ewa soon became my star employee and the feelings I had for her continued to simmer. As we spent more and more time together and I spent less time with my wife, Marie, I knew matters were certainly going to come to a head. I knew I couldn't pretend for much longer. When the attraction became obvious to even the likes of Mike, he encouraged me to have an affair, as he put it. He looked on incredulously when I stated I wanted to leave Marie for Ewa.

In truth, Marie had never been anything but a dutiful wife, who in many men's eyes would be seen as perfect. She had never once complained about my numerous nights out and frequent indiscretions. But from the start of our relationship, it seemed to me about two mates getting together. I never once tired of her company, and she gave me something I had never had before – a family. Mine had been a somewhat dysfunctional upbringing, with a stepmother who ensured I lost contact with grandparents and the like. Therefore, it came as no surprise to me that I was overjoyed to be made so welcome by her Welsh clan.

It wasn't just her father, Meryck, or her mother, Joyce, who instantly welcomed me into their hearts, but also aunts and uncles. They all seemed so at ease in their chosen lives, while embarking on home businesses conjuring homemade goodies from the laughter of their kitchens. This was something that was hard to leave behind, but by then I knew I had fallen for Ewa. There was no turning back. I knew at the time Marie took it badly, and who could blame her. Several years later we spoke, and I was delighted to hear that she had found love and a happy family and yes, she realised we had been better as friends than as husband and wife.

•

I discovered that Ewa was, in so many ways, the total opposite to me. Forthright in her opinions, I instantly knew she would not tolerate any of my usual nonsense. She had a youthful exuberance for life, coupled with a certain naivety and a razor-sharp mind that I admired. As we enjoyed romantic escapes to the Royal Crescent in Bath, I fell head over heels in love. In the years that were to follow, I always tried to be the best I could possibly be for her and in reality, she saved me from myself. By then – after years of hard living – I was closer than I realised to the edge of self-destruction, so this is something for which I will be forever grateful. However, if I thought my romantic ideal would be easy, well, I hadn't yet met my new mother-in-law!

Babs, as she was known, entered my life like a bull in a china shop. Shortly after Ewa and I moved into a new flat, just down from the hotel, I thought it would be a good idea to break the ice and invite Babs into the fold. If I thought my charm or even her beautiful surroundings were going to win her over, I was in for a rude awakening. Now, I know we all have horror stories about our mothers-in-law, and I had been warned that Polish mothers were big on religion, education and marriage, but all my best-laid plans vanished within twenty-four hours of meeting her. To compound matters further, I had naively thought that when it comes to family, the more the merrier, and had taken it upon myself to offer Ewa's sister a job. What I hadn't realised was that by combining her sister, Margot, with her mother, I was pretty much a lamb to the slaughter.

Instead of the idyllic countryside walks and the cosy pub lunches I had envisaged, the first day ended with me being summoned before a jury, in my own flat. If it wasn't bad enough to have been interrogated by her mother, even twenty-year-old Margot had thought it her place to point out my obvious failings. *That'll teach me for giving her a job*, I thought. It soon became apparent that, in Babs's eyes, I would never be deemed worthy of her beautiful daughter. In fact, just to rub salt into the wound, I was told that I was too old for such a beautiful girl. Too uneducated – my Swiss degree counted for very little; still married, which was not a great start, granted; and too poor. Yes, she had already checked my bank statement, which she had taken in secret from my desk. After the subsequent humiliation, I ended up staying in

33

one of the rooms at the hotel, while she lorded over it, both in my flat and by telling me how to run my hotel. So, all in all, I felt somewhat elated when she departed, but this wasn't before I had agreed that Ewa would go home for a year to finish her degree. But only on the understanding that should we make it through the year, we would then be allowed to get on with our relationship. In my eyes at least, what could possibly go wrong?

•

The next year went by with me taking frequent trips to Poland and Ewa joining me in the UK. Although I formed a good bond with Ewa's father, it soon became clear that it didn't matter how many lavish diners I took her out to, I would never be fully accepted by Babs. Not only was it taken for granted that I should pay for everything, but I was even on one occasion asked to pay to stay with Ewa! I don't know, but maybe her mother was trying to tell me something!

During our year apart, I had a spell working for the Automobile Association (AA), but as it didn't work out quite as I had envisaged, I decided to uproot my life and land myself in Bath. The problem was I had no home, no job and no income, but as soon as I arrived in Bath, something told me it was meant to be. As I checked into the Travelodge and marvelled my way around the historic buildings, I knew this would be home. I quickly found a flat there, next to Laura Place, and secured a job at the historic Pump Room. It wasn't long before I saw an opening for a general manager at the recently opened

Residence hotel. At the same time, Ewa returned, having evaded the grip of her mother, and joined me for our new life together.

Those early years were undoubtedly happy ones as we settled into our lives in Bath. Before long we moved into a period cottage on the outskirts of the city, in a small town called Corsham. Our new home, Pumblechook Cottage, was everything I had dreamed of, with its wooden beams, large open fireplace, apple trees in the garden and quaint country feel. Apart from the odd curve ball life threw at us, we loved where we lived and had a good set of friends. We by and large enjoyed our jobs and developed our already loving relationship, even if Ewa's mother still did her utmost to derail my best efforts.

In 2010 we married in a little church in Corsham and by 2012, Jack came into our lives. He had tried to pop back in as soon as he ventured out, but probably like the rest of the family he had decided that lunch was on its way! Babs had even been present at the birth. As we looked down at our very own *little miracle*, I hoped that Babs and I had buried the hatchet and little Jack would finally bring us together.

Although everything was falling into place, there was one matter that was persistently nagging at the back of my mind. I really wanted to start my own business and be my own boss. I had dreamed about it for years and now had to find a way to make it a reality.

Over the next few months, I started to investigate the opportunities around me. It soon became apparent that although our beloved Bath would be the perfect choice, our meagre funds wouldn't make this an option. During one day's research, I stumbled across the Isle of Wight and was captivated by the beauty of the island and the affordable prices. I researched the possibilities and was soon swayed by the inviting beaches. I started imagining a family life by the sea. Ewa knew that it had been my long-held dream and we started to plan our future. Deep down, I knew it would be a dilemma for her to be dragged away from her beloved Bath and, in particular, a job she had made her own.

Meanwhile, my mum had spent the last few years living in the mountains of Switzerland but being on her own, and now with a grandson to enjoy, she had jumped at the opportunity of joining our little family in the UK.

We decided to rent a bigger property in Corsham while we looked for a suitable property on the island and a separate house for my mum. Somewhere close by. Thanks to my mum's help, we had managed to muster up a deposit large enough to secure a property, but I soon became aware of the hoops I would be expected to jump through to secure a commercial mortgage.

After several months of repeated rejections, I approached Ian Taylor, who had by now set up the successful Abbey Hotel in Bath. With his help and a couple of phone calls later, the mortgage happened relatively quickly. It just went to show that the old saying 'it's not what you know, but who you know' was indeed correct.

In the meantime, Mum had arrived in Corsham, along with a very large lorry barely able to turn into the drive. If I thought family life was going to be easy, I had forgotten to take a few factors into account. The first obstacle came when Mum's ever-youthful Westie,

Zeus, spotted our near-blind cat, Cookie. Rather than the peaceful start I had hoped for, Zeus – delighted to be given the opportunity to make a new *friend* – had rushed past us and decided to chase a now terrified Cookie up the stairs. This resulted in the cat launching herself from our first-floor bedroom window. While I was somewhat horrified, Mum had nonchalantly brushed the chaos aside with the words, 'Well, they are just going to have to learn to get along'. Ten years later, and even with intense training, this still wasn't the case!

The other problem that soon manifested itself was that having two women in the house – each with different ideas on just about everything – probably wasn't going to end well. Their previous encounters had involved enjoying the delights of the slopes of sunny Switzerland and they had formed a good friendship. But being under the same roof, things had started to take a turn for the worse.

My mum has very old-school thoughts on everything from how to raise a child to the fact that a house should be always kept in a pristine state, and that everything should always have its place. This was something that had been instilled in me from an early age. Ewa is somewhat ... shall we say, *laissez-faire* about tidiness, and in tune with the more modern ways of motherhood. Namely, to panic about everything. In addition, Ewa is also probably the biggest hypochondriac I know. Although she would argue that I was exaggerating about her views on illness, I think friends would agree that if I was on my death bed, she would still be in a worse state! So, I was rather relieved when Mum completed on her house in Niton and the two women in my life were safely installed under two roofs.

2014 – Keats Cottage, Shanklin

'Keats cottage – Great food, amazing service,
highly entertaining.' —Jane McDonald

As I enjoyed an espresso and a brandy to ward off the
night chill and listened to a fox scurrying behind me, I
wondered if the past thirty years of striving for perfection
had all been worth it. I recalled the missed weddings,
birthdays, Christmases, the ridiculous hours and the
fractured relationships. Would I have had it any other
way? I guess not.

But, approaching fifty, the body was slowly creaking. The late nights and early mornings were starting to take their toll and the general public's ever increasing demands only served to add to the pressures. But what was certain, it had never been dull. I had memories and stories that would last a lifetime. My stories had been recounted so many times that my poor wife, Ewa, would look on in despair as soon as I opened my mouth. But no one could deny that I was what my good friend Pascal once described as 'the king of the blah de blah'.

I literally could go on for hours, but I always managed to have a captivated audience who would delay their day's activities just to hear one more story. Some of the tales and characters are so over the top, they sometimes seemed implausible even to me. For anyone who has watched the film *Big Fish* with Ewan McGregor, I guess my life reminds me of that. Sure, there might be the odd embellishment from time to time. But as the son in the film realises when he sees all the people from his father's *fantastical* past congregating for his funeral, even the most bizarre tale was based on truth.

Still nursing my brandy, I let my mind drift back to the island and the ups and downs of the past seven years, which had all started with such heady optimism as we embarked on the *world's most expensive journey*. I recalled our first website photo of the four of us and Zeus, our beloved Westie, posing for the camera. Looking full of hope and ready to conquer the world. It saddened me to think of what our photo would look like now.

Fewer smiles, I guess, as Ewa lived her life in Bath while Mum and I did our best to entertain yet another guest. Even Zeus had lost some of his usual lust for life and could barely make his way up the stairs. Like all of us, he too was getting older and even the daily walks weren't greeted with his usual enthusiasm.

Although we were determined to jump headlong into our adventure, even on the very first day the monumental task ahead of us became all too apparent. All around us, Keats Cottage, our new B&B, was literally crumbling before our eyes and while my mother and I could see the potential, Ewa's first reaction was one of reproach.

'What have we done?' she asked.

In truth, I couldn't blame her, and as we took in the sight of a building suffering from years of neglect, even Jack, who was still a baby, looked suitably unimpressed. Zeus had rampaged through every room and come back rather despondent, having been unable to find a spot he deemed comfortable enough for his usual afternoon siesta.

Trudging from room to room, we started to make a to-do list. After an hour we had already filled the first notepad. There was carnage everywhere – layers of plasterboard, cement, liberal helpings of black gloss. To make matters worse, the sash windows were all rotten and, in some cases, only held in place by newspaper. On turning on the water, we realised not only that the decrepit cast iron boiler was incapable of producing hot water, but also that the only water available came out in a sorry trickle.

I eventually saw the funny side when I decided to use our Saniflo toilet. The whole contraption was something of a death trap. I hopped on for what I thought would be five minutes' respite, but it turned out not to be such a wise move after all. The pump had a mind of its own and decided to jump into action before I had even finished. Fearful of losing more than my dignity, I was forced to evacuate.

The good news didn't end there. It transpired that the old owners hadn't been too honest about the bookings. There weren't any!

•

It soon became clear that it would be impossible to open before the new year and with the amount of work required, and for everyone's sanity, it was probably best for Ewa and Jack to decamp to her parents, in Poland.

The next nine months seemed fraught with one problem after another. It got to the stage where I was living alone with the cat, with just one electric socket, no hot water, cardboard in place of windows and just one plank of floorboard to navigate to get to my room. Maybe it wasn't quite *Grand Designs*, but I now fully understood the levels of stress involved. To be honest, it would probably have been better and cheaper just to have bulldozed the place to the ground and started again.

Our first mistake had been to trust in the local tradesmen. We naively thought they would be grateful for the business, but instead they had quite openly and without any remorse tried to part us from every penny we had.

There appeared to be seemingly endless methods of sending our stress levels through the roof, from the plumber who turned up six weeks later than promised to the electrician who charged £1,000 a week for labour and took an entire day to put up one single light bulb. Then we had plasterers who attempted to sabotage the building to generate extra work. Finally, a joiner – who we had booked in six months earlier and who at the time had been quite happy to accept a hefty deposit – decided once the scaffolding had gone up that perhaps the job of fitting our new sash windows was a bit too big for him. By the end, I think if anyone had uttered the words 'Sorry, mate, this is going to be a lot more than I first thought', I was likely to be joining the other more famous faces in Parkhurst prison.

Somehow, Mum and I managed to make it through the fourteen hours a day of back-breaking work, dealing with workmen who were too macho to address a woman, and copious amounts of paint, which by now was so embedded in my skin, I had given up trying to wash it off. By the time the skip company turned up and its owner had watched my mother and I struggle with several tonnes of junk while he stood idly by, nothing really fazed me – or perhaps I was too numb to be fazed.

I really didn't know what to say when the owner of the skip had the audacity to ask me for a tip. Was I mad, or was the rest of the population? By this time, I really didn't care.

•

Despite all the drama, Mum and I, even at our lowest moments, had never stopped laughing, even though some of the laughter was rather hysterical. The reason we worked so well together was that we both have an insane work ethic. We also have identical tastes, which is wise when your mother is the interior designer. And after years of training, I have the unique ability to agree with my mother when she is right – which, of course, is always.

When I look back, I don't know how we got through it, but we did. What is more, we never argued. After years apart from each other, I look back at our achievement in bringing Keats Cottage back to life with considerable pride. It's only fair to say that without my mum's artistic talent and sheer willpower, Keats would never have even got off the ground and for that I will be forever grateful.

After eight eventful months, I was dealt yet another hammer blow, this time by the council. When we first arrived, I had been assured that all small businesses were exempt from paying rates, so I was more than a little horrified to open a letter demanding full payment. When I finally got through to the relevant department, it transpired that as I wasn't actually trading, I was in fact liable for the full amount. I argued that it was currently impossible for me to trade and how was I supposed to pay with no income, but my pleas fell on deaf ears.

With my pot almost empty, I ended up taking a part-time position at the New Inn at Shalfleet. After a busy day, I would return to the endless jobs at Keats. Luckily for me, I met Bryan, who restored my faith in human nature. Bryan was the handyman for the New Inn group's pubs and, on hearing my tales of woe, he agreed to help me with Keats during the evenings and weekends. Thanks to him, we pushed through and managed to complete our project and looked ready to open on Valentine's Day.

During these final weeks, Ewa and Jack had returned from Poland. Much to my disappointment, rather than being excited by our efforts, Ewa seemed more concerned with the abundance of dust still in the atmosphere. I guess having recently become a mother, she was naturally protective of our little bundle of joy, but it wasn't the reaction I had hoped for, and it left me feeling somewhat deflated. In hindsight, this was perhaps the first indication of things to come.

CHAPTER 5

2015 – Opening for business

We finally opened for the Valentine's weekend of 2015 and welcomed friends from our previous life in Bath, including Tina and Keith, who had married just before our departure in a beautiful ceremony in the gardens of Longleat House. They were joined by one of Ewa's former bosses, Steve, as well as an array of guests from a variety of backgrounds. It was nice to be open finally, but I hadn't really paused for breath from the somewhat *intense* refurbishment, and this would later start to take its toll.

The B&B picked up pace. We attempted to offer great food and service, at affordable prices. We soon realised that if we were going to survive in what was a very competitive market, we would need to excel at all the aspects. Although only a relatively small place, the island is awash with accommodation, namely one hundred hotels, two hundred and fifty bed and breakfasts and a thousand self-catering offerings. That in turn meant we needed to be at the top if we were going to thrive. We also realised that with no parking, no sea view and no additional facilities – such as a swimming pool – we had to offer an outstanding service.

With Ewa's flair for marketing, our guests were soon enjoying our newly refurbished property. We had hit the ground running, but if the B&B was operating as planned, the same could not be said for the restaurant. We had taken out a loan merely to open the doors, so we desperately needed the restaurant to be a success too. As is often the case, the renovations stretched us to near breaking point.

We also knew that a chef would be too costly, especially as we could only seat twenty-four covers, and, in all honesty, we didn't have any idea of how many diners would come through the door. With this in mind, Ewa volunteered to become Keats's chef and we managed to recruit an eager helper, Neno, who was happy to be a jack-of-all-trades.

We decided to play to our strengths and produce a small but simple menu, featuring local produce. If all turned out to plan, we would then offer themed nights, based on Ewa's Polish background and my Swiss roots.

If I had any delusions that this would prove to be easy, it didn't take long for reality to sink in. The locals who had flocked to our opening never materialised and the tourists who peered through the window soon beat a hasty retreat once they discovered the restaurant was near empty. In our growing frustration I sent out invites for free meals, which even the Isle of Wight's illustrious critics Matt and Cat declined.

For months, I attempted to put on a show for the one or two booked tables to try and create an atmosphere.

This entailed me babbling on for hours, just so our guests would have any sort of experience. As we haemorrhaged our now dwindling funds, I even resorted to offering free tasters to unsuspecting passers-by. What I found amusing were the differing attitudes. The foreign tourists were delighted with the offering and nearly snatched our hands off. However, the good old Brits beat a hasty retreat to the other side of the road, clearly sceptical of what was being offered. Throughout this time, my only real disappointment was that although we sent our own B&B guests to numerous establishments, the compliment was rarely returned.

After a fairly agonising year, and with the constant financial pressure rising, a number of avenues started to open up that ultimately saved our fledgling business. Several local businesses tried us out and all of a sudden, the power of word of mouth took hold. I will be forever thankful to my now good friend Panos, the local barber, who saw something in us and helped us to establish our name throughout Shanklin. Alan, the local cab owner, along with his brother, started to frequent us regularly. Whispers abounded in the taxi ranks. We had also tempted the great and good from Visit Isle of Wight, who marketed the island to tourists, the owner of a tour company that offered golfing breaks, and the volunteers from Shanklin Theatre to come and give us a try.

This in turn led to us welcoming a whole array of editors and journalists, not to mention the likes of the cruise queen Jane McDonald and the comedy king Jimmy Carr. Our once empty restaurant now hosted the themed nights we had always hoped for and even my friend Marc – with his Michelin star in tow – agreed that, for pop events, he would delight our guests with his amazing dishes.

If it could be said that the business had turned the corner, the same could not be said for our relationship. Day by day the cracks started to deepen and after years of rarely arguing, we were now at each other's throats on a near daily basis. I think that anyone who works in catering would testify to the stress the job entails, and to live in each other's pockets 24/7 is not always a healthy environment. The problem was, we didn't appear to be able to find a solution. The situation was made worse by the fact that we were barely seeing Jack, who was by now spending most evenings with my mum. Every time we saw him, it appeared he had grown a little taller and as the years passed by and our little bundle had become a little man, I knew this was weighing heavily on Ewa's mind.

The other problem was that it takes a certain type of person to be able to cook in a restaurant. Such are the demands of the job that you must have a thick skin both mentally and physically. I think we all love to bake or conjure up a dinner party for half a dozen people but put yourself in a kitchen with a restaurant full of hungry mouths to feed and the situation becomes totally different. It's not just the heat, the scalded hands and the gruelling hours, but in today's world every diner is a critic and expectations have soared.

To her credit, the food Ewa was creating was exceptional and we started receiving rave reviews. You must also remember that Ewa was totally self-taught, with absolutely no background in cooking. If, to all and sundry, everything seemed perfect, this was not the case behind the scenes. Our daily rifts were becoming ever more frequent. In fairness, over the years I have seen several catering couples separate owing to this constant stress. I was determined to try and resolve the problem, even if our differing views wouldn't make this an easy fix. I was even contemplating the approach of two friends of mine – their answer to a happy working environment was simple. After thirty years working together, they just didn't talk to each other.

The biggest bone of contention was that our views on how to run the business were miles apart. For my part, I believed that sacrifices needed to be made. In order to pay off the debt, we should move heaven and earth to make it happen. Only then could we start to take the foot off the pedal and spend more quality time as a family. In my mind at least, knowing how hard it is to make a success of any catering business, the sacrifices being made were essential to ensure we had a roof over our heads and a legacy to leave Jack. It was never far from my mind that 50 per cent of all restaurants go under in the first two years and I was determined, after all these years of dreaming, that this wasn't going to happen. Unfortunately, Ewa's views did not match my own and she believed we should take every opportunity to spend as much time together as a family as we could, even if it resulted in the guests not receiving the level of service I prided myself on.

Now, I know I am very stubborn and take the need to give perfect service to the extreme. I remember also reading once about the French chef Bernard Loiseau, who committed suicide because he thought he was to lose one of his Michelin stars. At the time I knew this was extreme, although it was certainly something I could relate to. I also knew that we needed to change drastically, but in those initial years I didn't know how to. So, we were literally in a Catch-22 situation.

My second problem was my hatred of bad atmospheres. My motto is: if life throws a few curve balls, you just smile and get through it. So, even deprived of sleep and constantly exhausted, I would cheerfully walk into the kitchen each morning, hopeful for the day ahead. However, someone had forgotten to inform Ewa of this, and my once sweet demure bride had turned into someone who would have given Gordon Ramsay a run for his money. Her rationale was that if she was having a particularly bad day, I should just shut up and walk away. This wasn't made easy by the fact that she would follow me into the restaurant and remonstrate with me for any perceived failure. Mostly for talking too much! This in turn would aggravate me in such a way that I was now becoming as bad as her. I didn't like the person I was turning into. To make matters worse, Ewa was used to arguing and however bitter the comments, everything would be forgotten the next day. So, while she would sleep like a baby, I would toss and turn and stew over the comments made and this eventually led me to hit rock bottom.

If all was not perfect with us, perhaps our one saving grace was Jack. He continued to bring out the best in us and perhaps remind us of how the dream was meant to be. As the years flew past, our once small package had developed into a breath of fresh air. Although ever eager to please, Jack was painfully shy, but thanks to my mum's tutelage he was naturally well mannered. I'd always presumed that such behaviour was the norm, but my encounters with guests' children proved that this certainly wasn't the case.

I recalled a recent conversation with an old friend of mine where I suggested that as he had recently become a dad for the second time, perhaps he would appreciate a trip to the Isle of Wight and to bring along his family. 'Oh God, Woody. I wouldn't inflict that on anyone. My kids are simply feral.' The fact was, he really wasn't joking. To be honest, if I looked around on a daily basis, I would have to agree that this was the case with several children I had encountered.

But as I proudly took in Jack's development, what became strikingly clear was how he had taken on not only his parents' features but also their totally contrasting personalities. It was as though he wasn't quite sure which way he should behave and to some degree was almost torn. Add to this the potent force of his nanni's upbringing and I knew there would be interesting times ahead. Even he had decided that, in his early years at least, it was better to defer to his grandmother on all matters. Forty-two years his senior, I would still agree that this was the best policy.

If the work was gradually tearing us apart, our son went a long way to soothe away the tensions. On rare escapes, we enjoyed picnics at Queen Victoria's Osborne House, refreshing swims off the rugged coast of Steephill

Cove, trips on the steam rail and mackerel fishing off Yarmouth Harbour. If I felt any guilt at missing out on Jack's formative years, my worries were somewhat allayed by the knowledge that Jack had the best of what the island had to offer. For him at least, every day resembled a holiday. During these precious moments with Jack, Ewa and I both regained our smiles. Our differences and worries were put to one side, at least for the time being.

•

When he first emerged into this world, poor old Jack probably hadn't realised it would be so hard to *manage* his parents. I mean, which way was he supposed to turn? Was he supposed to be frugal like his mother? Or extravagant like his father? Cheeky like his dad? Or well behaved like his mum? Prudish like his mum? Or debauched like his dad? His daily life had turned into so many dilemmas, and it soon became obvious that handling the differing expectations was no mean feat. To give him his due, by the age of eight his ability to hit the right note with both his parents was a masterclass in diplomacy. I have no doubt that, given another eight years, he will be able to recount with considerable pride that his parents had managed to grow up *quite nicely*. But only under his watchful guidance.

By now, evidence of his emerging personality was ever present, and I was delighted that our once painfully shy child was turning into a charismatic young man. After some initial hesitation, he was now donning an apron and helping with the washing up as well as greeting the guests at breakfast. He had even turned his hand to housekeeping. But if I privately delighted in the fact that he resembled a mini-me, I soon realised that there was method in his madness and many things would come at a price!

It wasn't long before this once quiet child – perching on a chair to wash the dishes – was berating his father for his tardiness and exclaiming to amused diners that his dad really should stop chatting, as he was trying to get the dishes finished.

If the guests were highly titillated by the exchange, Dad was worried he now had two people to put him in his place. Remarkably for one so young, Jack quickly surpassed his father in the art of making money and knew exactly when a cute smile would encourage a tip. If I thought his line of attack was reserved for the clients, I was in for a rude awakening. Every couple of weeks, my mum and son would make the jams for breakfast. When he delivered them, I naively asked my son how much I owed Nanni for each jar.

'That will be 2p, please, Dad.'

I had stupidly been under the misapprehension that my son wasn't so astute when it came to finance, but this notion was quickly put to rights when I asked, 'And how much do I owe you, Jack?'

A smile quickly arose with the words, 'That will be twenty pounds, Dad!'

Now, you could put this down to either his mother's frugality or his father's extravagance. But as he was aged just five at the time, it certainly gave me pause for thought.

At about the same time, it soon became clear that Dad's influence might lead him down a dangerous path and that perhaps a more conservative route to his personal development might be beneficial. On one particular afternoon, I had decided to take Jack to the beach for an ice cream. As we enjoyed the sun and a Mr Whippy on one of the benches, a young lady in tight Lycra jogged past. Not an altogether unpleasant sight, I might add. Jack noticed her and exclaimed, 'Nice bum, Dad.'

As the woman turned round, I acted suitably mortified. She glared at me, and I had no hesitation in pointing the finger of blame at Jack. Jack found the whole exchange highly amusing, but seeing an *angelic* face, the woman's scowl soon became a smile and she jogged away into the distance. I tried to show my disapproval to Jack, but it was somewhat half-hearted. And to give the boy his due – she did have a nice bum!

As Jack grew, so did the business. Each year, we welcomed back familiar faces and an ever increasing number of new ones. Even after several years of trying, I realised that to many islanders we would never be accepted and would still be regarded as *foreigners* from the mainland. This statement was maybe a little bit of a generalisation and over the years we managed to make friends with a whole host of islanders. Nonetheless, I always found it a little disconcerting that in the company of islanders, not a single negative could be uttered about the place.

Over the years, I have employed two lovely ladies, both of whom are island born and bred, and when discussing a whole array of topics, I found them both extremely knowledgeable. But criticise the island in any way, shape or form and this would lead to a barrage of abuse and all rhyme and reason would totally vanish out of the window. Now, I'm all for a little loyalty to your hometown, but when I'm told Sandown Bay is the most beautiful place in the world, I'm sorry but I have to object. I also believe that the island has many beautiful qualities, but whenever any discussions arise that may in some way help to develop it, it seems half the island starts frothing at the mouth with indignation and telling anyone north of Yarmouth that basically they have no right to step onto *their* island. Not the wisest move when the island is dependent on tourism. Perhaps they would prefer that the island continues on its natural path as the UK's largest retirement village?

Even the great John Keats spoke of the strangeness of the islanders, who would not give him so much as a greeting, so at least I can say I'm in good company. In conclusion, I know countless numbers who love the island and return year after year, but I do fear that once the generation who love the chintz of the seventies and the island's old-school charm have died out, the new era may not put up with extortionate ferries and those who have not moved with the times.

CHAPTER 6

Putting the ghosts to rest at Keats Cottage

If I tended to tread carefully when venturing out of Keats Cottage, it did seem that fate had brought me together with the old building. Over the years, there have been many accounts of *ghostly happenings* and although sceptical at first, I certainly believe there are presences within those four walls. Strangely enough, despite all the remarkable occurrences, I have never once felt afraid – even when staying alone in the property.

For those among you who are tut-tutting and saying what a load of nonsense, I have to say I would normally agree, but there are moments I just can't explain. The first of these is that often when I enter a room, I feel like I have just been splashed with a drop of water. Without fail, I look up – dreading some problem with the plumbing – only to find nothing amiss. I have been told by those in the know that this is an indication of the spirit world trying to contact me. Well, you learn something every day.

Historical accounts mention a lady helping those in the kitchen. Now, I might just be a little superstitious, but my wife had never cooked in a professional kitchen before entering Keats and now she could cook for a full restaurant. Possible, you may well think, but what I found truly amazing was that with absolutely no practice in creating a new dish, it would turn out perfectly every time. After thirty years in the industry, and having worked with countless chefs, I didn't think this was possible.

There could be a plausible explanation, but it wasn't just me who had sensed something a little odd. The Keats' room is located at the back of the B&B and to all intents and purposes it is the quietest room. I found that, despite being a very light sleeper, I always slept like a log in this room and many guests came to the same conclusion.

This was taken one step further by one guest, who, after hearing my tales, told me he didn't believe in any of that nonsense. However, the next morning he came down to breakfast, rather pale and definitely not himself. He recounted his story: he also had an amazingly comfortable night, so much so that when his wife continually tapped him to get up, he told her he wanted five more minutes. After a while, he succumbed to this constant pestering and turned over, only to find that his wife wasn't next to him at all – she was actually in the shower and had neither tapped him nor asked him to get up!

If the sight of shadows or doors slamming for no apparent reason was slightly unnerving, what truly amazed me were the number of coincidences that seemed to occur on a weekly basis. Given the number of places I have worked, I expect there to be certain occurrences that may seem remarkable, but the sheer quantity and the depth left even me shaking my head.

Perhaps the most remarkable was that of a German family who were looking for a school for their two girls in the UK. Firstly, they had stayed at all the three hotels where I had worked in Switzerland. OK, I thought, totally possible if they liked to travel. Secondly, they were just looking at two schools for their children, the first on the island and the second in a small market town in Shropshire. When I asked where, they replied, 'Oh, you probably wouldn't know it, it's called Oswestry Grammar School.'

My old school!

'Where did you stay?'

'The Wynnstay,' came the reply.

My uncle's hotel!

'And where did you eat?' I asked.

'Oh, at a little restaurant called Sebastians.'

Two years earlier, we had in fact sat next to the owners of this restaurant at a friend's wedding in Devon. Now that's what I call a coincidence!

Looking back over the last few eventful years, if life has taught me anything, it is that one thing is for certain: there is no such thing as perfect. For as long as I can remember, I have been surrounded by good friends, had a lovely home and been in a happy relationship. The only thing that seemed to elude my *perfect* world was owning my business.

As I finally finished my brandy and contemplated calling it a night, I could only wonder if maybe I had wished for too much. Yes, I had the successful business I had always craved, but at what cost? Rattling around alone in Keats, with only the ghosts and my own demons for company, the cries of Jack's laughter seemed a distant memory and only added to my loneliness. What was the point of it all, if there was no one to share it with? In a world where we are surrounded by staged images of a picture-perfect world on Instagram, all anyone wants is for there to be someone to wake up to. Someone who is genuinely pleased to see you. The problem was that I had achieved everything I wished for, but in doing so, I had lost everything I had.

If I have been shown anything at all, it is that I really have nothing to complain about. I have watched guests with only months to live embrace every day with a smile on their face. I have seen friends battle with cancer, others drive to Great Ormond Street Hospital on a weekly basis to give support to their child, who would never know normal. So, my ups and downs were mere hiccups along life's rich path.

•

However, loneliness and depression had almost toppled me, edging me closer to breaking point. While the outside world saw me as the forever *cheerful chappy*, it only really hit home how low I had sunk when two friends from London had joined me earlier in the year. We hadn't met up for some time and, in my eyes, we enjoyed the weekend as we had on many previous occasions, with much laughter. But to my amazement they expressed concern even to leave me, and it was then that it really hit home how far I had actually sunk.

I probably would never have thought of myself as either depressive or lonely, but in reality, I had stumbled on such emotional times that I really wondered whether it was all worth it. This view would have appalled me in the past. I would have thought how selfish I was for even thinking it, but life – and being shown a window into other people's lives – had demonstrated how all our lives can dissolve in an instant.

Previously, confronted with evidence of abuse, I would have said, *'Well, why don't they just leave?'* Or if I saw e.g. a homeless person on the street, I would think, *oh, it must be drugs.* If I heard a story of someone who stayed with an addictive partner, I would ask *why?* But it's too easy to be judgemental. What I have learned is that it's very easy to have it all and then become bankrupt through no fault of your own.

So, after spending years obsessing over the moments when my own relationship started to unravel, I can now see that it has taken me all this time to start enjoying my own company again, without any feelings of animosity towards others or loathing that Ewa and I hadn't got through our differences as a team. At the end of it all, it was simple: my idea of *perfect* wasn't the same as Ewa's. I had wanted the business, the home and the family life, but I knew this couldn't be achieved without sacrifice and a great deal of hard work. Ewa wanted a much simpler way of life, and who was I to say whether this was wrong or right?

Over time we had grown ever more distant, to the extent that our daily arguments had turned increasingly sour. Try as we might, it seemed impossible to reconcile our differences and the whole atmosphere became strained. I was aware that Ewa was unhappy, but shocked to see the person I knew becoming someone who was totally alien to me. The situation had become intolerable and during those dark times, our only thread of hope was Jack. If Ewa showed her disdain by fiery outbursts, I sought refuge at the bottom of a bottle. Every night after service I was now drowning my sorrows in one or two bottles of wine. Hoping for a miracle, and that the next day would have an answer to our problems.

As is the case with me, everything goes to extremes. I either drink heavily or not at all. Even I knew something had to give or Jack wouldn't have a father, let alone a legacy. But even in these darkest moments, when I seriously wondered whether it was all worth it, I never failed to put on a *performance* at work to an audience who were oblivious to my suffering. As my hero Freddie Mercury sang, *the show must go on*.

•

In the end I knew a solution would have to be found and I knew that only I could find it. Ewa tended to bury her head in the sand and pretend that, contrary to the evidence of our now escalating arguments, nothing was really wrong. I understood to hide the problem would be futile. Should we continue on this path, we could well be making front-page news, but not in a good way.

I agreed to manage the B&B on my own, while Ewa concentrated on her old job. We decided that she should help me for a day and a night in the restaurant. This would give her far more time with Jack. Problem solved, I thought. Unfortunately, our trust for each other was now at breaking point and the compromise turned out to be too little, too late.

It was then that I realised the best option was for Jack and Ewa to return to Bath. Ewa could return full-time to her old job and give us the much-needed space to mend our relationship. But whereas Ewa was now flourishing in her newfound freedom, I found myself alone. Dependent on my mother's support and becoming ever lonelier and more resentful. All my efforts to sell the property seemed to hit one buffer or another.

So, as I now pulled myself out of my chair and hauled myself off to bed, I reflected on how grateful I was that the year of lockdown had allowed me to regain a semblance of my former self and an aim for the future. I asked myself, did I regret buying Keats? Hell no! Would I have done it differently? Probably not. Had I learned from my mistakes? I hope so, but those who know me best would say probably not. They would just smile at the thought of the next rocky adventure I was about to embark on.

Part Two

1990 – Switzerland, where it all began

As the train ambled its way out of Zurich Hauptbahnhof, I pressed my nose against the window and took in the beauty of my surroundings. Even after such a short time, I realised that I had entered an entirely different world. For a start, the train was on time – something that was a rare occurrence in the UK at the best of times.

I later heard that one train, departing from Zurich, had the audacity to be twenty minutes late. Such an occurrence was so unheard of that it had become front-page news in the *Zürcher Zeitung*! Oh yes, there is never a dull moment in Switzerland. That said, you couldn't help but admire Swiss efficiency. When I thought back on some of my UK journeys, stranded in the middle of nowhere and praying for the delayed regional service from Cardiff Central – with its two carriages – to even appear, my secret sniggering at Swiss professionalism was soon put to bed.

The other first impression that struck me, at both the airport and the Bahnhof, was how clean everything was, especially in contrast to the depressive departure lounge at Luton airport.

So, it was with these initial impressions that my adventure had begun. I had met up with my university chum, Andy, a couple of hours previously in the airport's smoking lounge. True to form, and with it being past the acceptable hour of midday, Andy had greeted me with a couple of small beers – *e staange*, to use the correct Swiss-German phrase. Now, you could hardly call these beers – they were half-pints made up mostly of foam – but it seemed an apt way to start our journey and calm our nerves, as Andy eloquently put it. For my part, I didn't want to dampen the mood and remind Andy that we were accustomed to celebrating with a pint just for making it to a lecture! But I guess at that moment we were like two kids in a candy shop, full of anticipation at what lay ahead.

As I sipped my *staange*, I took in my surroundings. In a strange way, those first few minutes summed up – albeit somewhat stereotypically – everything about Switzerland and the Swiss. I couldn't help but find it somewhat comical that here in our goldfish bowl of a smoking room, surrounded on all sides by glass, I could barely make out my neighbour through the fumes being exhaled. To the eyes of the outside world, this probably resembled some sort of opium den. This was in total contrast to the immaculate corridors and high-end shops, literally steps away. In hindsight, this is the quintessence of all things Swiss. The smoking room might be at odds with the clean mountain air, but it just goes to show that the Swiss think of everything.

Sure, smoking might still be hazardous to health, but in contrast to the UK, the lounge was spotlessly clean. I couldn't help but think back to my departure at Luton, where I'd had to walk miles to find a smoking zone, which proved to be no more than an open-air spot – surrounded by ashtrays that hadn't been emptied in weeks – and where it had been impossible to light a cigarette due to the howling gale.

Even in the squalid air of my fellow smokers, I could only admire the sense of sophistication surrounding me. While I grappled for the right word, it was in fact all around me: namely, money. The entire room was awash with Armani suits, Gucci bags, Rolex watches, all of which were adorning people whose very mannerisms exuded an air of confidence. One that only the very wealthy can portray.

Back at home, I felt at ease in my university attire but here, I suddenly felt conspicuous and certainly less than *dressed*. I had always loved to people-watch and was used to dealing with the *great and the good*, but what struck me here was that *everyone* seemed to be wealthy. Or was it just my imagination?

Andy was dressed in yet another of his hideous paisley shirts and was already downing his second *staange*. He was blissfully unaware of us being like two fish out of water.

We had met at university freshers' week and from that moment on I was swept away by the force of his personality and was constantly going down paths I wasn't too sure I should be. It wasn't as though I was some sort of shrinking violet or even that I was easily led, but somehow, I was now one part of three students whose antics were starting to be talked about all over campus.

The other member of our *brotherhood* was a Norwegian student by the name of Sven. Sven was a few years older than Andy and me, with smouldering good looks, not dissimilar to the lead singer from A-ha. His ability to play the guitar and his instant rapport with women made him, to me, the epitome of cool. Sven liked a beer or two and was not immune to some fairly wild behaviour. But unlike Andy, he ultimately realised that he was at university to study. Andy, on the other hand, although extremely bright, was starting to take a path that perhaps didn't bode well for either of us.

Shortly before our travels, we had enjoyed one of our now legendary nights at the Cyder House Inn in Godalming and indulged in one of our favourite pints, the aptly named *Grievous Bodily Harm*. However, this was not before Sven – in a more lucid moment – had the foresight to take me to one side and warn me that perhaps taking Andy along to Switzerland might not be the wisest move. Yet here he was in front of me, admiring his red locks in the mirror while humming another of his repertoire of tunes.

•

That past year had been something of a blur. One minute I was the model student, overachieving with my grades at A level, and the next I was blowing my student loan on wild nights out with my newfound friends at university.

Our hedonistic lifestyle had got so out of hand that a typical night out now meant cocktails in Covent Garden, followed by busking at Waterloo station just to pay for our train fare home. The absurdity of the situation was highlighted by the fact that Sven could play guitar and Andy could sing, while I could only be entrusted with humming and trying to appear sober – which was no mean feat. But any lucrative singing career was obviously to be put on a back burner.

I did content myself with memories of winning the school singing contest, aged just twelve, before a higher being had decided that the laws of gravity would prevail and any notions of being the next Aled Jones were quickly blown away. But if my contribution to the *band* was minimal, I did at least make sure we found our way home.

With my friendships now blossoming, what struck me most about the pair was that they had such a sense of adventure and an energy I had rarely encountered before. Even if this meant criticising the entire university campus. Not in any way deterred by the consequences and just for the hell of it, they had decided to write a column for the university newspaper. They thought it would be hilarious to berate the students for living off the government or their parents while enjoying a rather debauched lifestyle. The irony of the situation was that they were the ones guilty of this lifestyle. This in turn incensed a number of students to boiling point. Instead of being upset by the indignant rage of their peers, it only spurred them to write ever more scandalous pieces. Although I was not part of this particular conspiracy, I was deemed guilty by association and received the same scorn administered to my friends. If I was somewhat more sensitive to the criticism, they really didn't give a damn.

It wasn't long before this newfound lifestyle started to take its toll. To be honest, after a year that did not include a great deal of study, I fervently hoped that the more disciplined Swiss might be able to put me back on the straight and narrow. The pressing nature of my predicament became ever more widespread just a couple of weeks before our departure. After a somewhat overenthusiastic night at the Cyder House, I had staggered back to my flat, which was located by the canal and above the office of the owner of the canal boats. In something of a stupor, I had managed to misplace my keys and was now in no fit state to go any further. I had decided that my best course of action would be to clamber on board one of the canal boats and to try and get some rest.

This plan would have been all well and good if I had been clever enough to have woken up at a reasonable hour. Needless to say, I didn't wake up. That is, until some poor unsuspecting couple who had hired the boat discovered me several miles downstream, soundly asleep in their bed. What ensued was a vast amount of screaming from a hysterical wife, a long walk home and a rather huge rollocking from a not altogether happy canal boat owner. It was also the last time I ever touched cider!

After an eventful first year, here we were marvelling at the shimmering waters of Lake Zurich as our train hurtled past Pfäffikon, Thalwil, Lachen and Rapperswil. I had taken this route many times as a child, having enjoyed holidays with my aunt Rebecca and her banker husband, Jurg, as well as spending time with my cousins and my great-aunt in Lachen. As I took in the beauty of our surroundings, with the peaks in the background, my mind wandered back to those summer holidays taken with my family. It was always with a sense of awe that I marvelled at their extravagant lifestyles, in a world that seemed so alien to my own. Those hazy days were full of memories, from water-skiing off a pier right outside their front door to endless hours of fun in their Olympic-sized swimming pool. My brother and I had gawped in amazement when our cousins showed us their collection of games machines, which wouldn't have been out of place at a Blackpool arcade. It had certainly put our paltry Nintendo to shame.

If in those early years we were somewhat overawed, it soon became apparent that this was the world my mother had been born into. My mum, although overt in nature, had always kept her past hidden. It took years for her to really open up on the dramas of her life, which in many ways put mine in the shade. Her life had certainly been dramatic and after countless let-downs it wasn't surprising that her trust in people had been severely tested. Over the years, I came to realise that she had a whole array of friends who she had helped with some kindness in the past and who in turn would now do anything for her. But if she could take some form of comfort from her friendships, the same could not be said about her family.

I soon discovered that she had what could only be termed a dysfunctional relationship with her mother. This had been the case from an early age, as she was told very little about her father. Further disappointment followed. When she was aged just four, she was left in a sanatorium to recoup from a serious infection, with seldom a visit from her mother. The situation was made worse by the fact that the doctors didn't know if she would even live. It appeared to my mother that she was a secondary consideration to her own mother, who was reluctant to give up her whirlwind of social activities.

After a tumultuous start to her life, and having *survived* a succession of *stepfathers*, life hadn't dealt her the best of turns when it was decided by her mother that it would be in her best interests to marry the somewhat stabling influence of my father. Aged nineteen, and with her beloved grandmother departed, my mother made her way – albeit somewhat reluctantly – down the aisle.

When I look back at those early photos, it was apparent from the word go that my mum had an aura of vitality that my father would always have trouble keeping up with. Rather than opposites attracting, this was a situation that was never going to end well. The only real surprise to me was the fact that it took her twelve years to run off with her hairdresser, who in turn became my stepfather.

If she thought there would be support from her mother – who, incidentally, had been married three times – it quickly proved otherwise. I guess if she had chosen a man from a different profession, events may have turned out otherwise, but a hairdresser was not deemed appropriate. She was promptly disinherited and became the black sheep of the family.

From my own recollections, I had always found my grandmother a rather glamorous woman, whose character was a little intimidating. She had none of my mother's warmth. As a parent, hers was certainly the old-school style of the child being seen but not heard. I still vividly recall childhood holidays, when my brother and I – aged eight and twelve at the time – would visit her in her dreamy location amid the mountains. But if we thought it would be an avalanche of skiing, sledging and frothy hot chocolates, then we were in for a rude awakening. Instead of taking in the joys of the slopes, our holidays were more akin to a boot camp. Our gruelling routine started at six o'clock in the morning and followed a pattern of walking up a mountain for the next five hours. If we felt such efforts should be rewarded with somewhat gentler pursuits, we were clearly wrong. After a quick break, the same pattern would follow in the afternoon and another summit would be conquered. In truth, the most enjoyable part of the holiday was getting into bed, which seemed the only respite from our torment and aching limbs.

My mother – who would hate me for saying so – had inherited a couple of my grandmother's traits, namely an immense work ethic, an eye for beauty and an abundance of creativity. Although they were both stubborn and single-minded, my mother oozed fun, warmth, generosity and compassion, traits that I didn't feel my grandmother possessed. As for my grandfather – whom I had never met and who was never mentioned in polite conversation – it transpired that he was in fact an aristocrat, who had courted my grandmother by turning up to the store where she worked in a chauffeur-driven Rolls-Royce.

She was a *lowly* shop assistant with grand ambitions; she was swept off her feet and they were quickly married. However, this was not before his mother issued her own ultimatum: *her* or the inheritance. Whether wise or not, he chose to marry beneath himself and forfeited his inheritance. Unfortunately, this was where the fairy tale ended, as my grandfather was unaccustomed to having to make a living. He was forced to use his considerable charm in several dubious deals that didn't end well. Not one to be carried away by the romance of it all, my grandmother promptly abandoned him. His name was never mentioned again. One thing was for sure, my grandmother never forgave my mother for having the wrong father. It was only later that my mother discovered he was the only man my grandmother had truly loved. As I said before, you couldn't make it up!

•

In terms of the rest of my family, the extent of the riches at their disposal only became apparent when I turned fifteen. Along with my stepfather, my mum and my brother, I journeyed down from the UK to Switzerland in our little Ford Fiesta. As we made our way into my great-aunt's driveway, my brother and I became wide-eyed with amazement at the collection of cars parked neatly in a row outside her house. It was every boy's dream, an array of Ferraris, Lamborghinis and Porsches. More amazingly still, Mum's cousin, Hans Peter, had arrived by private jet from his home in Monaco and regaled us with stories from a world we really didn't understand. All the while, benevolent relatives showered us with one-hundred-franc notes. It was a far cry from the pocket money I received from my father, who still gave me my age in pence per week! Yes, you read it right, fifteen pence a week!

Perhaps my fondest recollection of that trip was of my great-aunt, Hedy, taking my brother and me shopping in her hometown of Lachen. She was greeted with such reverence from acquaintances that it wasn't dissimilar to watching a scene out of *The Godfather*. As we entered each shop, the owners would be so effusive with their welcome and shower my brother and me with all manner of freebies. If the owners were amazingly generous, this couldn't be said of my great-aunt, who after shopping had been joined by her friends and our young cousin, Sven, in one of the local restaurants. We waited patiently in the searing heat, while Hedy gossiped with her friends for hours. If we thought we were going to enjoy a little treat, we were somewhat deflated when we were forced to share one small Coke with three straws for the next four hours. I guess that's the way you stay wealthy! If I ever doubted her wealth, then I was certainly made aware of it when we entered her local bank. She proceeded through the foyer and straight into the manager's office without so much as a knock. If he was evenly slightly irritated, it didn't show – he merely got up and treated her like royalty.

Years later, my mum told me more of my family history. Whereas I had always known that my great-aunt was a little frugal, my great-uncle was known for his generosity. He was a larger-than-life character, known for his humour and love of the finer things in life. A fact that probably led to his early demise. They had started out in a two-bedroom flat and by his death they were the proud owners of numerous businesses and properties throughout Lachen.

Unfortunately, my great-uncle, Hans, died when I was very young, and I have no recollection of him. But I did hear that when he died, the funeral procession stretched for miles and was attended by many people who, unbeknown to my family, had been helped by him.

One story that probably best showed the magnanimity of my great-uncle stuck with me. On the day of his funeral, one man was seen weeping close to the front of the church. My aunt had never set eyes on the man before, so she went over to introduce herself. She discovered that this man was the proud owner of a vineyard that had been in his family for generations. He explained that after several bad harvests, he had been close to losing the business. One day when my uncle Hans was having lunch alone at his local restaurant, he noticed the man in a distraught state. He went over and asked if he could help, and this stranger told Uncle Hans of his predicament. Uncle Hans asked if the man minded if he came over to inspect the vineyard and look over the books. The man agreed, and when Hans went through the accounts and saw the pride the man had in his business, he realised that, through no fault of his own, this man had just been unlucky. It was then that Hans offered him a small fortune to put his business back on the straight and narrow. When the man explained that he would never be able to repay such a debt, Uncle Hans had told him that his only wish was to receive a case of wine with his own logo each year. My aunt was astounded – Uncle Hans had never mentioned the story or the man.

•

However, if my uncle's story was full of happiness, the same could not be said of his descendants'. The adage that money doesn't bring you happiness was clearly right, as millions were squandered. Theirs is a story of greed, betrayal, suicides, alcohol and drugs that wouldn't be out of place in a Hollywood movie. That said, I'm not sure my story would have been much different if I had been privy to such wealth at an early age.

CHAPTER 8

Learning the right path – a high-end apprenticeship

As I looked over at Andy, I realised that we had already arrived in Chur. From here, we disembarked to clamber on board the picturesque train to our final destination, Arosa. As we made our way up the three hundred and sixty-five turns to Arosa, it was as though we were part of some fairy tale, surrounded by magnificent pines, glistening lakes and brooding mountains, like those I had seen as a child in the *Heidi* books. The beauty of it all overwhelmed me and I couldn't believe our luck. We were about to spend the next five months of the holiday season in this little piece of heaven.

It was down to my grandmother that Andy and I had landed this summer apprenticeship in the five-star Kulm Hotel. I later learned that many had clamoured for this job and although at first this prestigious hotel had been reticent to take on two English students, my grandmother's force of personality had secured us the chance. It had, of course, helped that I possessed a Swiss passport. But as we made our way through the last of the turns, I couldn't help but marvel that two impoverished students were about to earn £1,300 a month, with free board and lodging and a £300 bonus just for completing the season.

As we passed by the lake, making out the swimmers who were plunging gleefully into the crystal-clear waters, we really felt like we had arrived in the promised land.

On disembarking from the train, we were informed that our luggage was already making its way up to the hotel. Andy was astounded by this typical Swiss efficiency and muttered, 'This is the life, hey mate?' For a second, I was worried he was about to break into song, which was not an uncommon occurrence anywhere he went.

Having navigated the Swiss timetable, we boarded the bus and made it up the only through road and were deposited outside the hotel. It was there that we were able to take in both the understated glamour of the hotel and the beauty of the mountains. Quite literally on our doorstep. We were then briskly and efficiently escorted by one of the porters to the ever smiling human resources manageress, who seemed genuinely excited to have two English *gentlemen* in her midst.

After the mandatory paperwork, we were given a tour of the hotel. If it seemed a little unassuming from the outside, it soon became apparent that this was a treasure trove of delights on the inside. What followed was an assault on the senses: chefs shouting out orders, wonderful aromas emanating from exotic-looking dishes, waitresses in traditional Swiss costume barging through swinging doors.

In total there were four restaurants in the hotel, ranging from Thai cuisine to a typical Swiss Stube, but it was in the main hotel restaurant that Andy and I would be working.

As we entered the glass double doors, I just gawped at the scene in front of me. The lunch buffet – which I later found out was one of the least elaborate offerings in the hotel – was so spectacular, I couldn't prise my eyes away. It was literally breathtaking. There were vegetables intricately carved into flowers, ice sculptures, dozens of cheeses, freshly baked breads, mouth-watering desserts. As I looked over at Andy, his expression of awe mirrored my own.

As I took in the amazing vista over the mountains, I happened to glance over at the guests and realised that for them this incredible work of art was just standard fare in their daily lives. By the time we made it through the opulent Thai restaurant, the Terrace restaurant – with its diners basking in the sun – the Taverna with its mouth-watering pizzas, then the hotel's own nightclub and the mountainside spa, we were like rabbits caught in the headlights, wondering how we would even find our way around.

Having made our way through the entire hotel, we were finally shown to the staff canteen, where we were greeted by numerous nationalities, who in the case of the pretty waitresses gave us furtive smiles. Others were openly sizing us up as to whether we were going to be threats in what was clearly a pecking order. But if I was a little anxious, Andy was totally oblivious to the stares and had found something altogether more interesting. Following his gaze, I too was open-mouthed and couldn't believe the scene in front of me. Numerous staff were crowded round the food trolleys, devouring the wonderful dishes we had seen in the restaurant just half an hour previously.

'Oh, my God, I think I've died and gone to heaven!' Andy exclaimed. The human resources manageress confirmed that any dishes not consumed by the guests were given to the staff. I was flabbergasted. It was like eating in a Michelin-starred restaurant on a daily basis and put to shame the meagre offerings I was used to back home.

Exhausted and exhilarated, we were finally shown to our chalet. Our home for the next few months. With two stubby beers in hand, we took in the mountain views, grinning like two schoolboys in a candy shop. Our room was not dissimilar in quality to the hotel rooms of the guests. To our amazement, as the manageress departed, she added that even the staff rooms were cleaned every day. For those who had lived in staff accommodation in the UK, this would be a real revelation and totally unheard of.

·

When I look back now, it was the Kulm Hotel that moulded me and made me into the person I am today. The good and bad. This quintessential Swiss hotel would set the standards of service I strived for and the levels of training I would hope to impart to others down the line.

It also illustrated the huge discipline required in an industry that can best be described as intense. Those early days showed me that charm can get you a very long way, but it also taught me that to succeed, you must ultimately be adept at playing the game of politics. The rules of the game will become clear as my story unfolds, but for now suffice it to say that thirty years later, it is still a lesson I have failed miserably to learn.

My other life lesson was not to try to live the life of your guests. A catering salary falls somewhat short of your guests' income. I suppose I am a little less frivolous with my money than I was in those early days. But even just a few years ago, a friend of mine, James, my trainee in my early years of management and who later became a successful general manager (GM) in his own right, said to me, 'Woody, you know your problem. You try and live a champagne lifestyle on beer money!' Fourteen years my junior and still much wiser than me!

The fact is that when you serve the rich and famous, their lifestyles do tend to rub off on you. For me, it's always seemed to be a case of lobster or beans on toast. Unfortunately, for me there has never been a happy medium!

The first day of work set the tone for our new lives in the hotel. As we lined up for our first service, dressed in the check waistcoats and green bow ties that indicated our lowly commis waiter status, we were soon to realise that anything deemed as substandard would never be tolerated.

Next to me, a Portuguese commis waiter was ticked off for not having shaved properly. He was sent home to shave and told by Herr Kuhl, the maître d'hôtel, in no uncertain terms, that any more misdemeanours would result in the loss of half a day's pay. This came as something of a shock, and I breathed a sigh of relief when Kuhl passed me by.

Later, I found out from another waiter that tardiness was never tolerated. 'Late' meant not by a single minute. It transpired that if it happened a first time, you were sent home and lost half a day's pay, the second time a full day's pay and the third time you might as well pack your bags ready for the flight home. I suppose this was the reason that I was always at least half an hour early to work for the next thirty years. At least one lesson learned!

Every aspect of the job was carried out to perfection, down to learning every ingredient on the menu before each and every evening service. With our limited O-level German, this took up a major part of our afternoon break, but we were keen not to encounter Kuhl's wrath, so we studied far more diligently than we ever did in university.

Owing to the numerous nationalities and differing personalities, Kuhl and his assembled class always struck me as a rather comical sight. Kuhl epitomised the very essence of German discipline and had an overwhelming air of arrogance. His number two was his exact opposite – Paul, a Frenchman, resembled a hyperactive bulldog. But his charisma and fluency in ten languages had the effect of generating the energy of the restaurant. He and I would later form a close bond. Then there was Tex, a Portuguese who made up the rest of the management team and condescendingly addressed Andy and me as *boy*.

Our main problem seemed to lie with the chefs de rang or head waiters, many of whom were either Portuguese or Yugoslav and had spent ten years acquiring their red bow tie status. They in turn regarded us as little more than upstarts. To my relief, we were made to feel at home by a contingent of Maltese waiters, all of whom seemed to have matching moustaches, and by an ageing Italian, Francesco, who with his chubby features and receding hairline was not your stereotypical Italian. We soon realised he certainly had the banter and, while he was no John Travolta, he was always first up on the dance floor. The rest of the ensemble consisted of French, German and Austrians, most of whom were pretty waitresses.

I realised there was a definite hierarchy. Each person had their place and woe betide anyone who stepped out of this rigid formation. Many of the red bow tie status waiters had endured the harsh realities that Andy and I were soon to encounter. If we had thought we would be hobnobbing with the rich and famous, then we were soon to have a rude awakening.

•

On our first day, we were set to work on the breakfast buffet. I marvelled at the array of freshly baked breads, the multitude of cheeses, fruit and meat varieties I had not previously encountered. There were plates of salmon and caviar and buckets of chilled champagne. There were even twenty jugs of exotic juices, catering for every taste. The only resemblance to an English fry-up was on one solitary counter, where a chef, resplendent in a tall white hat, would prepare speck[1] and eggs in front of the eagerly awaiting guests.

---

1 Speck is a type of cured, lightly smoked ham typical in South Tyrol.

As hundreds of hotel guests descended like wild hordes and eager children piled up their plates, it became obvious that there would be little time for tittle-tattle other than the obligatory *Grüezi*, good morning, and *En Guete*, enjoy your meal. The pace became so overwhelming that just to replenish the ever decreasing buffet was no mean feat.

Luckily, I still considered myself to be reasonably fit, which turned out to be essential. I was expected to run down several flights of stairs for one solitary item. In the bowels of the kitchen, a multitude of chefs would masterfully prepare immaculate plates of food amid a host of wondrous aromas.

Panting my way up and down those stairs, I was struck by the discipline in the kitchen. There was hardly a breath from the staff under the watchful gaze of the legendary head chef Herr Egli, whom I affectionately named Schnutzi Putzi on account of his enormous, well-groomed moustache.

Some weeks later, I had the gall to call him this to his face. A horrified hush descended on the kitchen. This was a man who ruled his domain with an iron rod. I don't know if it was due to my comical Swiss accent or because it was such a shock to be addressed in this way by the *crazy Engländer*, but much to my relief he roared with laughter. It was in that moment that I realised the importance of a good relationship with your kitchen colleagues.

Before long, I must have navigated those steps three dozen times and was sweating profusely. If I thought there would be any respite or acknowledgement for my efforts, this notion was quickly put to bed by Herr Kuhl, who was constantly berating me for my efforts. As I went about my work, I noticed from the corner of my eye that Tex and his band of cronies were openly smirking at my initiation. But unlike red-haired Andy, who was always quick to flare at any perceived slight, I realised I would just have to take it on the chin and buckle down.

•

Having tidied the buffet, we were promptly put to work in the restaurant. I was shocked to see the amount of food that had been left, piled high on plates. I hate to think what my mother would have made of it. I remember that when we were kids, we were not allowed to leave the table before every scrap was eaten from our plates.

Once restaurant duty was completed, next came the job of the two of us hoovering the entire restaurant. Even the commis waiters were now smiling, not out of any maliciousness but simply because the gargantuan task of hoovering what felt like a football pitch had now fallen to the two lowly newcomers.

While we were trying not to miss a speck, Paul, the assistant manager, had come over to inspect our efforts. He was laughing as he related a story from his cruise ship management days of the occasion when two Albanians had argued over who was responsible for the hoovering. The argument was resolved when one of the Albanians took it upon himself to chop off the other's ear. With Paul still bellowing with laughter, I let it be known that although Andy could easily *get on my nerves*, I wasn't about to do anything that drastic yet.

After just four hours of our shift, we were already exhausted and grateful for a pick-me-up coffee and fag. But as soon as these were dispatched, we were set the task of preparing the restaurant. Every single piece of cutlery had to sparkle, and no single chair or table could be out of line with the next. Once this mammoth task was completed, the symmetry alone was something to behold. We were even told to crouch down and check the exact alignment of every item. This attention to detail was something we soon understood to be the norm.

•

If Andy and I thought we were finally going to 'wait' on a guest, our enthusiasm was quickly dampened when Tex beckoned us over and, with yet another smirk, said, 'Come, *boys*, follow me.'

We were promptly deposited in an airless cupboard, where we were greeted by crate upon crate of cutlery stacked high to the ceiling. Obviously impressed by his own English, he departed with the words, 'You clean!'

For the next two weeks this room was to be our *home*, for both the lunch and dinner services. We endlessly polished cutlery while listening enviously to the contented laughter of the diners in the adjacent dining room.

In those first two weeks we went back to our room exhausted and somewhat dejected, but this turned out to be just the start of our short apprenticeship. After the Sunday night's service, Kuhl informed us that we were to report to his office the next morning at six o'clock prompt. Not sure what to expect, we had foregone our customary beer the night before, determined not to be late. Hoping we were not to be reprimanded for some perceived fault, we breathed a sigh of relief when Kuhl greeted us with a smile outside his office and then proceeded to escort us – bleary-eyed – through the maze of the kitchen. To our dismay, we were then introduced to the silver burnishing machine, which, Herr Kuhl told us, would be our new friend every other Monday morning at six o'clock.

As we had never seen such a device, Kuhl proceeded to explain to us the ins and outs of this contraption. If we thought our daily polishing had been a chore, we were now about to enter a whole new world of grief. All the cutlery had to be coated with polish, passed through the machine and then receive its customary buffing. But as we eyed up the now familiar crates, Kuhl – still smiling – took us out back and it then dawned on us that not only were we expected to clean our restaurant's cutlery to within an inch of its life, but also the cutlery from the other four restaurants.

With Kuhl's words echoing in my ears, I noticed Andy had turned puce with rage. The red mist I had seen on many occasions was starting to overwhelm him. He sullenly enquired, 'And when do we get a break?'

Still smiling, Kuhl replied, 'When you're finished.' And off he went. I honestly thought Andy was about to chase him and deck him.

So, I grabbed his arm and said, 'Come on, mate, we've got this.'

'Bastard,' came the reply, but at least disaster was averted. I knew we were being singled out for every menial chore, but I wasn't sure if we were personally on trial or if this was the usual initiation.

We set about our task, with little of our usual chat. Andy contented himself by humming along to music, while I watched the nearby ever smiling Thai chefs go about their work. I had been amazed by the artistry of the food the chefs produced in the main restaurant, but these Thai chefs produced works of art on yet another level. I later described what I had seen to another waiter, and he proceeded to tell me about the wonders of the New Year's Eve buffet, which spread like a train through four rooms and, on top of their usual work, took these chefs three weeks to prepare.

After fourteen hours of polishing, hands wrinkled like prunes, Kuhl passed our efforts as acceptable. Andy was still furious. 'I didn't sign up for this shit!' he later exploded. 'For God's sake, we are supposed to be training to be hotel managers, not some sort of lackeys.'

I let his tirade go over my head. As much as I tried to appease him, it had been instilled in me from a very early age that nothing comes easy in this life. My mother, who I would readily say is still nuts in her seventies, gets up after five hours' sleep and had taught me a work ethic that has stayed with me until this day.

Even aged sixteen, I was used to walking the dog at 5.30 a.m., joining my mum at work at 6.30 a.m. and doing my homework by 8 o'clock, and this was before I walked the two miles to school. In those early years, I happily accepted that many of my weekends would be taken up renovating our home and garden in Shropshire. Although it was hard work, I can only remember these as being long days filled with happiness and laughter.

So, after a bit of cajoling, I managed to persuade Andy it was in our best interests to buckle down and keep going. I also reminded him that we were earning a small fortune. If they wanted us to polish all day, so be it.

•

As it happened, a couple of days later our luck changed. I was walking through the foyer when I overheard an elderly lady saying that she had misplaced her purse. After a brief search, I found the purse behind one of the sofas in the lobby. She was clearly grateful, and we spent several minutes exchanging niceties about my background. But as the director of the hotel, Herr Ziegler, approached, and not wanting to risk any trouble from neglecting my duties, I bid her a cheery farewell. I noticed the inquisitive look from Herr Ziegler as he joined the lady. It was only later that I found out she was a regular at the Kulm and spent several months of the year making the place her second home.

I was never sure what had passed between Herr Ziegler and the lady, but that evening, after another bout of polishing, Herr Kuhl summoned us over. I wasn't sure if he was happy about the situation, but it became evident that I had made an impression on both Herr Ziegler and the lady. Albeit somewhat reluctantly, Kuhl informed us that from the following evening we would be working on one of the stations. Elated, we went down to the restaurant's pizzeria and treated ourselves to a calzone, accompanied by our now customary boot of beer, which although it was a litre and a half always seemed to be downed in one. Hence our nickname of the *crazy Engländers*. We applauded our mini success, which turned out to be the first of many stepping stones on our eventual journey.

CHAPTER 9

Swiss tipping culture

The next evening, buoyed by our success, we made sure we were immaculately attired, knew the menu off by heart and had learned all the table numbers. But if I thought life was going to be any easier, I was soon to discover my next hurdle. That night I was teamed with Voyo, a Yugoslavian waiter who was very much part of Tex's gang. He was very rigid in his application of – in his words – *the hierarchy*. This was where it soon became apparent that we were not going to be singing from the same song sheet. According to our roles, it was expected that he would chat with the guests and take their orders, while I was expected to take the chits[2] back to the chefs in their different stations around the kitchen. From there, I was supposed to carry the plates on highly polished silver platters and leave them on our station, where Voyo would take the plates a couple of steps and present them to the guests with a flourish. The two rules, which Voyo made abundantly clear, were that apart from the customary 'En Guete', I was not allowed to linger and talk to the guests. Secondly, I was

---

2   In service, the name given to the order pads.

never, and he repeated never, allowed to take the plates from the station to the guests. This was far beyond my job description.

However, it wasn't long before the whole stack of cards came tumbling down. Firstly, the guests were surprised to be served by an Engländer and desperately wanted to converse with me. Even though I would be at pains to beat a hasty retreat, this obviously upset Voyo. Secondly, I became anxious because Voyo wasn't exactly the fastest *tool in town* and was letting the food go cold on the trays. Naturally, I broke all the rules and served the guests. At the end of the service, I watched as a clearly agitated Voyo approached Kuhl to vent his disapproval at the expense of his disobedient trainee. As it turned out, Andy had fared much the same with his head waiter, Antonio, who was another of Tex's gang. Antonio had now joined Voyo in a heated debate. I could tell by Kuhl's expression that he was trying to appease the pair and expected the worst, but Kuhl seemed unperturbed by the situation.

That night also taught me another valuable lesson in how the hierarchy worked. With the chef de rang inevitably giving out the bills for the guests to sign, it was they who received a discreet note slipped into their hands. Alternatively, the guest would hand over a far larger sum to a member of the management team, a tip deemed sufficient for the whole of their stay. It was pointed out to me that any tips had to be deposited in a box and the amount recorded in a black book. Paul was quick to point out that should a tip be pocketed, this would lead to instant dismissal. As my gaze ran down the pages of the black book, the sums were quite staggering. There were literally hundreds if not thousands of francs being deposited on a daily basis.

'How does it all work?' I enquired of the ever friendly Paul, who had by this time taken me under his wing.

'Basically, it's a points system dependent on your position. The higher up you are, the more points you get,' explained Paul. Of course, the argument went that the management were given the most as they had worked hard for their positions. But given their salaries, I was amazed that from a team of around thirty, the three managers took the lion's share of around 50 per cent. Not bad, considering the pot usually easily surpassed 20,000 francs a month. If this was to leave me somewhat aghast, what followed next left me reeling.

Over the next month, the guests seemed to take well to the somewhat outgoing Englishmen and in fact handed over most of the tips to me, further fuelling Voyo's anger towards me. As I proudly jotted down my daily takings, I noticed that my fellow commis waiters barely made an entry. The sums I was depositing exceeded that of the chefs de rang, which was totally unheard of for someone in my position.

If I thought these efforts were going to be rewarded, I was in for the shock of my life. When it came to receiving our monthly envelopes, I was well aware that I had deposited the regal sum of 2,000 francs into the pot. As I eagerly ripped open my envelope, my face fell as I counted out five paltry ten-franc notes. It was then that I realised that my one point in the hierarchy was all that mattered. That night – a little wiser – I went down to the

Taverna for my customary boot of beer with Paul and moaned about the unfairness of the situation.

'But Paul, it's just not fair. I wouldn't mind if it was a small amount, but surely there must be something I can do.'

'Yes, there is something,' he replied, smiling. 'Just don't get caught.'

•

My first month with Voyo was a constant roller coaster of highs and lows. I was delighted to be let loose on the guests and fascinated to encounter all manner of people from so many different walks of life. My interest was piqued by the way in which people thought. I was aware that what I may have considered completely unimportant might be deemed by the guest to be the most essential part of their stay. No two guests are the same and I was soon shown that it was crucial to anticipate their needs. Many of my guests were happy to chat along with me, but one couple made it clear that I was there merely to serve them and general gossip with the minions was not on the agenda.

Every night, this ageing couple would be the first to arrive for dinner. Both would be immaculately attired, as if ready for a ball, she resplendent in a glistening array of diamonds and pearls. Voyo informed me that they had been coming to the Kulm for over thirty years and spent at least two months every year at the hotel. I noticed from the outset that not only did they not converse with the hired help, but they barely acknowledged each other. I suppose that's the joy of married life. Although they were clearly wealthy, their existence seemed so joyless. Each and every night of their extended stay, they requested the same table, the same aperitif, the same half-bottle of wine, even the same tomato juice as a starter, declining the more appetising dishes on offer. The adage that wealth doesn't bring you happiness couldn't have rung truer.

Their attitude was in sharp contrast to the lady whose purse I had found. Although alone, she had a *joie de vivre* about her that you couldn't help but find infectious. She would happily chat away to all and sundry and was always the centre of the party.

It was on one of those first mornings, finally away from buffet duty, that I happily greeted her at the door of the restaurant. While ticking her name off the list, I noticed that several of the suites were booked under her name. Knowing that she was another long-stay guest, I couldn't understand why she was coming to breakfast alone. When I mustered up the courage to ask her why she had so many rooms, she happily told me, 'Oh, my dear, it's just in case any of my friends decide to join me. But of course, they have such busy lives.' I realised that this dear lady was spending thousands of francs on rooms that were barely used. I couldn't quite make up my mind if she was just overly generous or if, behind the facade, she was slightly lonely. Constantly astounded by the world I now lived in, I was even more taken aback when, a short while into her stay, she came over to me with a huge smile and dropped an envelope into my hand. Apparently, she had asked Paul if I would receive the tip she was about to hand over and he had informed her that the tip would be shared. So, she had taken it upon herself to think of a much more novel gift. I opened the envelope and was stunned to see a ski pass for an entire season. The look on my face probably gave her the most joy of her stay. She was one guest I would never forget. It was also my first lesson that it does pay to be nice!

•

By the end of that first month, my relationship with Voyo had fractured beyond the point of no return. He'd told me for the umpteenth time to stop talking to the guests and I was constantly furious that the plates weren't being delivered to the tables on time. Something had to snap. Determined not to vent my growing fury in front of the guests, I had stormed into the kitchen, literally barging through the swing doors into a bemused Andy. 'That fucking arsehole bollocks me for talking to the guests, while he lets the fucking food go cold rather than doing his fucking job!' I yelled at him. Andy, somewhat surprised that his usually patient friend was now on the edge of hysteria, tried to appease me, fearing I was heading either for a fight or out of a job.

'He's not worth it,' he whispered above the din of the kitchen. After my moment's rage, I managed to make it back into the restaurant, with my best fake smile etched on my face – inwardly, I was seething.

But two things happened after that evening. Firstly, unbeknown to me, Herr Egli, the head chef, had overheard my rant and was either impressed by a commis who showed some spirit or was just happy that I wouldn't put up with his food getting cold. I never did quite find out. But for whatever reason, the second thing that happened was that neither I nor Andy worked with Voyo or Antonio again. Much to the relief of both of us.

From the next day on, Andy worked with the amiable Ratko, while I was paired with a flamboyant Australian named Eric. Eric was well into his forties, but he thought he was still in his twenties and was constantly hoping to ensnare some poor unsuspecting waitress with his charms and his beach-blond waves. He certainly had the banter, but to my surprise he always cut a lonely figure in the staff canteen. It appeared that either his ageing gigolo persona was not greatly appreciated or that, like his English counterparts, he just didn't fit in. Andy and I took to him immediately.

In that initial season, it wasn't just us at war with some of our colleagues but also the outbreak of the Yugoslav Wars, which brought about other tensions in the staff canteen. Former friends sat apart and, even in this little mountain resort, there were noticeable frictions among the differing parties.

If all was perhaps not always rosy away from the guests, I was grateful that I was no longer spending my days perpetually arguing with Voyo and was taken under the wing of the charismatic Eric. It turned out that my new role involved serving all the drinks in one half of the restaurant. With close to one hundred and fifty thirsty customers to serve, this was no small undertaking. It was made even more challenging when the guests would all arrive at pretty much the same time.

Fortunately for us, many of the guests, particularly the Swiss, would leave half their wine and half their water for the following night. This was certainly not a notion I was familiar with back in the UK and to this day I can't remember any occasion when I have left some wine over for the next day. Being able to deposit the wine on the table in advance turned out to be a lifesaver as it gave us a little respite in what was always a full-on service. With the more relaxed Eric and the autonomy the role afforded me, I started to enjoy the work once again, even if it still had its demands.

Of my apprenticeship with Eric, I can still recall a couple of events that are etched in my memory. On one of those first evenings, one particular guest ordered a red wine that was priced at around 500 francs, a small fortune to me. To be honest, I was scared to touch it, let alone open it. As this was my wine apprenticeship, I was hoping that Eric would take over, but unfortunately, he was already tied up with other guests. Being accustomed to opening bottles in the normal manner, I was horrified to learn that bottles of this age needed to be opened in a basket and then decanted over a flame, so that there would be no sediment poured into the glass. This was well past my university education, but after a quick explanation about the finer points from Eric, I thought, what could possibly go wrong? As it transpired, the answer was a lot. Trying to overcome my nerves, I went over to the table, pretending I knew exactly what I was doing. What Eric had failed to tell me was that with a wine of this age, the cork tended to disintegrate, and that pulling it at an angle made it even more difficult. I was determined not to be beaten and went about the task as manfully as I could.

Several minutes later, with the cork refusing to budge, I realised that panic had set in. I was sweating profusely and had also turned crimson. With a final flourish I proudly produced the cork, only to realise that half of it was still lodged in the bottle. Now I was reeling at the prospect of having destroyed a five-hundred-franc bottle of wine. And God only knew what Herr Kuhl's reaction would be.

Unfortunately, this turn of events had turned me into a caricature, not dissimilar to Mr Bean. After several more minutes, I managed to retrieve the remainder of the cork without it being permanently laid to rest at the bottom of the bottle. If I was in any way apprehensive, the jovial German guest had found the whole scene highly amusing. He simply roared with laughter and the rest of the table burst into a smattering of applause. When I finally managed to dislodge the offending cork, I took my leave. My dignity was barely intact, but I vowed never to be put in that situation again. I spent many spare hours practising on empty bottles.

My second recollection was of the week when we had a delegation of the top salesmen from one of the high-end German car manufacturers. I soon realised that this week had to go without a hitch. Herr Grandjean, the food and beverage manager, and his sidekick, Herr Mariacher, made one of their rare appearances in the restaurant to ensure everything went smoothly. The whole atmosphere became tense. Florists buzzed through the foyers, chefs busied themselves in hushed silence and even the usually affable Paul seemed irate at the merest blemish on an already immaculate restaurant. Andy and I realised that the best course of action was to keep our heads down and stay out of the line of fire as much as possible. Even Kuhl had lost his usual arrogance.

As we lined up after breakfast, Kuhl went through the evening's service and menu with a fine-tooth comb and constantly harped on about the importance of that evening's gala. The preparations meant that there was no break that day, but the opulent glamour of the restaurant made all the extra effort worthwhile. As Andy and I readied ourselves in our immaculate white jackets with gold braiding, we were already relishing the festivities ahead. We couldn't wait to see the spectacle that was about to unfold.

The evening was to be a six-course tasting menu accompanied by bottles of Perrier-Jouët champagne varying in price from a modest 50 francs up to several hundred francs a bottle. The gala dinner was for three hundred guests and half of these would be served by Eric and me with five different champagnes. So, as the evening started and a band struck up, the anticipation was clearly palpable. In the end, exhausted and foregoing our nightly trip to the taverna, Andy and I had slumped into our beds, eagerly recounting the night's events.

On the final day, we all breathed a sigh of relief, and when the final guest had departed, I reminisced enthusiastically to Sabrina, the receptionist. As we chatted, I jokingly said, 'I don't know what all the fuss was about.' She smiled and handed me a copy of their bill. The amount exceeded two million Swiss francs!

'That's what all the fuss was about.' With that, she returned to her duties.

CHAPTER 10

Settling into the Kulm Hotel

As the season wore on, we finally managed to buckle down into a routine and our only real concern was remembering which of five uniforms we were supposed to wear on any given day! Although it was clear that we would never be accepted as anything but those *boys* by Tex and his cronies, a discernible shift had taken place with Herr Kuhl. The charm of the English boys was now being discussed throughout the hotel. Kuhl had realised that this had not gone unnoticed by either the management or the guests. This shift in attitude made our lives a great deal easier. But if we seemed to have a little more latitude from certain quarters, we never took anything for granted.

It was also true that we knew it was wise not to upset the management duo of Grandjean and Mariacher and by and large we kept our distance. As with all Swiss hotels, the top positions were always held by Swiss nationals. There were no complaints there as the standard of life, not to mention the salary, far exceeded anything any of us could dream of. I later met several Sri Lankans, who cheerfully told me that they were doctors back home and were now more than willing to wash dishes for hours on end. If there was any cause for resentment at their lowly positions, never once did I encounter anything but a happy smile and a friendly greeting. It wasn't long before my admiration grew even more, when I discovered that many of them had worked tirelessly for thirty years, saving every penny, and had never once led a lifestyle approaching what was fast becoming my norm. I would love to tell you that I acquired this discipline, but that would never be the case. I often think about them, retired at fifty and sipping cocktails in the pool back in their homelands.

Over those few months, I realised that I had a way with people. A way that put them at ease, and an ability to adapt my personality to suit each guest. Over time I learned when charm was appropriate and even realised I could push the boundaries to the limit without causing offence. Not only had Kuhl realised the effect Andy and I had on the guests, but it had also come to the attention of Herr Ziegler – the general manager – who was always ready with a cheery word.

In that first season, a mutual admiration emerged that later developed into a lifelong form of friendship. After many of our raucous nights out, we would often see Herr Ziegler busy at his desk, although it was well into the early hours of the morning. It was due to this dedication that he had become the youngest director of a five-star hotel in the whole of Switzerland. On a couple of occasions, I had been called into his office to help him with his correspondence and had been rewarded for my efforts. If at that time I had rejoiced at having the *ear* of the director, it would ultimately lead to my downfall. A very hard lesson learned, but that came much further down the line.

•

After a somewhat hard initiation, the season passed by, with Kuhl having warmed to the two Englishmen. We struck up friendships with Clara, Ziegler's Spanish PA, as well as Sabrina, Kuhl's fiancée. Arosa became my second home, and I came to love this beautiful sleepy village at the top of the mountains. Most afternoons, we would while away our breaks by swimming in the icy waters of the lake, enjoying the summer sun on our backs.

With Kuhl's growing approval, I was now entrusted, along with a chef de rang and a chef, to take the guests for picnics in the mountains. There, the chef would prepare feasts on the barbecue, while we would chill beers in the nearby stream. It came as a welcome break from the rigours of the restaurant and gave me a chance to mingle informally with the guests. Herr Ziegler also took all the trainees walking from Arosa to Davos across the tips of the mountain, where the scenery was breathtaking. After a lunch fit for a king in one of the secluded mountain restaurants, we then walked all the way back. I had gone to bed exhausted but mesmerised by the whole experience. On those days, life couldn't have been much better, and I knew my decision to work in catering had been the right one.

•

What I came to love about the Swiss was their efficiency in everything they did. Trains ran to precision. Recycling was already years in advance of our own. No car was allowed to be driven through the resort after eleven o'clock at night and baths could not be taken in flats after ten o'clock in the evening, so as not to disturb the neighbours. It was a criminal offence if you failed to register with the canton when moving from one county to another.

I discovered that my grandfather, although married to a Swiss, would need to reside in the same house, in the same canton, for ten years before gaining citizenship. Military service was compulsory for anyone below fifty and went on for several weeks of the year. Considering the country was neutral, I couldn't believe the number of Swiss who not only possessed guns but had nuclear shelters underneath their homes. My uncle had also warned me not to fall foul of speed limits as the Swiss didn't just hand out the usual fine and a loss of licence, they even fined you a significant percentage of your wages. My uncle Jurg, who by then was vice president of a Swiss bank, had told me how he had been driving back to Zurich and was anxious to get home. He had been well over the speed limit. The police not only took his licence but fined him 10 per cent of his annual salary. A costly mistake. Fortunately for me, I hadn't yet learned to drive.

You couldn't help but admire the way of life. I would say that the Swiss are more than a little conservative, and many thought that Andy and I should be placed in some sort of straitjacket. Others seemed to like the excitement we brought. We noticed that everybody spoke English, which did somewhat curtail our attempts at what can only be described as one ugly language.

If our work routine now conformed to Swiss standards, the same could not be said of our after-work curriculum. Usually finishing work around ten o'clock in the evening, we then had the temptation not only of the resort's two nightclubs, but also the delights of our female colleagues. Our nightly ritual consisted of a swifty or two in the hotel's taverna, followed by a couple of games of pool at the casino's pool hall. Finally, we would arrive at either Nuts disco or the aptly named Kitchen Club. What I loved about our new haunts was that, because of their diminutive size, we knew everyone from the bar manager through to the guests and the employees from other hotels.

Whereas in England I rarely received a second glance, despite my best efforts at strutting my stuff, it seemed Andy and I were always surrounded by a whole bevy of beauties. The only downside was that it was the start of the nineties, but the Swiss clubs thought that good taste was being stuck in the seventies. There was no end of ABBA hits and YMCA. At first, we begged the English DJ to play some *decent* music, but were constantly knocked back with the reply, 'Sorry, the management won't allow it.'

We moaned like two disgruntled teenagers to Werner, the bar manager, 'Why can't we hear any decent tunes?' It was then we realised that, in Switzerland, anything goes when you have money.

'But of course, you can have any music you like, if you buy a bottle of champagne,' came the reply.

We scanned the drinks list and gulped at the 250 francs asking price.

Then in unison said, 'Let's do it.'

From then on, we were the first on the dance floor and the last to leave the club. I never could understand how we arrived back at university just as broke as when we started. But unlike the Swiss, we seemed completely unable to nurse a beer for an entire night. Our revelry usually finished around two o'clock in the morning, when we staggered back to the hotel and were quickly sobered by the mountain air. We usually had a couple of colleagues in tow, who by now were taking it in turns to keep up with the Engländers.

On one particular night, we had crept past Herr Ziegler's window and could still make out the dim glow of a desk light. Trying to be as quiet as possible, we made it back to our chalet only to realise that we had left the keys inside. Luckily for us, we had left a window open. Unluckily, it was on the first floor. Not deterred by our predicament, we tried to get up on the escape ladder, several feet above our heads. What harm could it do? With me balancing precariously on Andy's shoulders, we spent several minutes swaying miles away from the ladder. Giggling like kids, we were greeted by Herr Ziegler, who in turn didn't know whether to laugh or cry. We put on our best impersonation of being sober and finally made it to our beds at three o'clock in the morning. At 6.30 a.m., I was dressed and greeting guests for breakfast with an ever-happy smile. As Herr Ziegler wandered past, he noticed my rapport with the early risers, smiled and shook his head.

•

Around this time, Andy started seeing one of our work colleagues and I started dating a rather charming German housekeeper by the name of Sylvia. While most enjoyable at the time, the next turn of events was to signal the demise of mine and Andy's friendship. You see, Andy thought it was quite acceptable for him to play away from his supposed girlfriend, but on one evening I had received an offer from a rather beautiful blonde waitress. I am ashamed to say I had been flirting with her incessantly at the oddly romantic setting of the pot wash. That night, we all spent the evening at the club, and I secretly evaded Andy's and Sylvia's watchful eyes. Said waitress and I hopped into a taxi to rendezvous back at her staff quarters.

All was going rather well, until Andy decided to burst through the door. Unfortunately for me, I was already in the first throes of passion, with my trousers down to my ankles. He then proceeded to remonstrate with me for my selfishness. Of course, that kind of put a dampener on both my libido and that of the beautiful blonde, who was less than impressed by the intrusion. As Andy's tirade threatened to wake the whole staff block, a hasty retreat was probably the best course of action, even if my trousers round my ankles made a dignified exit a tricky prospect. You could argue that Andy had my best interests at heart. But to my horror, as I furtively returned to

Sylvia's room, lo and behold, who should be sitting in her chair but my erstwhile friend Andy. Not content with ruining a potentially memorable moment in my life, he had decided to blurt the whole thing to Sylvia.

What transpired was that Sylvia forgave me, but Andy and I spent our final weeks in the mountains exchanging barely a word.

When we bid a fond farewell to the beautiful Arosa, with at least our bonuses in our back pockets, I knew this was just the start of my love affair with Switzerland. Arriving at a grey Luton airport, I wished I hadn't returned, and returning to Guildford and the university confirmed that my heart wasn't in it. I knew the importance of having a degree, but by this time, rather than attending lectures, we were both either working in the local Trusthouse Forte or frittering our meagre funds on nights out.

Sven had warned me it wasn't going to end well with Andy. Sven was my one calming influence and as he was paying for his university course himself, inevitably his nights with us became fewer. To complicate matters further, from the moment we first met, Andy and I had gambled between ourselves on just about everything we did. From golf to darts, pool to tennis. The problem being that at the beginning, Andy mostly won. I in turn paid out. However, the tide turned, and I started to win. Unfortunately, Andy didn't deem it essential to pay his dues. One evening, working at the Trusthouse hotel, events escalated and during an after-work drinking session with a colleague, Andy and I – both clearly drunk – descended into a row. Egged on by our colleague, who was ex vice and should have known better, we engaged in a full-scale fight. Even though the fight probably resembled a couple of old ladies with handbags, this wasn't the wisest move as the staff canteen was on camera. It wasn't one of our finest moments.

In the early hours, without a word being uttered and still fuming at the night's events, we staggered back to Guildford station and hopped onto the train for the short ride home to Godalming. Before long, Andy was happily snoring away, and as the train came to our stop, I tiptoed past him and closed the door behind me without an ounce of remorse. Several hours later, a rather irate Andy screamed down the phone from sunny Portsmouth. What is more, he had no cash on him. As he yelled obscenities at me, I pressed pause and curled back into my duvet with just the hint of a grin.

A couple of days later, I rang my mum, checked out with my tutor – the affable Freddie Lawson – left Andy a note and never saw Guildford again. That was the end of *the riddle and the rave,* and, like Guildford, I never saw Andy again. Another lesson learned.

CHAPTER 11

Back to Switzerland with a new plan of action

Once home, I came up with the plan to return to Switzerland and earn enough money to enrol in the prestigious Swiss hotel management school, Les Roches. A few weeks later I was back *home* in Arosa, starting out for another season in the higher position of demi chef de rang, along with a slightly higher salary. This time I had my eye on the prize and started to save diligently, so I could return to full-time education.

•

After that second season, Helen, a colleague of mine, mentioned that she and her partner spent their summers working in the beautiful Ermitage Hotel in the sleepy village of Küsnacht, situated on the banks of Lake Zurich. This small luxury hotel radiated understated opulence. There were two restaurants, the casual beach club, with picturesque views of the lake, and the more refined Michelin-starred restaurant, which saw a whole host of diners disembark from their luxury boats and amble down the hotel's pier to enjoy the immaculate gardens and decadent food. In the centre of the beach club there was a circular bar, where the well-heeled residents would come to admire the lake's glistening waters.

Whereas the Kulm had a more family feel, the Ermitage was an adults-only playground for the more discerning clientele. Through Helen, I secured the position of chef de rang or head waiter. The staff were much younger than the more regimented team at the Kulm Hotel and there was less feeling of a hierarchy. Each waiter oversaw their own station and with that came the added reward of keeping your own tips, which was a huge bonus.

The restaurant manager was the amiable Herr Fuchs and even my German supervisor, Andrea, although formidable, turned out to be less intimidating than the foreboding figure of Herr Kuhl. The rest of my small crew were the outlandishly garish Sibi, who cut a comical figure with his long locks, eighties-style perm and matching *tache*. Then there was Andreas, a suave Italian, two sweet Finnish girls and an Austrian, another Andrea.

The kitchen was some hundred metres away from the terrace, so you quickly became adept at carrying large trays, full to overflowing, balanced precariously above your head. Should you forget one single item, you were rewarded by having to make it all the way back to the kitchen, and with so many guests this was not a situation you wanted to find yourself in. Another problem was that although the Michelin-starred restaurant had the same number of seats inside and out, the beach club, while seating over a hundred on the terrace, had only thirty seats inside. This meant that if the weather changed, there was bedlam as there wasn't enough seating to go round. It also transpired that the contract I had signed stated that should the weather be good, I would be expected to work any hours the management deemed fit.

That summer turned out to be one of the hottest on record, so time off became something of a luxury. I started in the morning at ten o'clock and finished at around midnight, with a small break in the afternoon. Although the work was gruelling, it was enjoyable and very rewarding.

My workmates, without the stuffy formality of the Kulm, made life enjoyable, but the icing on the cake was that my tips easily doubled my salary, such was the generosity of the clientele. If I thought I was doing well, I almost keeled over when I spoke to the barman who looked after the prestigious beach club bar. It turned out he was well known among the affluent bankers and the ladies who lunch. He spent the day schmoozing the jet set and the early hours as head barman at the infamous club The Kaufleuten. This pattern of work meant a 10 a.m. to 5 p.m. shift at the beach club and a 10 p.m. until 3 a.m. stint at the Kaufleuten.

'Aren't you exhausted?' I enquired.

'You get used to it and besides, I can then travel for several months of the year.'

'But why the two jobs?'

'Oh, that's easy,' came the reply, and at the end of just one summer season he showed me exactly how good he was at looking after those guests with their very deep pockets.

'Come, Dave, I want to show you my season's tips.'

Not knowing what to expect, I followed as he led me, smiling, into the hotel's car park. 'Jump inside, we'll take it for a spin.' He opened the door to his brand-new Porsche Carrera.

'Not bad for a season's tips.' He beamed. I realised then that I still had a long way to go.

Returning to my little room on the outskirts of Zurich, it was now a ritual to deposit my stash of tips in a little tin marked *school*. There was one week that would forever make me smile. During service, if the phone rang it was our job to drop everything and deliver any requests for room service. The terrace was invariably full, so this was something of a nightmare. The last thing you needed was to disrupt your flow of service and race around the hotel.

Well, it so happened that for five days we had an Arab princess staying at the hotel. On her first day the phone rang and my supervisor, Andrea, was busy and said, 'Can you take a tea up to room thirty-three.' Funny, I can't remember my wedding date, but I can remember a room number from thirty years ago!

Cursing my luck, I made the fruit tea and bounded up the stairs, praying that my guests wouldn't miss me. When I made it to the room, I was greeted by one of the most beautiful women I have ever seen. Trying to compose myself, I asked the princess to sign for her three-franc pot of tea. Astounded, she signed the chit and slipped me a hundred-franc-note tip. At first, I thought it was a mistake, but she ushered me away with a smile and explained, 'That's for you.' Buoyed by my success,

I decided to keep it under wraps from my colleagues. A few hours later, the phone rang again.

'I can't believe it, she wants more tea,' announced Sibi, exasperated.

Trying to act nonchalant, I quipped, 'I've got time if you like?'

Unaccustomed to such enthusiasm for room service, Sibi was happy to delegate the chore and sure enough, another 100 francs came my way. I can happily report that this princess stayed five days, received three cups of tea from me a day and was happy to part with 100 francs a visit. You do the maths. That week still makes me smile but I was wise enough not to divulge this information to my colleagues until after the season had finished!

The work continued with never a quiet moment and now the team had a daily ritual of swimming in the lake next to the restaurant, both in our afternoon break and at the end of the service. Those icy waters were the only respite for our aching limbs. I have to say that our little team usually created quite a stir. Sibi was not dissimilar to Liberace in appearance and thought it quite reasonable to shock the neighbours with the most outrageous pink thong, complete with fluffy codpiece.

But if my afternoons were awash with campness, my evenings were taken up with two burly German chefs by the name of Mike and Marco. These two shared the apartment next to me and couldn't have been more opposite to the effeminate Sibi. To me, this is the beauty of catering – the people you meet are so diverse and would never be described as boring.

I had always thought of myself as fairly observant,

but there's the odd occasion when it becomes clear that I really don't have a clue. Take Andreas the suave Italian, for example. He could only be described as your stereotypical Italian love god, who never once seemed to be without an entourage of adoring women. When he suggested a night out at one of Zurich's clubs, I readily accepted. My imagination got carried away at the thought of all the lovely ladies he attracted. Besides, surely, he couldn't manage all of them? But then again, he was Italian, so who knows?

We had agreed to meet outside one of the clubs and I was genuinely excited about the evening ahead. Maybe owing to this excitement I didn't really take in my surroundings, even when we happily chugged away at a couple of beers at the bar. The atmosphere was electric and, noticing a couple of rather cute young ladies, I suggested a go on the dance floor. In my defence, the lighting was rather low, but Andreas seemed pretty impressed with my old schoolboy moves of trying to rub my bum as close as possible to the *babes* next to me. These moves were rarely successful in my school days, so you can imagine my delight when not one, but two pairs of arms were wrapped around me. Roll over Italy, here comes the next love god, I thought. It was then that I noticed the *babes* had a little more to them than I expected. As John and Mark introduced themselves, I made my excuses and beat a hasty retreat to the bar, followed by a clearly amused Andreas.

'Why didn't you tell me it was gay night?' I asked, trying to compose myself.

'I thought you knew,' he replied with a smile as one

hand slipped onto my thigh. 'And anyway, don't you think it's about time you came out?'

While I almost choked on my beer, all images of hot Italian women quickly dissolved in front of my eyes. It took me several more minutes to dissuade a clearly aroused Andreas from taking his advances any further.

As you can imagine, I kept my distance from Andreas from then on, but this didn't deter him from trying to convert his latest recruit. Now, I have lots of gay friends – my son's godfathers are gay – but I can't understand why gay men have obviously found me attractive. Surely, they can see the heterosexual manliness coursing through my veins?! It's funny that the image of yourself obviously isn't what you portray. Many years later, a good friend of mine, Tina, told me, 'All the girls in the office thought you were off limits.'

'Oh, because of my girlfriend, Ewa?' I replied.

'No, because we thought you were gay.'

Inwardly, I wondered how this was possible. A couple of years later, I saw myself on telly and, not recognising myself, I croaked, 'Bloody hell, I sound gay,' and put on a voice several octaves lower. So, forty years too late, I worked out what all the fuss was about. As they say, 'Every day is a school day'.

CHAPTER 12

Good-time Charlie and falling
in love for the first time

At about this time, I noticed the rather beautiful Daniela, who worked up on reception. As she made her daily trips down to the kitchen, I did everything possible to ensure she noticed me. With my limited Swiss I did my best to impress, much to her amusement and the amusement of the chefs who were eavesdropping. Most of the time, my words were a jumbled mess. My usual *blah de blah* had clearly deserted me.

I realised then that, for the first time in my life, I was truly smitten. She had such an aura about her. Eyes that sparkled with a mixture of adventure and naivety. Her hair was all silk curls and her smile left me weak at the knees. But what shone out was her intelligence and zest for life. She was one of those people who lit up a room with her infectious laughter but never realised how beautiful she was. If I was taken by her, so were many of my colleagues. One day, Mike the chef miserably informed me that he had blown his chance by turning up late for a date. While I inwardly rejoiced at his news, I knew I would need to be on my best behaviour to earn her affection. I informed Nina, the Finnish waitress, that although I'd had a lovely week with her friend Tina, who had visited Nina on holiday, I couldn't possibly continue the holiday romance and suggested it probably wasn't the best time for Tina to return from Finland. But guess what? Tina turned up. So, not the best start to my romance with Daniela.

While Tina spent the week with her friends, I stayed far away from temptation and started what turned out to be a magical time with Daniela. What ensued was a fairy-tale romance. Romantic all-night strolls along Lake Zurich, weekend breaks to the glorious mountains of St Moritz, trips to Lugano and Locarno in the laid-back Italian part of Switzerland. These turned out to be my favourite parts of the country. We swam in the lakes and snacked on shellfish. We dined in glamorous restaurants and sipped mojitos in the sun. As the season ended, we decided we would try living together in the mountains of Arosa. Daniela secured a job as receptionist in the Park Hotel, and I managed to get a promotion to the rank of chef de rang in the Kulm Hotel.

Everything started out wonderfully, with our relationship going from strength to strength. Daniela had managed to secure us a lovely apartment in the middle of town. It was a little too close to the Nuts nightclub but at least it meant I wouldn't have to rely on staff accommodation.

Work began and it couldn't have got off to a better start. Paul, the assistant manager, had my back and I still had the confidence of Herr Ziegler, the hotel director, while Kuhl pretty much left me to my own devices. Friendships were struck with chefs, and Herr Egli made an exception and allowed me to tag along to a chefs' party, although this did end with me and the handsome chef Salvatore performing our own rendition of *The Full Monty*. Considering the conservatism of the Swiss, this went down pretty well with the entire restaurant. Twenty years later, the poor restaurant owner still remembered me and happily retold the tale of that infamous night to anyone who would listen.

I was still enjoying fairly wild nights out with Paul and recall that, rather than paying 20 francs for the three-minute taxi ride to the club, we travelled down the only road in Arosa hanging on for dear life to the back of the hotel's baggage trolley. We parked it outside the club, much to the astonishment of those waiting in the queue.

•

In the restaurant, I was now in charge of my own commis, a French guy whose easy demeanour was certainly a breath of fresh air compared to my experience of the previous two seasons. Although fun to work with, he made it clear from the outset that he didn't regard the role as a job for *life* as many of those who spent their whole lives working in the hotel did.

Around this time, and towards the end of a shift, Herr Kuhl mentioned that the suave head barman needed help in the panoramic bar. He always worked alone in the guest bar and many guests would make their way to him for after-dinner drinks. Many of the requests were for cocktails and he would soon be overwhelmed, so he asked if I could help him out. I obliged and it wasn't long before he was teaching me a whole host of cocktails. I don't know if he had a bit of a soft spot for me, as many had suggested, but I couldn't help but admire this suave man who had such rapport with the guests. I helped him on many occasions after my shifts ended and for a mere hour's help, he would discreetly slip me the princely sum of 100 francs. This wasn't far off what I was earning per day.

•

These were probably my happiest times at the Kulm and apart from the odd deserved slap from Daniela for returning home late, life couldn't have been better. By this stage, I was being invited out regularly by guests for both dinner and after-work drinks.

I realised a certain amount of charm could go a long way and it wasn't long before I came to understand just how far I could go, even with the cheekiest of comments. One evening, we were practising our silver service skills and I spent the evening parading around the restaurant with a rather large platter of vegetables. As I prepared to serve the potatoes, one shot through the air and landed *plop* between a poor unsuspecting guest's breasts. Apologising profusely, I came out with the first thing that came into my head. Smiling, I asked the guest if I could be of assistance and help to retrieve the offending item.

Kuhl had overheard the comment and was literally ready to hand me my P45, but to his astonishment and mine, the lady literally purred, and her husband roared with laughter. Much to Kuhl's annoyance, these guests became friends and even made Herr Ziegler aware of the esteem in which they held me. Although I have many faults, the ability to assess who I can and can't say things to has stayed with me throughout my career!

•

However, a succession of events was ultimately to burst my bubble. Perhaps my overconfidence led to my downfall? I was already aware that there were a number of people who were unhappy at my rapid promotion. But I had so much support that I went around somewhat oblivious to the daggers that were already being sharpened.

My first problem was Charlie. Charlie was a Dutchman who worked in the hotel's terrace restaurant. With his languid walk and lopsided grin, he was without doubt the most laid-back individual I have ever met. Considering we all worked in the cauldron of a very busy hotel, I don't think Charlie ever overly exerted himself. Charlie's parents owned a restaurant in Amsterdam, but he was not ready for the burden of accepting his inheritance. Charlie spent half his time as a snowboard instructor and if this failed, he would resign himself to a stint of waitering. Once he'd earned enough, he would spend the rest of the year getting quietly stoned in a hammock on some beach in Thailand.

It wasn't long before we started to enjoy the odd Grolsch or two in Rhondos, Arosa's only pool hall. Unfortunately for Daniela, this was located thirty seconds from our flat. The lovely thing about the Swiss and pool is that they invariably think they are rather good and are all too happy to part with Daddy's hard-earned cash. We quickly realised there was a golden opportunity to at least recoup some of our beer money. We had a good deal of success, but it wasn't long before I realised that Charlie outshone even me when it came to self-destruction.

I remember one night we had cockily challenged these two guys to pool and stupidly agreed to play for beers. We opened up a lead and managed to consume eight of our favourite Grolsch. With our bravado increasing, we failed to realise that our opponents had barely consumed a drop. Do you think sense prevailed? Of course not. By this stage we could barely see the table, never mind the balls, and it wasn't long before we managed to lose every penny in our pockets.

Although I didn't realise it at that moment, this was the start of my downfall, through no fault of Charlie's. It started one night in the Nuts nightclub, where it soon became obvious that Charlie was smitten with the attractive new English DJ. He spent the night drooling, while I, not wanting to invite the wrath of Daniela, decided to make an early night of it. Not thinking much about the night's previous events, I went into work as usual. Barely had I entered the door when I was accosted by an agitated Grandjean, the food and beverage manager. He had always reminded me of one of the two professors from my early *Tintin* books, but I quickly became aware that humour wasn't at the forefront of his mind.

'You two are always as thick as thieves, where the hell is he?'

At first, I didn't know what he was on about and asked, 'Who are you talking about?'

'Charlie, of course.'

'I really don't know,' was my honest reply. Now, I knew I had left Charlie in the club and although he was laid back, he always made it to work on time. So, when he didn't turn up on either that day or the next, even I began to get concerned. Much to our growing alarm, we couldn't find him anywhere.

To our relief, he waltzed in on the third day with a huge grin and not an ounce of remorse. He was accosted by a food and beverage manager who was clearly ready to explode.

'Where the hell have you been?' came the roar. To my amazement, Charlie didn't even make an excuse. He merely grinned like the cat who had got the cream.

'Well, I woke up to the most gorgeous girl I have ever seen and after the night I had there was no way I was leaving her bed.'

A deathly hush descended. Grandjean stormed off. With a smile, Charlie joined me for coffee. It was his first offence and because we would have been left short-staffed, it was decided that Charlie wouldn't be sacked but also wouldn't be allowed a break for the rest of the season. Rather than being upset, he took it on the chin. It was clear by the smile in his eyes that he spent the rest of the season reminiscing about those two wonderful nights.

To give you a true perspective of Charlie's character, after we left the Kulm I didn't hear or know where Charlie was for almost a year and a half. Into my second semester at hotel school, somebody I knew informed me that he had been in a bar in Montreux and had bumped into someone who knew me. Lo and behold, two days later, Charlie rocked up at my front door.

After a good night's catch-up, it became evident that as usual Charlie had no idea what he was going to do or where he was going.

'Can I stay with you for a bit?'

My school accommodation was somewhat cramped so I wondered how we would manage but agreed anyway. After lectures, I returned to a very happy Charlie, who was clearly dying to tell me his news.

'I've got a job,' he announced happily.

Pleased that he had found something, I asked, 'And where is that?'

'Oh, I'm in charge of running the bungee jump.'

'Oh fuck' was all I could think of at the time.

Charlie, of course, didn't take it personally.

Charlie stayed a month, sleeping head to toe with me in my single bed, while he spent his days *working at the bungee.*

One day he mentioned that he could save me 100 francs if I fancied a complimentary bungee jump. So, with a friend in tow, I decided to take him up on a tandem jump. As we lined up, Charlie greeted us as if he were some sort of emperor on his throne. His lopsided grin was even more in evidence than usual, and it was then that I realised he was completely stoned. An American lady in front of us was clearly apprehensive about the impending descent. As Charlie strapped her in, rather than reassure the poor woman he merely smiled.

'Well, if the straps round your legs don't work, at least you've got the other one around your waist.'

Obviously not thrilled by the observation, off the lady went, hoisted by the crane with her clearly audible screams of terror ringing out.

'Going well then, Charlie?' I enquired. I remember the thrill of the jump. Along with the thought, *please bounce*. But to this day, I am still petrified of heights and flying, something I never was before. Not long after that, Charlie departed and I've never seen him since, but I always like to think that he's lying somewhere in his hammock, with that lopsided grin of his.

•

My next problem came with Eric, my rather laissez-faire commis. Eric thought that turning up on time was not in his remit. After a multitude of warnings, Eric failed to learn his lesson. Grandjean informed him that, as he was incapable of making it to work on time, his services would only be required in the evenings. This meant his salary would be halved. Rather than being upset, Eric was delighted. Now he could spend half of the day snowboarding.

Not long after, over a particularly busy Christmas period, Kuhl asked me to work a forty-eight-hour shift, with only a couple of hours' rest.

Towards the end of the shift, another commis and I, bereft of sleep, had a fit of the giggles while clearing away the remnants from dinner. Herr Mariacher, the assistant food and beverage manager, passed us and was clearly not amused. I explained that we were just exhausted and apologised.

However, this cut no mustard, and he declared, 'We are all tired.' This came from a man who spent a large part of his day in the staff canteen playing *Space Invaders*. I was stupid enough to mention this. I tried to apologise but from that day on my card was marked and I received my first warning.

•

As the season drew to a close, Kuhl – who had presided over the restaurant for over a decade – rather than be elated that he was moving to a better position at a new hotel, became increasingly arrogant with both the guests and the staff. He was also aggrieved because I was still on good terms with his jilted fiancée, Sabrina, thinking that I should have sided with him and his new love, who I never had time for. Whereas before he had taken delight in having been part of my rapid development, he now thought I had garnered far too much favour.

Two weeks before we were due to finish, I made the fatal error of turning up late. As it was my first time in three seasons, it didn't really faze me too much. However, the usually jovial Paul nervously told me that Kuhl wanted to see me in his room, which was something that never happened. After three seasons enjoying his constant backing, I was still not overly concerned. When I knocked on his door, I was surprised to see Kuhl lounging on his bed in his underpants. With a coolness only a German can impart, he casually informed me that my services were no longer required, with the parting words: 'You should never have thought yourself bigger than me.'

Stunned, I made it back to the restaurant and saw the apologetic looks on the faces of my friends, who obviously knew of my fate. From there, I was led into Grandjean's office. It wasn't long before I was fuming. Kuhl had blatantly lied and said that it was me and not Eric who had been late nine times. I knew I wouldn't be able to appease him. He felt the same way as Kuhl, if not even more strongly. My final lifeline came with Herr Ziegler, the director of the hotel. I tried to reason with him and state my case, but this is where hierarchy in a Swiss hotel will always win. Although he knew Kuhl was wrong, he wouldn't go against a man who had served the hotel so admirably.

With two weeks to go, he agreed to pay my salary in full and gave me my end-of-season bonus. He wrote me a glowing reference and even told me that there would be a job once Kuhl left.

I know that over those three seasons I did a whole host of things that could have merited my dismissal, but I also did whatever it took to make those guests happy. By the time I left, I was inconsolable at what I considered to be a gross betrayal. I declined the offer to attend the end-of-season staff party. I left the Kulm a little wiser, with amazing memories. But if I thought for a moment I would ever be able to play the game of politics… Well, thirty years later I'm still hopeless.

On the plus side, even after all this time, Herr Ziegler still remembers my time at the Kulm Hotel fondly, as do I. We still meet up for lunch to reminisce about those times that forged everything I now know.

The Lipp Brasserie, Zurich

After Daniela and I left Arosa, I attended interviews at the Palace Hotel in Lucerne, the iconic Badrutt's Palace in St Moritz and the Dolder Grand in Zurich. Thanks to my glowing reference I was offered jobs in all of them, but they were unwilling to give someone the title of chef de rang before an initial season's training. By this stage, my main aim was to return to hotel school, which was to cost me 30,000 francs, so taking a reduction in pay wasn't an option. After several phone calls, I landed an interview at the Brasserie Lipp, just off the famous Bahnhofstrasse in Zurich.

I didn't really know what to expect, but the restaurant turned out to be yet another of Zurich's institutions. It resembled the classic French design of the Lipp in Paris, but what astounded me at that first interview was the sheer numbers ploughing through the doors. I was informed that on average there were five hundred evening diners. The menu was classical French and centred around such favourites as platters of fruits de mer, where the seafood was flown in fresh each morning.

CHAPTER 13

Over a thousand oysters were consumed in a single day. The vast menu also included choucroute au saucisson, bouillabaisse, steak tartare and moules marinière. The testimony to this menu is the fact that, apart from the specials, it hasn't changed in thirty years and nor has the number of diners.

Apart from the main restaurant, there was an up-market expat bar, known as The Lion Pub, which was like a gentleman's club in London, and the Jules Verne Panorama bar, fourteen floors up with stunning views of surrounding Zurich. The crowning glory of the whole interview at the Brasserie Lipp was not only that I got the job but also the salary involved. I knew it was better than I was previously used to, but the extent became clearer when I started.

•

Embarking on my first week's training with an older waitress named Ruth, it soon became clear that this was no ordinary job. The pace was relentless and after just one day my feet were so sore, I could barely walk. The restaurant was headed by the amiable Herr Bratschi, and my colleagues certainly made me welcome. Not only were they multinational but so were the guests. It wasn't uncommon to try to converse in three different languages at one time. Even if I wasn't fluent, I certainly gave it a go.

I soon became aware of the need for speed as each waiter was responsible for twenty-five covers that even for lunch were full twice over. If this wasn't hard enough, the evenings were even harder – you served somewhere approaching seventy covers. In all of this, the only help you received was that someone prepared your drinks for you in the dispense bar. The only other place I later worked at that came to close to these numbers was the Bluebird in West London, but even then there were two waiters per station.

The beauty of the whole operation lay in the fact that although it was extremely hard work, the financial incentive was huge. At the age of just twenty-one, my base salary was the same as my previous jobs – around 2,500 francs a month. Where it went to another level was that there was also a commission element. A monthly revenue for the restaurant in excess of a sum equivalent to £12,000 saw us earn commission of 12.5 per cent. As a typical month would see sales exceed £30,000, this meant a substantial commission. On top of this, there was no service charge and we kept our own tips, which usually exceeded £100 a day.

In the space of eighteen months, I was able to save the 30,000 francs needed for school, live in Zurich and enjoy a lively social life. As you can imagine, when I returned to England and my assistant manager's salary didn't make it to £10,000 a year, it came as quite a shock.

What made this system really work was that if, say, the manager required someone to help for an extra shift, then the commission alone meant the staff would jump at the chance. If there was a flip side, it was that mistakes came at a price. For example, my trainer, Ruth, was once in such a hurry when she used the old-fashioned manual card swipe that she failed to realise the number impressions hadn't made it onto the paper. As the guest was a 'walk-in', there were no contact details, so there was no way to retrieve the money. This one error cost her over 1,000 francs.

The same could be said if you made an error ordering drinks or food. If either item was prepared without the mistake being realised, the staff member covered the cost. We quickly learned to tot up bills in our heads to avoid mistakes. This has stuck with me ever since. It made me think twice about everything I did, but if you made a mistake once, you certainly didn't do it again.

This system is the best I have worked under, but it's only successful with a business that is guaranteed to be full. That is the reason catering is seen as a career in Switzerland, unlike in the UK. Two of my friends went into banking and finance after our Lipp days and they both said that it took several years to surpass the amounts we were earning back then. There are two testaments to the extent to which the system works. Firstly, on my return to the restaurant two years ago, six of the team I worked with nearly thirty years earlier were still employed there. Although these staff are only fifty, they should be retired soon. Secondly, I remember enthusing about the whole concept to the then private owner of the restaurant. He explained that the generous incentive encouraged up-selling, which increased sales. With little staff turnover, everyone won. He aimed to pay all the restaurant's bills by the end of November, then all the turnover for December was his.

'Not the profit, the actual turnover?' I asked, astounded.

'Yes,' he replied, smiling.

No wonder he was smiling: December's turnover exceeded one million Swiss francs. Not bad for showing your face for dinner, I thought!

•

If I had become more disciplined with my work, then the same could not be said for my social life. During my eighteen months at the Lipp, as well as working in the restaurant, I spent a considerable amount of time working in the Lion Pub because of the large English-speaking clientele. It was here that I teamed up with the ever jovial Brummie John and a Swiss guy called Urs, who resembled a huge Viking. The pub resembled an English pub but only in what could be described as a *Swiss way*. There were quite a few Brits working in the banks and they would quite happily down a few pints before staggering home. The Swiss financier, on the other hand, is a totally different kettle of fish and drinking is something that is definitely frowned upon. So, whereas the English would approach drinking with their usual reckless abandonment, the Swiss financier would order a tiny one-decilitre carafe of wine. Now, to me, one decilitre is not even a taster. Consider too that the price will far exceed the price of a bottle once drunk in quantity. It amazed me how many guests nursed their tiny carafe but before long had managed to consume fifteen of these and fared little better than their English counterparts when trying to make it through the door.

The second thing that surprised me, other than the £8

pints and the £20 burgers, was what would occur on the weekends. By and large, our clientele during the week were businessmen or ladies who lunch, but on weekends we were crammed with Swiss youths, swilling cocktails and enjoying the novelty of an English bar. On my first night, I was astounded to notice that, although the bar was packed, rather than take payment at the bar immediately, my fellow barmen would slip a chit in a glass showing the amount the table owed. Now, although not yet in the league of the English, the Swiss youths certainly had no problem running up a tab of several hundred francs. To my astonishment, even with such a packed bar, not once did we have a problem getting the bill settled or have so much as one table just walk out. Can you imagine telling Bob in the UK he really had had ten pints rather than the two he was claiming? It would be total mayhem.

The Swiss also showed that if there was a problem, they were quick to resolve it. In one instance, it wasn't a guest but an employee. In the Jules Verne bar, there was a very charismatic French barman – at the time, one of the best-known barmen in Switzerland. As a long-standing feature of the Jules Verne, he had many followers who would queue to get into this diminutive bar. One day there was a huge commotion. Apparently, the general manager had been a little suspicious about the revenue declared from the bar, so they sent someone undercover to see what was afoot.

Unbelievably, they saw that every night the head barman brought in a bottle of his own spirit and when the customer paid cash, he failed to ring it in. A shot of gin was around £14 and there are twenty-eight shots in a bottle. Although caught red-handed, the barman was moved on quietly with minimal fuss – as is the Swiss way. The guy was an institution, and the restaurant didn't want the scandal.

He moved straight into another plum job in a different establishment, but the management had estimated that his one bottle a night had cost the restaurant around 300,000 Swiss francs. If he didn't pay for his crime, then we certainly did. Both bars were subsequently fitted with devices that registered every pint poured and every shot served. Every last bottle of Coke had to be accounted for and if there was one error, it came out of the tips.

It was in the restaurant where I met Marco, another outrageously camp friend, and Don, a Canadian who has never left Switzerland and who ended up as one of my life-long friends. It always amazes me that after so many years, we still regress to the twenty-year-olds we once were, albeit a little greyer and – in my case – a little plumper, but the friendship has never altered. While my aim was to attend hotel school, Don was studying for his Master's in business and finance – no mean feat, considering our staggeringly long hours and our nocturnal after-work activities.

Our days usually ended with the three of us enjoying drinks in a dingy bar down the Bahnhofstrasse, which was about the only place to stay open until three o'clock in the morning and to serve a pint that was under £10 a pop. Our nightly sessions hit such an extreme that, rather than incur the wrath of Don's poor wife, Sidonia, and my neglected girlfriend, Daniela, for returning home so late, we resorted to camping out on the tables outside the restaurant. It was there that we would be discovered the next morning. At least we were never late for work!

•

If Don heeded the warnings of his wife, I would still find willing accomplices in John the Brummie and Urs the Swiss Viking. Both had partners, but they also knew how far their better halves could be pushed! My nights out with Don were curtailed after an occasion when we returned to his home, somewhat late and a little merry. I had happily passed out on his sofa but was soon awoken by the sound of glugging water and a very irate scream. Trying to open my eyes, I was confronted by the hysterical sight of Sidonia and a Christmas tree that had toppled over and was now spewing water everywhere. I protested my innocence, but Sidonia clearly didn't believe me, and Don was soon under a strict curfew. It took a long time but after thirty years, I have finally been forgiven for my alleged crime. Don still sends me a yearly picture of an ever larger Christmas tree with the caption: *Imagine the damage you could do with that*. It was probably the only time in my life that I was actually innocent.

As home was too far to go back to for afternoon breaks, it had become my norm to have a bite to eat and a few pints in either the Oliver Twist pub or the English pub. Like the Swiss, I was now alternating between pubs as I worried about being perceived as some sort of reprobate. In the afternoons I was joined by Al Kadri, a fellow waiter who had escaped the conflict in Lebanon and arrived in Zurich as a refugee. As he recounted his epic tale, I was amazed to learn how the Swiss allowed him entry but only if he stayed in one canton and worked at least ten years at the Lipp. His is an inspirational story of success. Thirty years later, he still lives in Thalwil with his first sweetheart, a Norwegian, and their children, and continues to work in the restaurant. He is still full of stamina and his greeting is as enthusiastic as ever. Although he might have joined me in the afternoons, he was wise enough to know which side his bread was buttered and always made it home after work.

When I look back now, the perils of catering are obvious, as is the strenuous nature of the job. The incessant pressures of a demanding clientele and the ridiculous hours can soon lead down a slippery path of either drink or drugs. I have always been too scared of drugs – or perhaps, knowing my own addictive personality, I've been clever enough to stay away. But drink was now playing a major part in my life.

The thing about catering is that it's very hard to calm down from the unceasing buzz of the day. It didn't matter that after a day's work you could barely walk, most people needed something to take the edge off. When I look back at my high jinks, I put them down to youthful exuberance – primarily because even if I was consuming over ten pints on most days, I could still do my job with only a few hours of sleep. Of course, you only look back on the good times, whereas in reality I was on a dangerous path – even at that early age. It wasn't until I reached my thirties that I had some semblance of control and that was only really because by then I was a manager. In truth, I had to reach the age of thirty-five and meet Ewa before I was firmly put on the straight and narrow.

CHAPTER 14

Girls, girls, girls

After a couple of years of being besotted with my first true love, Daniela, two events happened that would throw my world into turmoil. Firstly, back in Zurich, I met a German waitress named Katja and, secondly, I went to hotel school in the Swiss resort of Crans-Montana.

Now, I have to say the scenery was tempting in so many ways. Sixty-six nationalities in such a confined space were a little too much temptation for me to handle, and my antics were to get me in a whole heap of trouble that seemed to magnify every time I tried to extricate myself from a problem.

My first faux pas came shortly before I was due to leave for hotel school. Several of the team from the Lipp were enjoying some after-work drinks at the Oliver Twist pub, in the old part of the city. One thing led to another, and I ended up going home with Katja. Now, to my credit, I came clean with Daniela and after many tears she decided to forgive me. Daniela, I have to say, was the kindest person I had ever met, and I still feel remorse for the way I behaved. Perhaps if I had met her ten years later and not been at the stage where *my cock ruled my head*, as my mum so eloquently put it, the outcome may have been far happier. Sadly, I was far too immature and selfish at that time to realise what a great person I had.

Unfortunately, Katja moved into a flat close to Daniela and me, and the next couple of months became a little strenuous, as I really didn't know which flat to call home. As a result, I moved out of both flats. However, things never turn out quite how you expect and Daniela – rather than walking away – decided that I might be worth saving. Rather than accept defeat, Katja – on hearing that I didn't think we should carry on the relationship – began sending a whole array of gifts to me at hotel school, as well as turning up unexpectedly on my doorstep on more than one occasion. You would have thought I had learned my lesson, but instead I tried to become intimately acquainted with as many nationalities as possible.

By this stage, my mum, who adored Daniela, was fielding numerous tearful calls, mostly asking where the hell I was. Katja, rather than backing down, became even more persistent, while I embarked on two further relationships, which only added to the stress. The ridiculousness of the situation became apparent when I hooked up with all four of them in three different cities in the space of three days. Were those days fun? Yes, they were, but ultimately, I was weak and they deserved better.

•

If I was certainly more *worldly wise*, both my naivety and my curiosity were to get the better of me on more than one occasion. During my early days at the Kulm Hotel, I had travelled to Zurich for a night out with a friend and spent the evening at my favourite haunt, the Oliver Twist.

Now, at the end of the evening, in rather a jovial frame of mind and enjoying one last cigarette before I made it back to my hotel, I sat content at an outside table, watching the world go by. To my amazement, a rather cute Asian girl joined my table and enquired if I would like some company. Thinking how nice it was that even in a big city like Zurich, Swiss people made such an effort to have a chat, I accepted. As we introduced ourselves, my only real concern was that the poor girl might be a bit underdressed, as the evening was turning chilly, so of course I chivalrously offered her my jacket. As the pub was now closing, she suggested going back to her flat for a drink, which I thought was a little forward since we had only just met, but hell, why not. You only live once. So, we proceeded to her flat, conveniently located just a couple of minutes from the pub. Once inside her apartment block, I was amazed at all these couples passing by who looked so happy, although, strangely, even the gents were giving me curious smiles. I guessed the Swiss really were a happy nation. She made us both a drink and started to gyrate provocatively in front of me. But rather than oozing sexuality, it seemed a tad rehearsed for my liking. Looking back, it was something more akin to Mrs Brown with a handbag. Noticing my distinct lack of interest, the once sweet girl seemed irritated by my lack of appreciation for her dancing skills.

'Well, aren't we going to get down to it?' she enquired.

Now, this was too forward even for me. I mean, I'd only just met the girl. It was only when she uttered the words 'It will be a hundred francs for straight, anything else will be extra' that I finally clicked. Thinking she may not be very impressed by the twelve francs fifty that were left in my back pocket, I made my excuses and bolted for the door, followed by a volley of shoes hurled in the direction of my head and the threat of calling the police. As I said, in some ways I was still very naive.

•

Not only did my naivety cause some fairly interesting moments, but so also did my inquisitiveness. On one of my frequent visits to Zurich, I noticed a rather interesting cinema named the Stüssihof that apparently screened a number of adult-rated films. I watched as a string of businessmen exited the back door, clutching their briefcases and looking round furtively as if hoping they wouldn't be spotted by some acquaintance. Well, judging by the clientele, I couldn't see myself being bundled into the back of a van, so I thought, what the hell. My curiosity piqued, I flipped through the *Zürcher Zeitung* newspaper and discovered there were in fact three such cinemas in the city. I decided to check out what it was all about on my next visit. We certainly didn't have such places back in the UK.

On my return, with my stomach in my mouth, I plucked up the courage to walk along to the Kino Walche, as it seemed far enough away to spare me bumping into anyone. Nearing the door, I practically jumped out of my skin as someone I knew honked their horn and offered me a cheery wave. Now a total bag of nerves, I pretended I was heading in a different direction and continued to circle the cinema while I regained my courage to enter this *forbidden zone*. Being a young male with a pretty healthy appetite, I did not want to be perceived as part of the dirty mac brigade, but even so I couldn't help my curiosity.

I approached the cashier, perspiring slightly, and it took me several minutes to hand over the notes, my hands were shaking so much. The receptionist, who was probably used to seeing everything, barely gave me a second glance and continued to feast her eyes on the latest women's weekly. Still shaking, it took me several attempts to put my ticket in the turnstile. Head down and praying there wasn't someone else I knew, ignoring passing stares in the corridors and the moans that seemed to be resounding from every wall, I breathed a sigh of relief when I finally made it to the back of the cinema. I cowered down to watch the movie.

Thankfully, the cinema was almost pitch black. I settled down to watch Ron Jeremy in action and thought that if he was the world's biggest porn star, then perhaps there was hope for the rest of us. But if I thought I was in for a relaxing film, it turned out the gods thought otherwise.

Although there was a multitude of seats available, one suited and booted gentleman decided what the heck and sat right next to me. With a smile, he gave me the usual Swiss greeting, *Grüezi*, hello. Not wanting to appear rude, I smiled back and returned the greeting. I settled back down to watching the film, but the man now appeared to be fumbling around under his coat. Almost tempted to ask if he had dropped something, my eyes almost popped out when— well, let's just say it wasn't his keys he had out and appeared more than happy to display to all and sundry. Taken aback, I escaped to another seat as quickly as I could. As far away from the gent as possible. I never did see much of that film, because what ensued was a classic game of musical chairs. It seemed as if it was only me who didn't gain pleasure from exposing myself in public.

Abandoning any hope of watching the film, but determined to carry on regardless, I noticed several cubicles at the back of the cinema where I might be alone with my thoughts and finally enjoy any number of movies in peace and quiet. I was even happier to discover that the cubicle door could be locked from the inside.

Any illusions of peace were quickly dispelled by a succession of discreet knocks on my door. It seemed that, as the new arrival, I had prompted a whole army of advances that I had definitely not bargained for on my arrival. I made it abundantly clear to the suited and booted gentleman that I was terribly sorry, but he wasn't of my persuasion, and I was then accosted by a somewhat rounder lady, whose suggestions only made me wonder, *does she really think that's possible in a cubicle of this size?* I was certainly no athlete and although I admired her perseverance, I doubt either of us would have made it out alive.

If I thought matters couldn't get any worse, I was totally exasperated when I heard yet another knock on the door. *Bloody hell, is this a queue for Disneyland?* I wondered, but lo and behold it was the receptionist, who informed me that I had triggered the alarm by not putting any money in for the film. Now at my wit's end, I bypassed my newfound *friends* and made swiftly for the exit. *Welcome to the land of erotica*, I thought. As I have said before, fantasy and reality are certainly not the same thing.

•

Even now as I look back, I can only ask myself, *what are the rules?* I mean, there are no clear guidelines as to what is and isn't acceptable behaviour. Are my experiences just the same as any young male or have I pushed my luck a little too far? I guess every individual is different. As a youngster, you may revel in your exploits to your friends and embellish your prowess, but you certainly wouldn't go to your parents for any advice. Even now, when Mum starts to tell me about her colourful past, I roll my eyes and say, 'That's more than I need to know, thanks, Mum.' At the age of fifty, I guess I still couldn't be sure how discussing my adolescent trip to an adult cinema would be construed. Was I some sort of deviant or was it perfectly normal?

On that matter I probably needn't have worried, as Mum happily recounted a tale of her own to me. Apparently, in the not-too-distant past, she and a friend had decided on a trip to London and rather than the usual shopping spree, they decided to check out the delights of Soho. I can only imagine the hilarity of the situation as they walked into a sex shop like a couple of giggling schoolgirls – not least as I perceived her friend as rather conservative – and grimace at the thought of my mother looking in amazement at the objects of pleasure flashing before her eyes.

When one rather exuberant item caught her eye, she exclaimed, 'Bloody hell, there's no way that thing would go anywhere near me.'

Her otherwise demure friend had my mother in hysterics when she replied, 'Oh, I'd never have had a problem with that. My gynaecologist said you could drive a double-decker bus through mine.'

I realised two things after that: firstly, I would never be able to look at her friend without remembering the story, and secondly, perhaps the apple doesn't fall far from the tree after all and my antics weren't quite as bad as I imagined.

•

When it comes to my experiences with the opposite sex, I would never entertain the notion of relating any gory details to friends; it just seems plain wrong to talk about wives and girlfriends in that way. So yet again I ask myself, would a friend be surprised or appalled by my antics, or revel in them? All I know is that one person's *fun* is not the same as another's, but as to whether it's right or wrong, I still can't tell you the answer.

Take the taboo subject of anal sex. I have known girls who would coyly ask if I fancied giving it a try. Others who've said, 'If you go anywhere near there, I'll snap your bloody fingers off.' And one who thought it was as natural as having a cup of tea.

When the subject was broached with one friend, he was incredulous that such a situation should ever arise, but happily recounted the tale of how he enjoyed three-somes with a girl and a friend of his. I'm sorry but the thought of having my friend's hairy arse anywhere near me makes me recoil in terror, as does the thought that his libido might be in any way superior to my own. Yet again, what is right? Each to their own, I suppose, is the answer.

•

Few members of the opposite sex really tell you what it is they deem acceptable and what clearly isn't. That said, I knew one girl who would settle down on the sofa with *Debbie Does Dallas* in much the same way as most people would watch a rerun of *Emmerdale*. I have also known one of my more adventurous partners ask me whether I was into watersports, and who was perhaps less than impressed when I replied, 'Oh, I've always fancied the idea of taking a canoe out on Lake Zurich.' It's not always easy to tell what's really in someone's mind!

Even when you think you finally know your other half, your best efforts may not be quite as enticing as you had imagined. I have always considered myself a considerate lover and having taken on board female friends' advice that it's not all about *wham bam*, and finally learned where all the erogenous zones are – without having to consult a diagram – I did my best to impersonate Casanova and provide what I thought was one of my better performances. After forty-five minutes of well-thought-out foreplay, my erstwhile partner chirped up, 'For God's sake, will you stop faffing around down there and just get on with it.'

That's the problem with the Brits: we just aren't great at communicating our feelings. If she had expressed her desires clearly and at least forty minutes earlier, I wouldn't have ended up with a face so beetroot it looked like it had been attacked by a Brillo pad. When it comes down to it, I think our female counterparts really just want to humour us and let us believe we have some sort of clue about what's really going on.

Trying to impress a somewhat younger lover, I couldn't understand why after five minutes her enthusiasm had waned. When I enquired after her well-being, she replied, 'Oh, you finished me off ages ago.' Even then, it didn't dawn on me that my prowess had warranted the joyful shriek in my ear and I thought perhaps it had something to do with the chocolate bar I had inadvertently left in the bed and which was now firmly stuck to my arse! Thirty years of trying to understand the workings of the female mind and I still might as well have been seventeen.

CHAPTER 15

Hotel School, Switzerland

Having saved the fees, I ventured into the world of hotel school, in another scenic setting – the world-renowned resort of Crans-Montana, well known for its skiing and famous golf course. Although glad to have the opportunity to study and determined to make a better fist of it than my first efforts, nothing had prepared me for the world I was about to enter.

The school was the epitome of everything Swiss. Set in the tiny village of Bluche, it was approached via the tiny funicular up the mountain from Sierre. The school had thought of everything, and I was amazed to see that the kitchens were decked out with state-of-the-art induction cookers. These hadn't yet appeared even in the most prestigious hotels. We were decked out in uniforms and our three-year course consisted of a year in service, a year in the kitchen and the final year in management. This was punctuated with a six-month stint in one of the Swiss hotels. With my newfound enthusiasm, I couldn't wait to start and certainly didn't want to waste the 30,000 francs I had worked so hard to obtain.

The one thing I hadn't anticipated were my fellow students. While I had been working, I had always felt that I totally belonged in that environment but at hotel school – bar a few exceptions – I felt like a pea out of a pod. A handful of other students were also paying the fees themselves, but the majority seemed to come from a world much more privileged than my own and on the whole, I felt like I didn't belong.

As just one example, an Indian guy reluctantly had to send his maids home as the school didn't think a maid service would teach him much, considering his first week would be spent washing up in the school canteen. Two other students were expelled from both the school and Switzerland when an arsenal of weapons was discovered in their rooms. Hadn't they realised they were in a neutral country?!

It wasn't long before the extent of the wealth at the disposal of many students became evident. One night, I went to a casino in Montreux and watched a fellow student blow the equivalent of my allowance for the whole semester in just an hour. More often than not, I returned to Zurich at the weekends to enjoy familiar surroundings and people more on my wavelength.

However, I did make friends with Anjay, my room-mate, a Kenyan who certainly had the same eye for the ladies as I did. Even after all our ups and downs, twenty-eight years later we are still friends and, although our bodies may have grown older, our characters have remained the same. The rest of my cast included Bryan (a hyperactive American), Ollie (an Australian who was never short of an opinion) and Graham (a Scotsman who spent most of the semester as champion of the games machine).

It was probably only in my final semester that I really enjoyed all the school had to offer. I managed to pass my service year with a distinction, mostly because I learned everything from working rather than from the course. The kitchen year proved a little more testing and although these days I can rustle up a mean breakfast and tell you how something should look and taste, I'm damned if I can remember the hours I spent making a consommé or practising how to fillet a whole animal from scratch.

In between semesters, and to my relief (not least because I needed the money), I was able to complete both my apprenticeships back at the Lipp. Although I passed the last term with a merit, I missed out on the elusive overall distinction by 0.1, due in part to my frequent trips to Zurich. But in general, I was satisfied with my results.

•

When I look back at those days, it is perhaps not with the same euphoria that most of my fellow students seemed to feel. As I have said, I never felt as if I belonged. Was it all worth it? Now, that's a difficult one. Sure, I acquired a lot of knowledge, but like most things, you tend to learn more on the job. I think if I had stayed in Switzerland and made a concerted effort to master that 'beautiful' language and let my Swiss passport open doors, then my diploma would have meant a great deal.

Unfortunately, although it was a box ticked, I was soon to discover it was never really what you knew, but who you knew. With three great references from three world-renowned hotels, I thought I would walk into one of the top establishments back in the UK. But to my shock, I was rejected by big names such as Chewton Glen, the Four Seasons and the Savoy without so much as an interview. Bad timing? Overconfidence? Maybe. But I wasn't really surprised when fellow students with lesser grades and certainly limited experience found their way through similar doors. Doors have also opened for me through people I know, and I guess that's the way the way the world works. But I sometimes wonder if the money could have been better spent. Although, knowing me, I would have found a whole host of ways to squander it anyway!

•

Switzerland will always hold the fondest of memories for me and over the years I have considered moving back. Ultimately, I have stayed in the UK, and I guess there is always a reason. I still go back and catch up and reminisce and have even had the odd job offer or two; but although the remuneration has been highly tempting, I have always thought it would be a step back. Anyway, where could I get a full English or a Yorkshire pud? Priorities!

Part Three

CHAPTER 16

2019 – Life and death

I guess I have been lucky when it comes to witnessing the demise of a loved one. I simply haven't been there when it has happened. Grandparents have come and gone but I have been spared the heartache, as it has always occurred while I've been in some other part of the country. My one consolation is that they have been surrounded by love and I think that is all anyone can hope for.

When I hear of all those unfortunate souls who have lost loved ones through this Covid crisis without so much as a farewell hug, my heart goes out to them. My grandparents all lived to a ripe old age and for my own part I'm just happy that after so many years apart, I did at least get to have some part in their lives. At least towards the end.

As I get older, death and illness become much more prevalent and as the years tick by I've become increasingly aware of my own mortality. Over the last few years, my existence in my B&B has been a window into other people's lives. I have seen immense courage in those who have clearly suffered and watched as friends have lost loved ones, but I still smile when I think back to my own family's visits. There was so much laughter from cousins, uncles and aunts on those rare occasions when we were together. One occasion turned out to be the last time I saw my dear uncle Geoff, but I can still imagine him smiling down and wondering just what the hell has happened to the world we live in.

I have been humbled by the number of people who have enjoyed their *last days* at my little abode. One such family are joined by their friends every year and have told me that the father – who is terminally ill with cancer and has so far cheated death – wants the last holiday he remembers to be at my B&B. The reason I do what I do is to have made that small difference in someone's life. I couldn't be a doctor or a nurse, but if I can give someone one special memory then that's all I can really ask for.

I have friends whose children have suffered from the day they were born and whose daily existence revolves around trips to Great Ormond Street Hospital. I know others who have cheated death and those who stoically carry on as though cancer were nothing more than the flu. Friends have struggled over the early loss of a parent or been fitted with a pacemaker by the age of fifty. But I have found that those who have the most reason to bemoan their lot are usually the ones who rejoice in everything they have.

For my own part, years of stress, relentless hours and a generally unhealthy lifestyle have made me look at the damage I'm doing to myself. Maybe I should heed the advice of my doctor, who constantly berates me for not slowing down. But I guess I really don't know any different.

If there was a turning point, it came when I was taking part in a business breakfast at the nearby Royal Hotel. I got up to make my speech and noticed the sip of tea I'd just taken was running down my chin. Chiding myself for clumsiness, I took another sip, with the same result. It was then that my neighbour suggested I look in the mirror as *my face didn't look quite right*. Charming, I thought. As I took stock, I realised that one side of my face didn't match the other. With a quick visit to the GP, I was rushed into A & E and admitted to the stroke unit.

After four days of convalescing, it was decided that my *disarranged* face was due to Bell's palsy rather than a stroke. I realised I had been fortunate. But to be honest, I really didn't want to leave that hospital bed as it was the best rest I'd had in years. I was to miss Doris the tea lady even more. While I heeded the doctor's advice to rest, by the next day I was back at work – still with a face that couldn't quite align itself. But if I thought I was never to confront death – or at least, not for a long while – the powers above had other plans.

The day started out much like any other. Of course, it had taken umpteen bellows of 'Jack, it's time to get up!' for my son to even raise his *angelic* little face from the pillow. And of course, he was on yet another go-slow. I knew it was a trait inherited from his mother, who was also fond of her lie-ins, but how on earth did it take one small child so long to get ready in the mornings? It never ceased to amaze me how we as parents would be frantically running about, even with the day barely begun, while our son would nonchalantly go about his business without a care in the world. I could only think back with fondness to those days when I was much the same. When my parents had said these were the best days of my life, I never listened, but of course they had been so right. I could only think, wouldn't it be lovely not to have to worry about mortgages, bills, relationships – or even getting your blessed child ready for school.

'Dad, are my teeth clean?' Jack asked, producing a set of pearly whites that wouldn't have looked out of place in an Oral B commercial.

The ritual clean had now become something of an obsession; my best attempts at good parenting and his nanni's advice had clearly backfired. It had all begun with good intentions to get our six-year-old to brush his teeth properly. I had warned him, 'You don't want to end up looking like your father, do you?' Whereupon I would show him – much to his disgust – my denture for my two missing front teeth from a rugby mishap. Although I had tried to sound rather heroic – relaying tales of my battles on the rugby pitch – my son was clearly not convinced. He was happy to tell all and sundry that 'Dad hasn't got any teeth because he never cleaned his properly'. So much for the devotion of one's son, I thought, somewhat crestfallen by this apparent lack of parental appreciation.

So now we had to wait while our son took his dental hygiene to another level – he was quite prepared to add an extra ten minutes' brushing to the dentist's recommended daily allowance. If I thought we were starting to make progress and he might actually make it down the stairs, I had forgotten that we still had his shower to contend with! The soundtrack to this ritual was an off-key rendition of Nickelback's 'Rockstar', which featured a few lyrics – not from the original – that Jack was obviously delighted with. By the time I had managed to extricate the imaginary air guitar from a clearly amused Jack, I might just as well have taken the shower with him.

'Jack, will you move it!' I would bellow, trying not to swear, as this would inevitably end with me being reprimanded by my wife, eagerly egged on by our visibly overjoyed son.

In Jack's defence, I must confess that I too am partial to luxuriating in the peaceful confines of the shower. But with condensation now dripping from the bathroom windows and a haze of steam permeating the entire house, the joy of having a son just like me was starting to wear thin.

Breakfast would be yet another trial. Jack had recently watched – and taken to heart – a documentary that had shown the benefits of chewing every morsel as though one's life depended on it. 'Look Dad, it's all gone,' he'd say, thrilled with his efforts and instructing me to look into his empty mouth after every single mouthful. God, how I loved these bloody self-help gurus!

By now I would be repeatedly looking at the clock, thankful that Jack's mum had managed to get his breakfast ready, his school bag packed and his project assembled. But as I pushed him towards the door, I would notice that his shirt was still untucked, his hair resembled Boris Johnson's – or Doris Bonson, as my son liked to call him – and his shoelaces were still untied.

'Jack, you haven't got your hat and scarf,' his mum would remind him. Even if I was already perspiring, I didn't like to say it was like the Sahara-bloody-desert out there, because of course a mother always knows best. This obsession with having our son dressed as though he were about to depart on a trek to the Himalayas had reached such a point that I now deemed it appropriate to put *a certain picture* on display in the centre of our restaurant. The scene depicted a recent outing with two of Jack's girlfriends, who were around his own age. As it was a beach trip, they were attired in bathing costumes and accessorised with a towel, whereas our son had a woolly hat, scarf, puffer jacket and gloves. But if I thought the picture would have the desired effect, I knew this was yet another argument I was doomed to lose.

Finding the car was always problematic as I continually forgot which of the three possible locations I had actually parked it in. I would like to put this down to age, but it would be a lie. I remember once parking in an underground car park in Switzerland and, on returning, I was proud to have remembered the level and the space our car was parked in. Only to discover the car was missing. It was only after a few minutes' panic and after contemplating ringing the police that I realised we were in fact in the wrong car park. So, nothing much has changed. The daily ritual continued with me uttering a few choice words as I yet again tried the wrong spot, only for my dear son to pipe up, 'I knew it wasn't here, Dad.' Trying to pretend he wasn't Bart Simpson, I was by this time dragging him to the next option.

Once we made it to the car, the next hurdle was always the car seat. With little help from my son, I strained and yanked at the offending item and would now be freely perspiring as we were *running* late. I would finally manage to attach the right clasp into the right socket. The makers of car seats had obviously not had dads in mind when they decided how to construct these contraptions. Or, failing that, they had a very warped sense of humour. Just to improve matters, my angelic son would then have the audacity to remark, 'Dad, you do know we're going to be late, don't you?'

As I hit the pedal to the floor, Jack, delighting in the speed but ever the model citizen, would declare, 'I don't think Mum would be happy about you doing fifty in a thirty zone, do you, Dad?'

A response was neither expected nor required, as Jack would now be in full 'Bohemian Rhapsody' mode. It amazed me that everywhere we went, we were accompanied by a new song, yet after weeks of rehearsal, I'd had to sit through his entire nativity play without him singing a single note. This was because Jack spent the whole play trying to untangle himself from his fellow angel's wings. Taking centre stage in front of once bored parents, Jack towed the poor angel next to him across the stage floor, my dear son oblivious to the commotion he was creating while his *proud* father looked on aghast.

Glancing back in the mirror, I didn't know whether to laugh or cry as I noticed that Jack had managed – even with all his chewing – to leave half his breakfast on his brand-new school jumper.

'Dad, doesn't this tank go any quicker? We really are late now,' he'd say, checking his smart new watch. Oh, how I rejoiced when his teachers taught the little angels to tell the time and now my own cherub would tap his watch and look at me as though he were the parent every time I was late.

'The big hand is at one now. That means we're already five minutes late, Dad.'

'Your time-telling is really coming along well, Jack.' I'd beam, secretly wanting to throw the damn watch out of the window.

Now with *the tank* at full capacity, we neared the school. My mother – clearly delighted that I was now in a midlife crisis and knowing I secretly harboured a desire for something sporty – had thought it would be amusing to provoke my son into winding up his father by calling our rather domesticated choice of a Dacia *the tank*. Of course, this was after she had initiated him with glory stories of her own open-topped MGB, making Nanni far more glamorous than middle-aged Dad. So, *the tank* had stuck.

Although we had decided on what I considered a sensible type of car, my son was clearly not impressed, so I in turn told Jack that 'the boys' would be getting a sports car soon.

'But where will Mum and Nanni sit? he enquired.

'We can always stick them in the boot,' was my reply.

Jack thought this over and obviously deemed the scenario totally acceptable, so Dad's middle-aged dream might come true after all…

•

As the other parents were returning to their cars, Dad finally made it to the classroom with the doors just about to close, only for Jack to make his final contribution to the morning's events by chirping, 'Dad, have we left my project in the car?'

'Shit,' came the reply. But not before his teacher had heard and given a look that suggested Dad might well be spending his morning in detention. Trying to regain my composure, I smiled and, while pushing Jack through the door, added, 'I'll be back in one sec.'

His teacher was obviously not impressed and raised her eyebrows. Dad raced back to the car to retrieve Jack's project. Unfortunately, by the time I returned his carefully prepared *winter wonderland*, it resembled more of a wasteland, much to the annoyance of my son.

An hour into my day, I was actually looking forward to work. But as I drove back, I remembered something else that was nagging at the back of my mind. The previous night, I had tried to ring my mother at home but had received no reply.

This was not an uncommon occurrence as Mum tended to fall asleep on the sofa, snuggled up to her beloved Westie. As I made way back into Shanklin, I smiled as I recalled the numerous evenings when I had stayed over and would try to get them off to bed as they were both clearly snoring, only for my mother to startle awake and declare, 'I was just resting my eyes.' But as I parked and was yet again diverted to voicemail, a sixth sense set in, and I started to worry that something untoward had happened.

I asked Ewa if she could look after breakfast, dashed back the way I had come and made it to the sleepy hamlet of Niton. I prayed that my mother would be outside on her patio, enjoying her fifth cigarette, or *breakfast* as I jokingly referred to it.

When I arrived, I was initially relieved, and perhaps a little annoyed, as Mum was outside her cottage, struggling with the rubbish.

'Oh, my God, Mum, are you okay?' I remonstrated. 'You haven't been answering your phone.' But as I came closer, my euphoria disappeared. I noticed her eye was swollen and closed and she seemed totally disorientated.

'Right, we're going straight to A & E,' I told her.

As usual, she waved me off with the words, 'I'm fine, and anyway the bin men are coming.'

Taking the bins off her, I noticed that her Westie, who usually yapped at my heels, was uncharacteristically subdued and there was a distinct smell of vomit pervading the house.

'Mum, you're not okay, you've been sick.'

'Have I?' came her reply. 'I'll be fine. Don't make such a fuss.' I can't say I was surprised by the response. I remember my mother telling me about her grandmother, who, after twice being given the last rites, had deemed it unacceptable to die before she had cleaned her windows, because 'what would the neighbours think?' So, stoicism seems to have run through the family.

'Mum, we're going right now.' I tried to sound outwardly in control, but inwardly my whole world was screaming, 'Please, don't let anything happen to her.'

As Mum struggled to keep her balance, I ushered a bemused Zeus back inside and eventually bundled Mum into the car. But, naturally, not before she had rummaged in her purse and in typical Mum-style had attempted to pay me for the journey to the hospital.

'Mum, for God's sake get in the car.' The words came

out as a whisper. Rain started to fall, and I watched as Zeus scratched at the door to get to his beloved owner. As I fastened her in, I was just relieved it wasn't another child seat. We sped to the hospital, where I dumped the car and rushed frantically into A & E.

As we made our way into reception, I remembered all the reasons I hated hospitals so much. The overriding smell of disinfectant. The sombre faces, coming at you from all sides. And then there were the poor parents, who comforted their little ones whose limbs seemed at odds with human nature. Perhaps it was the feeling of fear, mingled with sadness, that made me want to bolt straight back through the door we had just entered.

As I recounted the events of the morning to a very patient receptionist, I thought about the fact that our being in this hospital was fast becoming a recurring theme. Two weeks previously, Mum had come in for a routine cataract operation, but whereas the first operation had been successful, this second one had left her complaining about blinding headaches. I clutched her hand and waited for a doctor to come, and prayed it wasn't too serious. Little did I know that things were about to get much worse.

Having waited tensely for hours, it literally felt as though my mum were ageing before my eyes. I squeezed her hand, and I knew she was outwardly trying to be tough, but I could see the fear etched on her face. This woman was unrecognisable from the force of nature that I loved so much.

She had always been there for me through all my triumphs and disasters, despite having to contend with so many of her own demons. Two broken relationships, one so bitter it had resulted in the loss of friends and family – even the support of her own mother. The second, to *the love of her life*, had been even more scary. Her life with my once beloved stepfather, at first so idyllic, had become her torment as he was free-falling into a downward spiral through alcohol. A free fall from which he would never recover.

As Mum stirred in the bed, she attempted a smile, but she seemed dazed and confused.

One doctor had already come and gone in a two-minute whirlwind, stating before he exited the room that she'd had a stroke and needed a scan. Not quite the bedside manner I had hoped for.

Shocked, I tried to reassure my mother, hoping the swelling was nothing more than a minor problem from her cataract operation. But deep down, I knew this wasn't true.

When we bought Keats Cottage, a run-down shack of a place, it was my mother who had the vision to turn it into something magical. Over the years, a whole array of friends told me how she had transformed their own homes, which in turn transformed their lives. As I looked over at her, I felt blessed that – despite all the upheaval – we had at least managed to share so much laughter together.

As she stirred, my childhood came to mind. I recalled her working night and day to give my brother and me a chance in life as we grew up.

I knew even then how lucky I was. Even when she arrived an hour later than all the other parents at school, I just smiled because I knew the sacrifices she made were always made with us in mind.

CHAPTER 17

My mum exercises her charms

Over the past six years, we had enjoyed our time to-gether. Time we had never had in the previous twenty years. Although I was busy with the restaurant and often saw her only fleetingly as she passed through with either Jack or a whole host of goodies, we did enjoy our yearly trips to foreign climes. Once a week, to escape the pres-sures of work, I would arrive in her enchanted garden, where we would while away the hours with a bottle of wine. As the light faded, I would make out the glow of yet another cigarette and would recount my tales of woe into the small hours, with Mum listening patiently.

I was jolted out of my reverie by the entrance of another consultant, whose brooding good looks and jovial smile brought my mother momentarily back to her normal self. My mother had a sexuality that she liked to call *mysterious*, whereas I would just label her a flirt. But there was no de-nying that a lot of grown men became putty in her hands.

On first appraisal, you could say that my mother is pretty reserved. Almost as if she is working you out. Some might argue that she is somewhat aloof, but once she accepts you, the ferocity of her spirit seems to leave men weak at the knees. My friend Don would always look wistful whenever her name was mentioned and I would have to stop him as he started, 'If only she was a couple of years younger...' Of course, I have encountered this often, and remember in my early years thwarting many an overeager man's advances with the words, 'You stay away from my mummy.'

If, aged five, this was the start, then it continued into my twenties when my mother met me in Switzerland and joined my friends and me to go nightclubbing. It might have been dark, but they were quick to think she was my sister, which of course delighted her. Now, in our later years, she feeds on the fact that people think she is my wife, which she finds highly entertaining, while I am less impressed by their assumption.

Even after all these years, I notice a wry smile as a text arrives from yet another man trying to curry favour. My mother is no fool, and although she likes the attention and the odd holiday here and there, she puts her foot down if she thinks they are getting too comfortable and trying to move in. 'Don't think I'm washing another man's pants again,' she is quick to say.

Over the years, more stories have come out. One involved a holiday with her sister in Jordan, after which she mischievously told me about her *holiday romance*. Squirming at yet another revelation, I had muttered, 'Oh God, Mum, I don't want to hear this.'

However, she was now in full flow and couldn't help but let me know with a huge smile on her face, 'Oh, he was a bit younger than me.'

'How much younger?' I had enquired.

With an even bigger smile, she'd replied, 'Oh, a few years younger than you.'

Obviously delighted at my overt shock, she had become more serious when she added, 'I did give him a fake address and telephone number though.'

Good old Mum, you couldn't help but admire the woman.

•

Meanwhile, the consultant was now informing my mum that she had in fact had a bleed to the brain. I don't think either of us really knew how to react. The copious amount of paracetamol was obviously having no effect, as she was clearly struggling with the pain while simultaneously trying to pretend she was fine.

'*Susy*,' – he and my mother were, of course, already on first-name terms – 'your situation is a little more serious than we can deal with at St Mary's, so we're going to fly you over to Southampton.'

Little did I realise this was to trigger a string of events that I would later recall in something of a haze. Knowing Mum was going to be airlifted and assured that I would have enough time to collect her belongings, I dashed back and threw together any essentials, which of course included her sexy thongs as she needed to *look her best* wherever she went. I dropped her poor bewildered Westie off with Ewa before hurriedly setting off back to the hospital. As I turned to wave goodbye, Zeus was already clawing at Ewa in an attempt to escape. She told me later that although he had pride of place in her king-sized bed, the accommodation had proved not to be to his liking, and he had subsequently peed over my rather unimpressed wife.

Visibly shaking, I made it back to the hospital where I found, to my horror, that the cubicle in which I had left Mum was empty. In a panic, I frantically stopped the nurse I'd been conversing with for half the day. Initially, she didn't remember who I was when I demanded, 'Where's my mother?' I was somewhat relieved to discover that Mum was already on her way across the Solent.

By the time I'd dashed to Cowes, dumped the car on double yellows and hot-footed it onto the Southampton ferry, I was already surviving on adrenaline.

•

After the sleepy vibe of the Isle of Wight, Southampton and the hospital were an assault on my senses. A taxi dropped me at the entrance, and I was somewhat overwhelmed by the sheer size of the place.

I navigated my way past a group of pale patients who were happily blocking the entrance, attached to an array of drips while sucking away at cigarettes as if it were their last. Which it possibly was! All around were children who were obviously suffering but were still managing to beam up at their parents as though they didn't have a care in the world. Elderly patients waddled around in pyjamas with a look that suggested they were thinking of happier times. Kind volunteers helped the lost and anxious to reunite with loved ones.

The whole scene was at odds with the world I knew. I had never really had to confront death or illness. But now, as it surrounded me on all sides, I realised how irrelevant many of my other worries were. Who really gave a damn if the steak was medium rare rather than rare, or that the cappuccino only had one shot rather than two, or that the bloody carrots weren't al dente enough, or the duvet's tog count wasn't quite up to scratch. All these daily troubles seemed so irrelevant compared to the suffering that now faced me.

The ground floor of the building resembled more of a shopping mall than a hospital. With its abundance of restaurants and shops, it took me a while, plus the help of a kindly volunteer, to navigate to the neurological department.

After meandering through several corridors and trudging up the final four flights of stairs, I finally saw my bewildered mum, sitting upright in bed, clutching her bag as though her life depended upon it. My heart went out to this now frail figure who I barely recognised. I realised that for once it was me who was going to have to be strong for her and not the other way round. As I reached Mum, she was already chatting somewhat incoherently to a consultant, who looked as weary as my mother. He went through her options, and it felt as though time were standing still. As I struggled with the medical jargon, Mum was now clutching my hand as hard as her bag.

Before I knew it, the doctor was holding out a pen for me to sign a consent form, as Mum was not deemed fit enough to make the decision on her own. Seeing my hesitation, he added, 'If you don't sign, she won't make it. The operation really is your only option.' It was then that I really became anxious. The rock in my life seemed to have dwarfed before my eyes.

True to form, she momentarily sprang to life and in her usual way declared, 'Well, we better get on with it then.'

Funnily enough, two months later when I recounted these events, she recalled little of the two weeks we were about to embark on.

•

The operation was scheduled for the following morning. I tucked Mum into bed and couldn't believe that two days previously we had been playing squash together. It also dawned on me that I had nowhere to sleep that night. As I trundled my way back towards the entrance, where a helpful nurse had mentioned that I might be able to use a room within the hospital grounds, the corridors were pretty much deserted. With funds and energy levels low, all I wanted was a bed and a wash. I could only imagine what was going through my poor mother's head.

•

I checked in with night security and made my way towards the gated complex that would prove to be my home for the next two weeks. It took several minutes for me to navigate the multitude of locks and make it into the room. The duvet was threadbare, the light flickered and there was a chance I would have to share the room, but never was a bed so welcome. I slumped exhausted on to the pillow, pleased the day had finally ended, and hoped the next day would be a little better.

Hospital trucks outside my window and multiple pings of my phone woke me. I scrolled down the list of familiar names, but right now I just wanted to make it back to the ward. So, I took a tepid shower, said hello to the landlady and grabbed a coffee in the foyer before retracing my steps to the hospital.

Mum was awake but I noticed she was still clutching her bag and I was told she had refused any attempts to get her to eat the previous day. 'The coffee is awful and I'm dying for a ciggy,' she remarked as I settled into the chair beside her. She rolled the one eye that was still open. 'And they kept asking me the same bloody questions all through the night. How is anyone supposed to rest?'

It took me some time to realise that the nurses asked the patients their name, address and date of birth to determine if they were relapsing. Mum was clearly not enamoured and was answering like a petulant schoolgirl.

'It's for your own good,' I pleaded to no avail. I soon discovered the validity of these questions when I overheard a sweet old lady talking to her brother in the next bed.

Outwardly upbeat, the nurse asked her, 'Now, my dear, can you tell me what day it is?'

'What a stupid question,' the old lady replied. The brother smiled tentatively. 'It's the day after yesterday.'

A sharp answer, I thought, as the nurse nodded her encouragement.

'Okay,' she continued, patience personified. 'Do you know what year it is?'

'Well, that's easy,' came the reply. 'It's 1946.'

Now my interest was piqued.

The nurse nodded affectionately. 'Who is this, my dear?' she asked, pointing at the old lady's brother.

'Well, considering he comes in every day, surely you should know him by now. That's George, my husband.'

Half smiling, half welling up, the gentleman turned to me and explained that her husband, George, had died twenty years ago.

Now the questioning made sense.

I turned to my mother and asked, 'Mum, do you know who I am?'

'Yes,' came the reply. 'You're still the same silly sod you were yesterday.'

I allowed myself the hint of a smile. Perhaps it wasn't going to be so bad after all.

•

Before I knew it, Mum was whisked away by her exhausted-looking surgeon, with me trying to offer a few words of encouragement. 'I love you, don't cause too much trouble,' I said. My words trailed off behind the fast-moving trolley.

Over the next few hours, I took stock. Nervously waiting for an update. Fielding texts from anxious loved ones who wanted to come and visit. Mum had made it clear before surgery that she didn't want any visitors. She obviously didn't want anyone to see her in any way diminished.

The one person who couldn't be dissuaded was her sister, Rebecca, who was now berating me for not returning her calls. I tried to explain that I hadn't really had a lot of time, energy or even a signal. But I could tell by her rambling that this wasn't really cutting it. It transpired that Rebecca had already booked her flight and car from Switzerland and was arriving in two days' time.

'Shall I book you a hotel, Gotti?' I asked, panicking as I recalled her last visit to the UK, when it had taken two room moves for her to be satisfied. And that had been in the Savoy! I frantically tried to recall if there was a *posh* hotel in Southampton, or even a Hotel du Vin.

'Oh, these things really don't matter at a time like this,' she chided. 'I'll just stay where you are.'

I couldn't help but smile, imagining my rather glamorous godmother, resplendent in her designer gear, joining me in my shared accommodation and using the communal bathroom, where it was difficult to tell the difference between the toilet paper and the bath towels.

'We'll sort it when you get here,' I suggested.

•

After guzzling multiple coffees, I made it back to the waiting room. Not long after, the phone rang and I was ushered through the electronic doors into the intensive care unit.

As I made my way through the throngs of bodies, hooked up to all manner of devices, I felt like a *voyeur* in a bad movie. Only this wasn't a movie.

However, by some miracle, my mother appeared to be the only one awake from her ordeal. She was merrily chatting away to her ever-attentive Portuguese nurse.

I spent the day with her and, much to her annoyance,

attempted to get her to take on as many fluids as possible. The nurse informed me that the following morning she would be discharged to a ward, where I could wait for her. I assumed we were over the worst.

•

The next two weeks seemed to pass by in a blur, as one day rolled into another. During this time, I encountered so much that has stuck vividly in my mind: the kindness of strangers, the bravery, the pain and the comedy. Newly acquired friendships and the worst in human nature. It all happened in those two weeks.

•

Having waited patiently on a stool for seven hours, surrounded by my mother's belongings, I was finally taken through to her. If I thought this was to be an emotional reunion, I was clearly mistaken.

After those endless hours of waiting, I was greeted by my mum exclaiming, 'Where the hell have you been? I suppose you've been chatting up some nurse, rather than thinking of your poor mother.'

The mother I loved had overnight turned into someone unrecognisable. And I don't mean in a good way.

'Have you been looking after my purse?' she erupted. 'Anyone could have stolen it, you know.'

I tried not to laugh as I looked over at the ninety-year-old lady who had yet to raise her head, never mind make off with my mother's crown jewels.

The nurses then gave me the unenviable task of trying to get my mother to eat something and take on the copious amount of liquid that would aid her recovery. This proved to be near impossible. What ensued was a sketch not dissimilar to *Little Britain*, when Andy turns his nose up at everything, saying, 'I don't want that one.'

•

I knew that my mum had a deep fear of hospitals from a very young age and did my best to remain as patient as possible. Whereas she would constantly berate me for my efforts, she would then turn into Mother Teresa whenever a doctor or nurse approached.

For fourteen hours a day, I patiently tried to administer bed baths, take her to the shower, give massages and make countless trips for *proper* coffee, freshly made smoothies and other requested goodies that were now piling up around her.

It was the least I could do after all the years of sacrifice she had made for me. I carried on with a smile on my face, although inwardly crestfallen that none of my efforts had hit the right note.

On one ward round, I took the doctor to one side and explained the situation, asking, 'I don't recognise my mother at all. Is this normal after such a procedure?'

He listened patiently and nodded. 'Oh yes, this is perfectly normal, and sometimes their previous personalities never return.'

'Oh joy,' I mumbled and returned to Mum, who was turning her nose up at another hospital meal.

'Would you eat this shit?' asked my usually polite mother. Thinking of my diet, which currently consisted of sandwiches and coffee, I replied, 'Happily.'

•

In between the anxiety and the stress, there were moments of frivolity that will be forever etched on my memory and which my mother will not be pleased for me to recount.

The first came when – in an attempt to get her to actually eat something – I decided to surprise her with her favourite Swiss chocolates.

These were instantly refused with the words, 'I couldn't possibly eat any of those.' As she stubbornly looked on, I decided the chocolates shouldn't go to waste and offered them round the ward to grateful recipients.

Obviously not impressed by my generosity, Mum berated me, exclaiming, 'Always trying to impress others, but not looking after your poor old mother. You're even giving away my chocolates.'

After this, my mother's fellow patients were too scared to accept a second, so I left the rest of the box on the side and tried to see the funny side of the situation.

In the morning, the ninety-year-old lady next to my mum was clearly happy to see me and even more delighted to be offered another chocolate. I could see Mum was trying not to rise to the bait but, seeing that most of the other chocolates had disappeared, I asked her if she had enjoyed her midnight feast.

Indignantly, she replied, 'But I haven't had any.'

Both her fellow patients and the nurses couldn't help but smile. Her mouth, nightie and bedclothes were totally covered in chocolate.

As I mentioned before, my mother could be described as pretty flirtatious, but in her current drug-induced state she probably wasn't at her most alluring. Daily, a technician would pass by who incidentally came from Shrewsbury – not far from where I grew up. It was his job to fit electrodes to my mum's head to see the patterns of her inner workings. For this to work properly seemed to require rather a lot of lubricant and gel. Mum, whose hair now resembled the mad professor from *Back to the Future*, was oblivious to her current state and was still trying her most seductive approach.

However, with her hair in electric shock mode, her speech slurred from all the morphine and the remnants of her chocolate binge still in evidence, it wasn't perhaps the look she was after. But even if the poor man wasn't titillated by my mother in her hospital stockings, give the girl credit – she had changed her knickers, which she was now happy to display to the increasingly nervous technician.

As his panic set in, the technician, clearly petrified by my mother's advances and eager to escape, asked, 'Is she always like this?'

To which I replied, 'You haven't seen anything yet.'

I don't think he ever did find the necessary spot on my mother's head, but for me it was a welcome relief to at least see a semblance of her former self.

•

It certainly wasn't easy to see someone with so much zest for life reduced to a pale imitation of her former self. Even I was a little indignant when one nurse asked me, 'Does she normally get around by herself?'

'You have no idea. She gets up at five-thirty in the morning after going to bed at midnight, and still runs rings around me,' came my reply.

My new home had become a window into other people's lives. I chatted to my mother's fellow patients, watched on in awe as nurses went about their business and felt saddened by the ninety-year-old lady whose daughters visited just once in the two weeks I was there. And who, after only five minutes, couldn't wait to beat a hasty retreat.

CHAPTER 18

Gotti lands

It was with a mixture of apprehension and relief that I greeted Mum's sister Rebecca at the hospital entrance the next morning. Yet another tidal wave was entering my life.

As I approached, she was already berating the taxi driver for his poor motoring skills, but luckily, he didn't understand too much English and was happily agreeing with everything she said. It wasn't long before – very much like my mother – she was devouring her second cigarette.

The two of them always reminded me of Edina and Patsy from *Ab Fab*. The farcical nature of the situation was made more apparent as my perfectly coiffured, immaculately dressed godmother leaned over a gang of pot-bellied, toothless wonders, clad in their hospital gowns and struggling to keep hold of their drips, to ask for a light.

She was blissfully unaware of the irony, but we were both brought to earth with a bump when someone decided he was not happy that two men in wheelchairs were happily smoking away while blocking the entrance to the hospital. The two men were *three sheets to the wind* and quick to inform him that he could 'fuck off' as they were going nowhere.

Instead of letting the matter lie, the man took umbrage and catapulted the two unsuspecting men past the two of us. Amazingly, they both kept hold of their drips and their cigarettes as their wheelchairs flew past.

'Welcome to the UK,' I announced.

We spent the next twenty minutes trying to find a toilet deemed clean enough for her perfectly toned buttocks. I could only be grateful that I had not subjected her to the horrors of my accommodation and had the foresight to book her into one of Southampton's better establishments.

•

My godmother was used to Swiss standards of cleanliness and was clearly not impressed that there was dust everywhere. Builders were all round us, happily drilling holes in every conceivable wall. Not the best way to recuperate from head surgery, I thought. Being British and not wanting to complain, I stopped my godmother, who was on the verge of trying to get my mother moved.

You could see the obvious distaste in my godmother's eyes as she surveyed my mother's surroundings. She was not at all convinced by my constant affirmations that 'she really is in the best place possible'.

In fairness, I did recall phoning when my brother's wife went into labour in Switzerland and being amazed to find that even my brother had an en-suite adjoining room, complete with à la carte menu – and he was only the father. Not quite the National Health Service!

Shouting over the din of the drills, Rebecca did her best to speak to my mum, but if I had hoped that seeing another friendly face would in any way be beneficial, I was quick to reject this notion. Mum was quite happy to berate her sister as much as she did me. To be honest, I was just grateful to be out of the firing line, even for two minutes. If I was a little upset by the abuse, her sister took it all in her stride, and we happily caught up while responding to Mum's ever increasing demands. In truth, I was grateful for the help and the company. I think it hit us both hard and I could clearly see the disbelief in my godmother's face. Just one month ago, they had been skiing at Rebecca's home in Kitzbühel. To me, they were always the naughty schoolgirls, thick as thieves, constantly misbehaving. To see them in such a situation was alien to both of us.

Just as we were getting reacquainted, Mum decided she needed to wash her hair and have a shower. We both carried her to the bathroom, and I was happy to let her sister do the scrubbing as I was by now getting a little too familiar with my mother's anatomy.

Seconds later there was a scream from Rebecca and, bursting through the door, I managed to catch my mother before her head hit the floor. Mum was unaccustomed to getting out of bed, so the strain had been too much. As we both waited anxiously for the nurse to help, I couldn't believe that my petite mum could weigh so much. Once she got back to bed and returned to her normal self – the new demanding version – we both breathed a sigh of relief.

Downstairs in the café, I delved into the seriousness of the situation and how I would cope once we got home to the B&B. As I looked over at my godmother, it seemed absurd that I had spent barely any time in her company in the last thirty years. We happily recounted tales of the early holidays I had spent with her as a child. In many ways, she resembled my mother – they both have a mischievous way about them – and I had forgotten how much I really enjoyed her company. In reality, hers was a world I had only skirted the edges of. A world of designer goods, fast cars, the right address and liberal amounts of Botox. It was a world in which keeping up with *the Joneses*, or should I say their millionaire banker friends, was everything. This life that once so enticed me had never seemed more irrelevant than it did right now.

It wasn't long before my godmother deemed my mother's wardrobe to be insufficient and we embarked on what my godmother did best – namely, shopping. My attempts to make her understand that I didn't really think it mattered to my mother what her attire looked like fell on deaf ears. I mean, my mother could barely recognise us, never mind worry about how she looked. Even so, I obediently followed my designer-clad godmother into the nearest and only clothes shop in the vicinity and even if she was not impressed by their offerings, she was definitely a woman on a mission. It was a wonder to behold and reminded me of a hound picking up the scent of a fox. By the look in her eyes, she was moving in for the kill.

This was a look I had seen as a thirteen-year-old child. On one holiday, she had taken me shopping on the Bahnhofstrasse. I had spotted a rather beautiful woollen jumper embellished with a hippo playing golf. To my amazement, she had followed my gaze and whisked it from me and into her basket. When we approached the till, I was already protesting at her generosity, but even I was dumbfounded when she didn't bat an eyelid at the one-thousand-franc price tag. For the next few months, I all but slept in that jumper. You can imagine my distress when my mother managed to shrink it beyond recognition. That beloved jumper still haunts me to this day!

'Gotti, she's in hospital, not on the bloody catwalk,' I appealed. It wasn't long before she was so laden with garments that even the disinterested shop assistants focused on her, obviously calculating their commission. As soon as an item was in her basket, I tried to return it to the shelves. She attempted to evade my eagle eye and hide thongs that were no more than dental floss and T-shirts adorned with the words *Sex Kitten*. All I could think about was that poor technician. Hadn't the poor man been subjected to enough?

By the end, despite all my pleading, Rebecca had managed to spend, in a paltry ten minutes, the equivalent of my entire clothing allowance for a year. She protested, 'A woman needs to feel good about herself.'

I didn't think that colour coordinating with hospital stockings and slippers was really a priority. But as we left the clearly delighted shop assistants, I think the pleasure of doing something *normal* was as much of a comfort to my godmother as it was for Mother.

Laden with our purchases – plus several treats from the food store – we made our way back to the ward. If we had more of a spring in our step, the same could not be said of my mother, who returned to her *Little Britain* mode, with the ultimate put-down, 'I don't like that!'

For a split second we were both crestfallen, but it wasn't long before our smiles returned, and we admired our creation – resplendent in matching hospital stockings.

All joking aside, I was so grateful not only for the help and the fact that Gotti was a buffer against my mother's constant jibes but also for her company; the road ahead seemed endlessly daunting.

Evenings were spent back at her hotel and after a constant diet of hospital sandwiches, I was overjoyed to revel in the joys of the hotel's restaurant.

With great sadness, I said goodbye to Gotti after three days that will stay with both of us forever. Not least when she said that she hoped her children cared about her as much as I cared for my mother.

On my own once more, I settled back into my daily routine of inedible sandwiches and copious amounts of coffee. This kept me going for the mammoth task of completing the numerous requests that started at seven o'clock in the morning and ended at ten o'clock each evening. During this period – watching through the window of other people's lives – I felt truly humbled and realised just how fortunate I was.

When I recount these tales to my mother now, she says she only remembers the incessant drilling of the builders. In truth, I think she remembers more than she lets on. Although she feigns horror at some of her hospital antics, I think a little part of her was glad to have had a little fun, at my expense.

I have so many vivid memories of those two weeks – the tireless work of the upbeat nurses, the occasion when one doctor was so stressed, he nearly administered my mother's dosage twice; overall, the ability of those who had gone through such adversity to see the best in everything. On the other side, I saw patients who were alone without the comfort of loved ones, and patients who would barge to the front of shop queues, considering themselves more worthy than their fellow patients. These were the memories that stayed with me.

The most defining moment came when Ewa and Jack visited. My godmother had said this was a bad idea, but I decided that it could aid Mum's recovery. It might possibly be the last time Jack would see his beloved nanni. When Jack entered the ward, his face was aghast. For an instant I thought that maybe Gotti had been right, but as soon as the curtain was drawn, I saw the obvious delight in both their eyes and my fears vanished.

Jack took over my role and showered his nanni with the same care she always gave him. I looked on in awe as he made sure she took her tablets and smiled as he gently placed the water glass to her lips, cleaned her teeth, read her stories and generally amused the other patients when he declared, 'Oh God, Nanni, what's happened to your pants? They're nearly as big as Mum's!' I think more than anything our little boy gave her the courage to fight on.

If that had been one of the highs, then my lowest moment came just a couple of days later, when Mum was unable to use the arm and leg on one side of her body. In a panic I called the nurse, who reassured me that she was fine.

'She can't be fine. Her eye is looking in the wrong direction.'

The senior nurse saw the commotion and she quickly ushered my mother back into intensive care. Another harrowing twenty-four hours. As I entered the next day, I was relieved when Mum demanded, 'And where the bloody hell have you been?'

'Right here,' I whispered with a tear in my eye, as I had honestly thought that night would be her last.

•

This experience had a profound effect on me – not just the multitude of emotions, but also the kindness of random strangers. I was awoken one night by the sound of someone creeping into my room. To be honest, with the room priced at £14 a night I was a little worried about who I'd be sharing with. My fears were totally unfounded as my first companion was a retired naval officer from Wolverhampton and my second a retired businessman from Jersey in the Channel Islands. It wasn't long before we shared hugs, tears, stories and meals together and the company helped us all through this harrowing time.

If I thought my situation had been hard, each told me that over the last twenty years they had made count-less trips to and from the hospitals dealing with their respective partners' multiple health complications. I was honoured to meet both their wives, and the love they shared was abundantly clear. I could only look on and hope that if there were ever the need, someone would care for me in the same way. It was their courage that put my own into perspective.

After those eventful weeks, I needed to return to the B&B as the season was soon to be in full flow. The nurses deemed it sensible for Mum to stay in for a few more days, but when I told her the news, the fear of being left hit her hard and, although she could barely get to the toilet unaided, she demanded to be taken home. I suggested that I would tidy her house – still in the carnage that it had been left in – and then prepare a room for her back at Keats.

That was the plan, anyway. The next day, I arrived back on the island and while happily throwing away remnants of her last night at home, from all over her house, I was informed by a nurse that my mother had passed herself fit and was ready to be discharged. Fortunately, an ambulance would bring her back to the island and she would arrive safely back the following morning. Having organised her home, I spent the rest of the day preparing Keats for the deluge of guests.

By the morning, I was happy in the knowledge that everything was ready for her arrival, but after seven hours' waiting, the hospital rang to let me know there hadn't been an ambulance available and my mother had spent the whole day awaiting my arrival.

With guests checking in, I explained the situation again and a couple of hours later the ambulance arrived. As she reached the doorstep, happily clutching her young driver, I looked at Jack with a tear in my eye and whispered, 'Typical Mum, I knew she wouldn't stay.'

As we settled her in, Jack squeezed my hand as my tears continued to roll and said, smiling, 'Are you okay, Dad?'

'I am now, Jack. I am now.'

Of course, in typical Mum-style, she checked herself out of Keats within two days and went back to the privacy of her own home. One week later, the nurse visited, expecting a frail old woman confined to her bed, and was instead greeted by the sight of Mum, on top of her ladder, cutting her hedge. She never could be told!

•

If I thought the year couldn't have got off to a worse start, then more was to come. Two months later, I waved Ewa and Jack off at the station to embark on their new lives in Bath. Yet again, I choked back the tears and wondered if anything else could possibly go wrong. Although the B&B was alive with the sound of guests, never before had I felt so alone.

Part Four

1990–1998 – The other halves

I guess you could say that I have always been curious about the opposite sex. Everything about them entrances me, but do I understand them? No. I would have to say that after fifty years I still don't really have a clue. Funnily enough, my fascination started at my all-boys' prep school, aged around eight. I can still remember sneaking my mum's Littlewoods catalogue into school, because it had several pages dedicated to the lingerie section…

During one afternoon break, I furtively made my way to the maze of rhododendrons and settled down to become better acquainted with my newfound *friends*. As I marvelled at a whole new world of delights, I was abruptly brought back to reality.

'Woodward, what the hell are you doing in there?'

Chastened, I emerged from the rhododendrons to be confronted by the one face I didn't want to see, namely my headmaster, Pease-Watkin. Now, this was a man who seemed to be in a perpetual state of rage and the last thing I wanted was to be in the firing line. So, I mumbled, 'Nothing, sir.'

Obviously not convinced, he asked, 'And what's that behind your back, Woodward?'

Luckily, as I produced the catalogue from behind my back, the pages flipped to the Black & Decker pull-out rather than the page I had been enthralled with, namely, *what to get your man for Valentine's*. Little did I know that this lucky escape was to set the tone for many years to come. Being in an all-boys' school, my knowledge of the opposite sex was pretty limited, but I deemed myself fortunate to be one of the few day boys. Otherwise, my sexual orientation might have turned out a little differently.

•

When I was twelve, my mother took me out of prep school and deposited me in the grammar school, which I'm pleased to say was mixed gender. Now, I still remember the delights of my first kiss with Michelle, who was one year my junior. After three hours of constant chatting, I finally mustered up the courage for that elusive first smooch. Our foray into courtship was less romance and more feats of athleticism that seemed to involve endless bouts of wrestling. The relationship was a happy time, with multiple break-ups and make-ups that certainly prepared me for the future. By the age of just thirteen, I felt I had the world at my feet.

Naturally buoyed by my success, I returned home with a cockiness only adolescence can bring. My stepfather – who never missed an opportunity to have a little fun at my expense – noticed the spring in my step and enquired with a mischievous grin, 'So, you know everything about sex now, do you?'

Fuelled by that first kiss, and giving what probably resembled a Del Boy shrug, I replied, 'Of course I do.'

Still trying to catch me out, he asked, 'Well, tell me, what's oral sex?'

Delighted to know the answer, I replied, 'Well, that's easy, it's talking about it, isn't it.'

With that, I bounced out of the room, my sexual education complete.

•

Those early teenage years seemed to be an endless stream of firsts: first kisses, first tentative fumbling, first of pretty much everything, in fact. I took delight in a whole array of what I felt were the most wondrous moments of my life. Redheads, blondes, brunettes, long legs, short legs, pert bums, generous bosoms, fair skin, exotic curves, sparkling eyes, coy smiles – I just couldn't believe I was privy to such an amazing world.

By thirteen, I knew that my antics might lead me into trouble. This was highlighted when my mother was called into the head's office, where he remonstrated with her about her son's errant behaviour. Mr Potter had regrettably caught me in a somewhat romantic embrace, lying on top of an equally eager girlfriend. My mother later advised me that if I was going to conduct myself in such a manner then it was probably better that my innocent fumbling wasn't conducted on the headmaster's desk!

At around the same time, I remember my dear grand-father Pop asking me, laughing, when taking me off for a game of golf at our local course, 'Are you a bum or tit man?'

Somewhat taken aback by the question, but mar-velling that there was life in the old dog yet, I replied, 'Definitely bum.'

The old boy was obviously happy with the reply and probably credited himself with providing some of those genes down the generations. I had, of course, remem-bered the poster in his study of a tennis player with rather a pert derrière.

•

By my late teens, however, I realised I really didn't under-stand the rules at all, and that fantasy land was certainly different to reality. I think we were aged fifteen when we went on a rugby tour to Holland and spent one enlight-ening day in Amsterdam. As the *boys* hit the red-light district, I wasn't sure if I was curious, excited or plain ter-rified by the sights we encountered as we ventured from one sex shop to another.

The Dutch were certainly more *adventurous* than their English counterparts and I discovered that my sexual education was still very much in its infancy. Used to the odd magazine stolen from unsuspecting fathers and distributed at the back of our school bus for our away games, I now realised that *Sexy Secretaries for the Mature Male* or *French Fillies in Stockings* were pretty tame offer-ings. Maybe I shouldn't pass judgement on those fathers who had a penchant for titles such as *Bouncing Boobs for the Over Sixties*. Surely on my return I could look at those fathers again without avoiding eye contact and turning crimson.

If I had thought this '*fantasy land*' was going to be exotic, I was in for a rude awakening. We hid ourselves in the back row of some seedy sex show, cowering behind the seats, eagerly awaiting the first act. As the act started, I was incredulous that ping-pong balls could be fired from a fanny at such velocity. Rather than being excited by the spectacle, what I really wanted to do was grab a bat and ask the girl if she was up for a game of mixed doubles.

The act that followed was pretty much centred around audience participation. As the young lady at the front gestured for us to come up to the stage, we cowered lower in our seats and shook our heads vehemently. If we were somewhat timid, the same could not be said about one old boy, who seemed to me like Lazarus rising from the dead as he jumped onto the stage. Apparently, expelling ping-pong balls was not her only forte, as she proceeded to insert a banana inside herself. As the old boy devoured said banana, I was just happy he managed to perform his act without losing his dentures and I realised, after the spectacle I had just witnessed, it was probably a bit too early for lunch!

On my return, my tentative probing into the female world continued unabated, but I still didn't know where the lines were drawn. What was acceptable and what wasn't? To make matters worse, the girls I dated didn't seem to give me any clues either. Or perhaps I wasn't so good at reading the signs? My friends seemed far more sophisticated than I, but I wasn't sure if this was macho bravado or whether they actually knew the *secret*.

As I turned sixteen, my overtures had progressed to taking romantic *walks* round the school's playing fields, nearly always leading to yet more fumbling, not to mention grass stains that might take some explaining. Although I took delight in exploring the female body, the question of the next step was something I was still unsure of.

In the meantime, I relished those outdoor pursuits, even when my games teacher, Mr Jones, called me over one day. Not one to mince his words, he complained, 'Woodward, it's a bit bloody difficult to umpire a bloody cricket match when all I can see is your arse bobbing up and down.'

Luckily for me, I hadn't yet progressed to the stage of removing my trousers, or my ticking off could have been much more severe.

Now, to say I was naive at the time would be an understatement, and years later several old girlfriends said that they were just as anxious as me. In these instances, I was happy that my enthusiasm had not got the better of me, but this was not always the case. I remember one girlfriend, who happened to be my tennis partner at the time, informing her whole class that she thought I was *frigid* for not taking matters further. Rather than feeling upset at being ridiculed in front of her class, I was furious that I had missed the opportunity to sow my wild oats. As I say, I just didn't know the rules.

Another short-lived romance had led to me taking a

girl home while my mother was at work. What ensued was a rather steamy shower and every act being performed apart from the main event. But I found out that *hell hath no fury like a woman scorned* when the young lady announced to her friends that I 'couldn't find a clitoris if it was marked out on a chalkboard'.

Well, I don't know about the chalkboard but that night I went home and – it being a time before Google – located a dictionary to find out what this bloody clitoris was all about.

•

In my final year at school, I did finally do the deed with a very sweet girl, who shall remain nameless. Our relationship developed, but we foolishly did not heed my mum's words; she had thought this sweet girl wasn't ready to embark on a physical relationship with me.

Just as my A-level results were due, we enjoyed a romantic holiday with her parents in the sunny climes of France and it was here that I finally lost my inhibitions. Looking back, my mum was right. We were too young, and she deserved better as I left her for university and went from one relationship to another. Now, I'm a big believer in karma and – should she be reading this – not long after, I was certainly paid back tenfold.

A couple of years previously, I had been dating a younger, part-Spanish girl by the name of Candy. Candy was the epitome of bohemian cool and, with her smouldering good looks, she turned many an eye. I guess we were both young when we dated, and our trysts were no more than my usual antics on the playing fields. However, when I went to university, Candy and I met up for drinks at Covent Garden and, being so much older, I thought that our relationship could be taken much further. Of course, when she invited me to that year's Grand National, I virtually bit her hand off at the thought of rekindling our relationship.

However, what I didn't realise was that we would be travelling on a bus with several of her fellow students from Shrewsbury College. The journey proceeded with the two of us enjoying each other's company, but I couldn't help but notice that Candy was sneaking furtive glances at another guy behind us. When we arrived at the course, we enjoyed the races alone, but it soon became evident that, like the horse I had bet on, I would be leading for the first circuit but would fall at the last.

We attended a ball, but rather than the romantic liaison I had envisaged, it soon became clear that the reason for her *older man* to be here was in fact to make this other guy jealous. What ensued was me strutting my stuff like a lone ranger on the dance floor while Candy made her move on the fabulously handsome student who had been sitting behind us on the bus. If I thought my night couldn't get any worse, I discovered, once the bus arrived back in Shrewsbury, that there was no way home until the next day, so most of us packed into the gigantic home of someone's parents.

Candy was whisked off by her new beau to one of the rooms and I was left to share a freezing living-room floor with several couples and barely a blanket between us. My last memory of that fateful night was when one amorous couple tried nudging me to determine whether I was awake. Feigning sleep, I valiantly dodged this guy's arse and balls, which were way too near my head for comfort, with my ears covered so I wouldn't hear his partner's ever increasing moans. I guess that's karma!

•

My late teens and twenties were exciting times as I stumbled from one disaster to another – all of my own making. Although I was more aware of the *rules*, I would say that these formative years highlighted a good deal of curiosity, an abundance of naivety and a considerable amount of extreme behaviour, some of which I regret and some of which was just too enjoyable to regret. Although not always my finest moments, I certainly have memories that will last a lifetime.

CHAPTER 20

2015 – *Four in a Bed*, social media and the dreaded reviews

Over the last few years, we have all seen the unparalleled rise of social media and all this entails. There is no doubt that it can be hugely beneficial to your business. But as the world now seems to be ever more divided, views are increasingly polarised, so ideals have been taken to an unheard-of extreme. We now must endure the faceless consumer who believes it is their right to say whatever they deem acceptable, although they are never held accountable. It is no wonder that with a media that promotes negativity, we are now in a situation where footballers have chosen to come off social media, presenters are scared to air their opinions, and everyone seems to be vilified for their views.

When we see female football presenters trounced, based purely on gender, for their opinions, rugby players receiving death threats, based on a perceived error, and celebrities hounded at every opportunity by a media hell-bent on destruction, we must fear for our future. As with everything, we seem intent on building someone up, only to delight in their downfall. Is this really the world I want my son to inherit? All around us we are perpetually bombarded by sexual inequality, homophobia, race issues, anti-vaccine, pro-vaccine, mindless violence, greed, rape, abuse in football, abuse in schools. Is it too much to ask for us all to get along?

In my own little world, I admit to an unhealthy addiction to the likes of TripAdvisor. I am the first to check through the reviews when booking a hotel or a holiday. But I find it strange how our morbid fascination is piqued by the one bad review rather than the countless other glowing reports. Herein lies the problem. On a personal front, the consensus is that if there is a negative review – when there are hundreds of positive reviews – we should just take it on the chin and ignore it. But what if this review is totally unfounded or in any way malicious? How, then, is it not possible to take it personally?

The problem, for me, is that TripAdvisor, Booking.com and the like refuse to remove any *false reviews* and argue that if all your other reviews are great, then the potential guest will see past this. They also counter that you, as the proprietor, can put your side of the argument, but this is something I have always stayed away from, the reason being that the public love the drama. Even if the guest is clearly an over-entitled dick and plainly in the wrong, we love to see an owner, visibly frothing at the mouth, bringing the guest down a peg or two. But does this really help, I ask? I can also assure you that no one for so much as a second thinks the poor owner might have endured sleepless nights because of someone who is plainly malicious and out for their five-minute shot at self-importance.

I recently read in an article that should someone we know receive a negative comment, 80 per cent of us really wouldn't care and 20 per cent of our so-called *friends* would actually delight at their friend's discomfort.

•

I do believe that constructive criticism can only be a good thing, but in many cases, it is also a personal thing. My attitude is that if someone mentions you don't have, say, enough sockets in a room, they may be one of those people who need to be hooked up to every device possible. However, if a second person mentions the same issue, then it is time to act. But don't think for one second that even the most inconsequential comment or review will go unnoticed by the eagle-eyed public. Say, for example, I receive a review of 9/10 and say this review states great food, great service, went beyond expectations, but there was some slight street noise, the potential guest reading this review will ignore the positives and be sure to request a quiet room away from the street. It's human nature, I guess, but of course it would never occur to the guest booking that the person who wrote the review might be a light sleeper used to living in the countryside with just one sheep and one cow for company within a five-mile radius.

Then comes the double-edged-sword scenario. When I started up, such was the state of our business that the only possible way was up. It was floundering so low that I had next to no business – not an ideal way to begin. With a ranking of 224 out of 226 B&Bs, it wasn't as though it could get any worse – and I think the two B&Bs below me in the rankings had in fact closed. Through a combination of hard work, bloody-mindedness and, of course, pandering to the needs of every guest, I managed to sustain a meteoric rise up the rankings. Fantastic, I thought; I had reached the upper echelons of the B&B world and finally had a thriving business with lots of happy and returning guests.

But it was then that the fun really began. I soon realised that even an average review could send you tumbling down the rankings and hovering among the also-rans. If you are in a big city such as Bath or London, this is fine; but on a highly competitive island, it's essential to be at the top.

My friend Marc – a Michelin-starred chef in his own right – applauded me on my success but thought it right to warn me, lest I should become complacent, that from now on my guests' expectations would double. Every Tom, Dick and Harry would have an opinion. Oh boy, was he right! If it is relatively easy to garner good reviews for a B&B, it's an entirely different story with a restaurant. The problem with a restaurant is that food is very much in the eye of the beholder – or on the end of their tongue.

When we launched the restaurant, our aim was simple: to produce a limited menu that was home-made using locally sourced ingredients. This, we found, was all well and good when we were establishing ourselves, but when we became the number one restaurant in Shanklin, everything changed. Some guests thought they would enjoy a Michelin-starred experience at McDonald's prices. Suddenly, everyone had an opinion and of course they all knew better.

When I recounted this to Marc, he smiled and said, 'Now you know you have arrived, and the expectations will only get higher and higher.'

I think you can finally say you've made it when you're in a situation where you are so full that the odd bit of negativity is like water off a duck's back. But then it is also easy to become overconfident and believe your own hype – and stop caring what your guests are thinking.

Over the years, I have marvelled at how social media and, in some ways, our fixation with celebrity have taken over. It seems everyone wants to be the next Gordon Ramsay, Jamie Oliver or even my old colleague Fred Sirieix, but what they don't seem to understand is that to be where they are today takes years of toil and dedication. They don't just whip up a quick pasta, magically appear on the telly and have millions thrown at them.

That said, I don't believe in the old-school style of cheffing, which at best could only be described as brutal; while at its worst I have witnessed acts administered by chefs that would today almost certainly land them with a lawsuit or, even worse, jail time. I do believe the younger generation need to grasp the fact that there is no such thing as a free ride. I now must resort to mollycoddling youngsters to even grace me with their presence, and I do wonder how they would have fared with some of the more volatile characters I have worked with over the years.

When I worked in Cheshire, the then head chef took offence at the constant badgering of the restaurant manager. He responded by seizing a blowtorch and, rather than caramelising the nearest crème brûlée, deemed it totally acceptable to singe the poor manager's hair to within a whisker of his scalp. To add injury to insult, the owner told the manager not to upset the chef! In no way was the chef even reprimanded.

On another occasion, a head chef in Switzerland was so incensed by one of his junior chef's efforts that he threw the unsuspecting chef head first into the nearby stockpot. I am sure it was more by luck than judgement that there weren't any contents simmering away. The young man in question came away with nothing more than a bruised ego. But back then, no one batted an eyelid.

Perhaps my overriding memory was from working in Preston, when a chef decided that one of his young protégé's efforts was not up to scratch. He bound the young lad with Sellotape and shaved off his hair and eyebrows. The final coup de grace was having a cucumber shoved *where the sun don't shine*. To my utter amazement, the teenage chef never uttered a word of complaint, merely dusted himself down and shrugged off the whole incident with, 'Well, I won't fuck up on service again.'

I can't ever condone such behaviour and these examples give you a taster of how intense a kitchen could be. So, whenever we critique a chef's food, please try to imagine the physically draining work, intense heat, cuts and burns and the huge dedication and commitment it takes to produce consistently amazing creations.

If the attitude of the young chef twenty years ago was the norm, then that cannot be said of youngsters today. I recently had a twenty-year-old chef break down in tears and accuse me of showing him no appreciation because I had the audacity to tell him – albeit very calmly – to scrap some cremated scrambled eggs and start again.

If I had to do a double take with this young chef, that was nothing compared to a young catering student I had agreed to take on. Her college required each student to supplement their course with some hands-on experience. Having done something similar, I was more than happy to help. The course tutor informed me that I was under no obligation to pay a salary, although the student had to work thirty hours a week. I was uncomfortable with this, so when I'd met the young lady and judged her more than capable, I suggested a proper salary rather than the suggested slave labour. Everyone's a winner, or so I thought.

The first day went without a hitch and I was relieved that it was turning out so well. However, after this, things went awry. The next day, clearly the worse for wear, she rang in sick. Okay, I thought, we all make mistakes, so I gave her the benefit of the doubt. On her next shift, she didn't even phone; she just failed to show up. And this continued for the whole week, so I concluded she didn't want the job. I phoned the college to discuss the situation and to my amazement the lecturer was clearly shocked – the student had informed her how well she was doing. Well, if you called a one-day-in-nine show-up rate a good total, I was clearly in the wrong business.

•

Apart from the odd magazine article, newspaper review and a rather nice mention by the late A.A. Gill for outstanding service, I have had very little interaction with the world of social media. To be honest, I am so old school that emailing and googling are pretty much my limit. If my wife, Ewa, can't sort out any impending crisis, then Jack, my son, usually saves the day and laughs at his father's technical faux pas. It has become a ritual to hear a sigh, accompanied by, 'Do you get it now, Dad?' It's not that I don't see the benefits but, with my limited patience, as soon as technology moves forward it leaves me behind. Even paying a bill online leaves me in a cold sweat; I usually believe I'm transferring my entire life savings into some offshore account, never to be seen again.

My only real foray into the world of *celebrity* was appearing on Channel 4's *Four in a Bed*. Actually, I tell a lie – my previous fleeting limelight moment came when I worked for chef Paul Heathcote and appeared on the evening news. Back then, I had spent the entire day training local schoolchildren in the art of service in front of a watchful BBC camera crew. After a pretty exhausting day, as well as countless interviews, the evening culminated in the schoolchildren and I putting on a dinner for Preston's VIPs; or should I say, the evening consisted of me doing my utmost to stop little Tommy unloading the contents of his tray down the Lord Mayor's back!

Over the course of dinner, I thought that after all those hours in front of the camera, putting on my most radiant smile and with my boundless charm and enthusiasm, a glittering career on the TV would naturally follow. Just before service, I rang my mother and informed her that my moment of stardom was imminent; she had to watch the news on telly that evening. Returning home and on a high from the day's events, I rang my mother, expecting adulation to follow. To my surprise, all I heard was my mother clearly trying to humour me.

'Oh darling, you did look so smart when you passed by.'

'What do you mean, passed by? What about all the interviews?'

'I'm sorry, darling, I must have missed that bit.'

Horrified by my mother's lack of enthusiasm, I curtailed the conversation and settled down to watch the recording. What was supposed to be my moment in the sun turned out exactly as my mother had said – just a two-second cameo. To make matters worse, my boss, Paul, had grabbed the limelight. I mean, for God's sake, he'd only turned up for the bloody dinner!

In truth, I hadn't been that deflated since my mother inadvertently recorded over my triumphant win at the annual pool tournament at my hotel school, Les Roches. Instead of now seeing my spectacular double on the black, I have to console myself with yet another episode of *Homes Under the Hammer*. When I was approached by *Four in a Bed*, I had no illusions of grandeur, just a hope that it might put our fledgling business on the map. Little did I anticipate the impact the show would have or how it would continue to help many years after it was aired. For those who have not watched the show, the idea is that four rival B&B owners visit each other, score each other's properties, pay what they think it's worth and decide if they would return. The establishment that gets the best price, in comparison to what they charge, is declared the winner.

Before the production crew turned up at Keats, I had been warned by several reliable sources that the editing could influence the outcome. Ewa thought I should have my head examined for even entertaining the idea, especially as it had only been six months since we'd opened the doors to our first guests. As far as I was concerned, so long as I didn't go down the path of Syed, a waiter who had worked with me at the Bluebird and then made a seismic hash of a hospitality project on Alan Sugar's *The Apprentice*, what could possibly go wrong?

Although Grant, the producer, was quick to put us at ease, it soon became apparent that the whole process would be anything but plain sailing. First, on each show, you are responsible for hosting an activity while the guests are staying at your establishment. This turned out to be our first major headache. Every idea we had, from a trip to the local vineyard to a day playing crazy golf, was immediately deemed too boring and shot down in flames.

When it was suggested that Ewa and I should attempt Polish dancing in the middle of the restaurant, I realised that the B&B experience came a distant second to the entertainment the show wanted to provide. Regarding strutting my stuff, I did stand my ground with a few choice words along the lines of 'if you think I'm attempting Polish fucking dancing in front of millions of people, then you can think again'.

In the end, a compromise of sorts was struck and as the weather was a little unpredictable it was agreed that, should the weather be poor, Ewa would do a blind tasting of Polish cuisine, and should it be fine, we would all attempt to catch lobsters off the sunny shores of Ventnor. What could possibly go wrong?

It soon became clear that for every show, there is a planned line of attack. They know which couples are likely to rub each other up the wrong way, who is likely to make a fool of himself and who is to be cast as the villain. The trouble with those editing the show is that, once they've decided how they best think events should turn out, they are pretty much like dogs with a bone.

Grant had decided that as I had worked as a hotel inspector for the AA, this would be one of the focal points of the show. During my interview, I pointed out that my time at the AA had been a mere three months. It could hardly constitute a career and I would prefer it to be left out. Although noted, it was obviously ignored.

My second insight into the show came moments before my guests were about to check in. The crew took it upon themselves to take a couple more shots of the rooms just prior to the first arrival. Having spent two days cleaning the place from top to bottom, the last thing I wanted was some camera person traipsing through my immaculately polished rooms. Grant tried to assure me that all would be fine, but was it my imagination that one of the cameramen couldn't quite catch my eye on exiting the room? I only had a split second to check one of those rooms, but when I did it was clear to me that the bedroom wasn't as pristine as I had left it.

This left me wondering. While watching other shows beforehand, I could never understand why the contestants would leave a mess in the rooms, knowing they were about to be critiqued. However, in many cases I now understand the look of incredulous disbelief on the host's face when a hair is found. Better still, in one episode the guest found a worm in the toilet and coincidentally had a phobia about worms. I mean, you couldn't make it up, and it certainly made me wonder how these things magically appeared.

This aside, Ewa and I had decided that our best plan was to be ourselves and see where it took us. We had no intention of becoming embroiled in any arguments and certainly no intention of underpaying, purely to win the competition. As the long day commenced, we were both apprehensive and excited. To be honest, the way I saw it, we were just doing what we did every day, with the addition of a couple of cameras being stuck under our noses.

So, when Donna – our first guest – arrived, I was just relieved to get the show on the road. As it turned out, Donna was a no-nonsense Leicestershire lass, who certainly didn't suffer fools gladly. As we opened the door, you could see we all just wanted to get on with the experience. I was repeatedly asked to reopen the door, with the greeting 'Hi, welcome to Keats Cottage, I'm David and this is my wife, Ewa', so it wasn't long before the world of *celebrity* began to wear thin. By the seventh attempt, I was just about to call it a day and I could tell that both Donna and Ewa were performing their welcome through gritted teeth.

By the time Chloe and her lovely mum, Lesley, arrived at Keats, there was quite a crowd gathering across the road. As is the world we live in today, we were soon being asked for selfies. An hour in and I was already feeling fatigued. Matters only got worse when we discovered that Martin and his partner, Sara, were running late. It transpired that while they were enjoying the delights of Shanklin seafront, Martin was unfortunate enough to have had the whole of the driver's side door of his car taken off its hinges as he attempted to get out. This was possibly an omen for the show, and by the time the effervescent Martin rocked up, I had really started to ask what we'd let ourselves in for.

•

As our guests went to scrutinise their rooms, the production crew added to the already mounting levels of stress by informing us that, as the sun was now shining, we would make our way down to Ventnor to enjoy the delights of lobster fishing. This came as something of a relief to me, as I was by now desperate to escape the confines of Keats. For poor Ewa, it was something of a let-down – she had spent hours preparing her fabled pierogi, as we had anticipated poorer weather.

Our motley crew made its way down to the shore in the sunshine, and I believed we were over the worst. But it wasn't long before the gods were to intervene again and although the sun made for a rather pleasant day, the same could not be said for the sea, which was becoming quite choppy. While our lady fishing guide – who wouldn't have been out of place in an episode of *Baywatch* in her tight red shorts and matching boots – was relishing the event, the same could not be said of Ewa, who was already turning a shade of green. The crew encouraged me to show my manly side and haul the pots from the depths of the ocean, but my competitive spirit was put to one side as Ewa emptied her lunch over the side of the boat, much to my distress and the obvious delight of the production crew. They were already contemplating a soar in their ratings. At least the seagulls who were lining up above my wife's head seemed happy with the outcome.

•

Once Lesley and I had escorted the still shaky Ewa off the boat, I asked Grant if they would be kind enough not to show the entire contents of my wife's stomach to the viewing public. To give him his due, he did feign concern at our plight, but was quick to remind me of the contract I had signed, agreeing that anything and everything could be shown. In hindsight, credit where credit is due; they were kind enough to omit the part where Ewa started wailing so much that even the seagulls took flight as she beseeched the crew to get her off this bloody boat and back to dry land! I guess every cloud has its silver lining.

After a somewhat entertaining afternoon, I whisked a still unwell Ewa back to the B&B, where she stayed for the rest of the day while I continued with the interviews. I then attended the dinner alone, trying to put on my best smile while Martin grilled me on how much I paid for Keats before stating that I was far too cheap for what I was offering. If that was his reasoning, then I thought I could at least expect an overpayment.

By the time the evening was over, and I had served Martin his 11 p.m. brandy, I was happy to flop into bed. As I started to drift away, I was already contemplating the next day's breakfast service and hoping the day might be a little less eventful.

The next morning went pretty much without a hitch, apart from Donna not enjoying her sausage. As we settled into our feedback, we were delighted by the high scores and the three *yeses* to coming back. So at least our efforts had paid off.

At the time I didn't appreciate it, but it was certainly beneficial to kick off the show first, because at this point everyone wants to appear friendly. It's only later in the show that tensions start to escalate, especially after poor feedback.

As we made our way up to Leicestershire to experience Donna's B&B, we were contented to have come out relatively unscathed and with friendships blossoming.

What viewers might not realise is that the whole experience is filmed over two weeks. We were promised to be only a short distance from the island, but this turned out not to be the case. You spend the night before your stay in an independent hotel before checking in to your competitor's B&B. Not realising the amount of travelling, we returned on the Friday night at the end of the first week to a full B&B. We had a full restaurant on the Saturday night and after serving our guests breakfast on the Sunday, we made the gruelling trip back up the motorway to Manchester.

As you can imagine, after that seven-hour journey I couldn't wait for the morning interview in the car, which entailed me chatting to the producer while navigating rush-hour traffic. This with a bloody camera stuck under my nose and a cameraman who was so long-legged I couldn't even change gear. By the time we reached our destination, I wished our Duster could miraculously turn into a James Bond car complete with ejector seat. If only!

To our amazement, Donna ran the whole B&B without any help. This is no mean feat. I know from experience that trying to cook *and* serve breakfast is not an easy undertaking. Breakfast turned out to be a little disjointed, but the food was faultless. Ewa and I had agreed in advance that the only criterion we would base our payment on was whether we would be happy to pay that rate as a paying customer, so we deemed any minor faults immaterial. With this in mind, we paid in full; but it became obvious that Martin was starting to grate on Donna's nerves. A storm was brewing.

Many people who watched the show have come up to me and said, 'Oh, wasn't Martin a horrible little man.' To be honest, although he could be mildly irritating and some of his views were cringeworthy, to the extent that I spent half the time praying he wouldn't put his foot in it yet again on national TV, there were times where he was actually good fun to be around. The producers preyed on someone who was easy to cast as the villain of the piece. Sara, his partner, was an absolute delight, and I could only marvel at her patience. I soon realised that this quiet lady was the rock in Martin's life. She kept everything together and wasn't the money-grabber certain quarters wanted to believe.

That said, I was flabbergasted by the vitriol that came Martin's way after the show. There were literally hundreds of unpleasant comments on his Facebook and TripAdvisor pages. What was more astonishing was that it appeared none of these people had ever met him or stayed at his establishment. How could they possibly pass judgement?

I guess I had never really considered the possibility of poor feedback, even though I had been warned about it. This siege mentality from certain quarters of the public is something that concerns me for the future. To be honest, when it came to celebrities, I had always thought that if they wanted to be in the limelight, then they should be able to withstand constructive criticism. However, the abuse that people are subjected to now seems to have passed the point of no return. I feel something needs to be done about it.

In Martin's case, I don't think he had properly thought about the reality of what he was letting himself in for. He obviously had no experience in hospitality and thought it would prove easy to attract celebrities to his affluent part of Manchester, which played host to countless footballers and in turn provided the opportunity to charge a premium. What he hadn't factored in was that his partner had a full-time job with British Airways while he really wanted to do as little as possible for maximum reward.

The point I tried to explain to him was that if he was charging over £500 a night, there really was no room for error and everything needed to be perfect. At those prices, self-check-in, cook your own breakfast and an additional service charge were not something he could get away with. He argued that he had not been overly critical of the cleanliness of the other establishments, but the problem was that his place really wasn't as clean as any of the others. At that price, he really needed to be ten times better. That was the whole point he clearly missed. To cap it all, after telling me I should think more carefully about the bottom line, he then proceeded to get a catering company to provide a breakfast that would have fed thirty people. His lack of prowess became ever more apparent when I had to show him how to make his own coffee! Martin, rather than taking on board Donna's comments, totally antagonised her by stating that he '… made the most money' and that 'Donna was too cheap to stay in a place like his'.

•

All in all, there were a number of positives from the show. Lesley and Chloe were a delight and deserved to be its winners, and I was overjoyed when Chloe returned with her partner to stay at Keats. Donna, I'm pleased to say, keeps in touch on Facebook. She let me know after she returned to her B&B that, thanks to the feedback from the show, she confronted her owner and asked for more help. He declined. She left and he ended up paying three people to do her job. As for Martin, I never heard from him again, but I wish them well.

The show has given me another tale to tell and is constantly repeated, so it continues to help boost business. Did I enjoy it? Absolutely. Would I do it again? Without a moment's hesitation. Would Ewa? Not a cat in hell's chance. But as anyone who knows me can testify, I love to blah de blah. For me, it was one of life's adventures, never to be forgotten. However, I did laugh at the tale one of my regulars told me. He had whisked his partner away for a romantic weekend and on the previous night, I had served them in the restaurant. They were well away from Shanklin, so you can imagine their surprise when the voice they heard, during their first throes of passion, was in fact mine. As he so eloquently put it, he then saw my ugly mug on TV, which put a halt to any further developments because his wife forced him to watch the entire episode. Oh, the life of a celebrity!

•

For those thinking of participating, I would say just be yourselves and you can't go far wrong. Be warned: once the editing is complete, you may well feel you are watching an entirely different show. There were several instances where events were omitted that definitely had a bearing on the outcome. There were also minor details that the producers took delight in going over again and again. The point I'm referring to is Donna not enjoying her sausage at Keats. She never once made an issue over the sausage, and stated that she wasn't particularly fond of sausages. Unbeknown to us, the producer went on about the offending sausage to such an extent that Donna repeatedly asked them not to bring up the subject again.

To make matters worse, I had no idea that Sausagegate was to be such a big part of the show. My only memory was of the crew tucking into breakfast and eulogising over the sausages. In my naivety, I had invited my butcher and his colleague to view the episode. Not knowing what was coming, you can only imagine my horror when the poor man's sausage was continually dragged up.

There was one evening when I mentioned to Sara that she was obviously the rock who kept everything together in their relationship. She was visibly moved, and I think with the whole show having been a bit of a nightmare for her, she appreciated being recognised. This was also not shown after the edit. I believe this would have gone a long way towards showing the softer side of a couple who seemed to me to be cast as *lambs to the slaughter*.

•

As for TripAdvisor, I guess you only really remember the amazing highs and the abysmal lows and, as my friends say, you really should just ignore it and carry on regardless. But my problem is that even if that person is obviously a pretentious wanker, I still want them to be won over and shake my hand at the end of it all. *Why?* you may ask. Simply because I believe that is my job. It is with pride that I managed my eight years without a blemish on my TripAdvisor record and won the coveted Red Funnel award for best B&B in my final year, but as they say, pride comes before a fall, and this certainly happened to me with one restaurant review that haunts me to this day.

You will always encounter someone who thinks they are superior to the rest of us or who likes to flaunt their wealth. There are those who want something for nothing and those who think they are better than the little waiter, who is privileged to serve them. The key is to play to their egos. Stay friendly but drop the subtlest hint that they aren't quite as grand as they think they are.

I have found that those who like to show off their wealth will change towards you if you happen to mention you are Swiss. Others who feel they are intellectually your superior might change their attitude if you mention a private-school education and a Swiss degree. It's all just a game in people's minds.

I have also realised over the years that the worst thing you can do is hide away from what can only be described as a bullying guest. They will love the fact that their abhorrent ways have won the day. I have watched many colleagues over the years shrink away from this sort of confrontation but, although I abhor conflict, my approach is to kill them with kindness. I would say that 95 per cent of the time, this line of attack tends to work. Often, guests will come down to breakfast in the foulest of moods, *ready for a fight*, but as soon as they see that all your other guests are relishing your best efforts, their attitude will totally change.

Many guests have told me that I have the patience of a saint. Because of this perceived tolerance, I have on many occasions been asked to serve a difficult VIP, but in truth I hate confrontation and do not believe that two wrongs make a right. I also believe that if a guest walks away unhappy – whatever the circumstances – I have failed to do my job. However, there have been occasions in my career where the mark has been overstepped and a put-down is the order of the day. One thing I can't abide is if a colleague is talked down to in an overly aggressive manner.

For me, service is about putting on a show and every guest is part of the play. While some guests might enjoy the attention, others will enjoy peace and quiet. The art is in anticipating their needs and behaviour before they even know themselves what they want. Daily, there may be a multitude of different situations that require totally different reactions. An East End wide boy might be sitting at one table, someone who loves a bit of banter and whose idea of fun might be to drop a coarse comment and expect a similar comment back, but that wouldn't go down too well with the lord sitting at the table next to him, someone who wouldn't have a clue if you asked him if he wanted a drink from the *near and far*, meaning bar.

This is where a good server is worth their weight in gold. For example, you might have a lady who enjoys a bit of flirtatious banter, but the art is knowing how far to take it before the husband either invites you for a *ménage à trois* – yes, before you ask, these situations do arise – or threatens to knock your teeth out. The point is, everyone is different, and you must be the master at responding to each of these differences. This is no mean feat.

•

Coming back to that one bad review that still troubles me to this day, you may well ask why. I know it shouldn't but ask any hotelier who really cares, and they will all say the same – it bothers them and, trust me, the consequences can be enormous.

While on the Isle of Wight, I had one guest who checked in on our Valentine's package. They lived on the island, but this was not uncommon as several guests came from the island, especially during quieter times of the year. Everything had started off well. As they enjoyed a complimentary drink, Nic, the guest, mentioned that he was a builder and had even done some work on our property years earlier.

We chatted on and I mentioned how my mother and I had in fact done a lot of the refurbishment ourselves. Nic's wife had even praised our efforts, stating that they wished there were more B&Bs like ours on the island. So, as I left them to their Valentine's afternoon, I had no inkling of how events would unfold.

When Nic and his wife joined the others in the restaurant, the place was already full. Sitting next to them was a group of regulars, enjoying a seventieth birthday party. Things seemed to be going along nicely, then from nowhere the night took a massive turn for the worse.

Our menu comprised five main courses, all home-cooked from locally sourced ingredients, and on the night in question twenty-four out of our thirty diners had opted for the duck. The quality of our food was something on which we had built our reputation, and all the guests had waxed lyrical about the duck. So I had no inkling about what would ensue until Angie, my waitress, came back, stating that Nic wasn't happy with his duck.

As I came over, the once gracious Nic and his wife were now in full flow and were announcing to the party next to them what a disgrace the duck was. These things happen and at the time I was not unduly perturbed. I apologised profusely and noticed only a single bite had been taken. A little strange, I thought, but I did what I thought was needed in the circumstances. Firstly, I offered him a new portion. Declined. Secondly, a different dish. Declined. A little perplexed, I offered him a complimentary dessert and drink. Again, declined. Thinking that their romantic night was not going as planned, I bit the bullet and told them their meal was on me. Surely that would make amends?

But if that was my initial reaction, I was certainly not prepared for his departing words: 'I hope your fucking breakfast is better than your dinner.' Not the gracious Nic I had first encountered. I knew something was seriously wrong, but I couldn't put my finger on it. I had dealt with many situations, but this just felt wrong on many levels.

As Nic and his wife left the dining room, I breathed a sigh of relief and went back to the kitchen to taste the offending item. For the life of me, I couldn't find fault with it. It just didn't add up. I returned to the dining room, and many of the guests tried to console me and told me the food was delicious. Nonetheless, I was still concerned that it wasn't to his liking.

If I thought my night was going to improve, alas no. Five minutes later, Nic and his wife came back into the restaurant, claiming they had been violently sick. Anyone with any common sense would know that in the time that had elapsed, and the fact that they hadn't touched their dinner, this was nigh on impossible. My patience was waning. I said I would check into this, but as so many diners were eating the same dish with no ill effects, I found their complaints difficult to accept. Nic accused me of calling him a liar, to which I replied that I would not be charging for his room, even though he had used all the facilities for the whole afternoon, and that perhaps he should leave. Ewa had heard the commotion and, having far less patience than me, told him in no uncertain terms not to come back again.

As I went to bed that night, I knew we had not heard the last of the matter. With a little trepidation, I went to check the reviews the next morning. If I had feared the worst, it was nothing compared to what was in store for me. The vitriol that greeted me was something to behold. What was truly shocking was that, firstly, he had posted attacks on every forum possible. TripAdvisor, Booking. com, Facebook. He went all out. Secondly, he had attacked parts of my business that had nothing to do with his stay and parts that he and his wife had previously complimented. Again, it was a mystery.

Obviously upset, I recounted the tale to friends, who told me to post a reply, but although I was sorely tempted, I had refrained from doing this for the past thirty years and was not about to start now. In fact, I was conversely delighted by the number of guests who had eaten that night and had taken it upon themselves to write their own comments and to refute Nic's claims on TripAdvisor. Oh well, there was some justice, I thought. But I was not prepared for how malevolent some people could be: lo and behold, Nic's wife wrote her thoughts on TripAdvisor. My doubts about TripAdvisor were proved when one year to the day of the event, Nic, for whatever reason, tried to slate me yet again.

At the time, I was understandably upset, as was Ewa. But, to me, what was more astounding was that when I approached the relevant media, showing that his review was incorrect and substantiating this from several other guests, they point-blank refused to remove his reviews. Therein lies the dangers of social media.

Now, to this day I don't know what the issue was, but so many thoughts ran through my head. All things aside, he paid not a penny and yet was still hell-bent on destroying my business. Two things happened because of that incident: I lost all faith in social media and my wife never cooked in the restaurant again.

CHAPTER 21

My first experience with the super-rich

As to my story, the latest twist in my ongoing saga came in the final months of my stay at hotel school when I met up with the very vivacious Sarah. As we had known each other for some time as friends, she was already privy to my exploits, but little did I know that this *force of nature* would put me in the shade.

Sarah could only be described as a bundle of dynamite. One that should have had a warning sign plastered to her ample bosom. Short blonde hair, tottering on high heels and with a fag constantly in her hand; her pent-up sexual energy was so evident that on first meeting her, my stepfather almost choked on his beer, declaring, 'Oh my God, boy, that girl is sex on legs.' He wasn't wrong. Another friend, who met us with his girlfriend, declared later that he was scared to be left alone in a room with her. Enough said.

•

After a tempestuous start, where I could barely keep up, I put an end to my other relationships – although, it has to be said, not before a trip to the beautiful island of Kos with Daniela and a weekend of fun with Katja in Holland. But when I made it back to the UK, I decided finally to put my house in order, especially when Katja turned up on my doorstep having secured a job at The Goring Hotel in London.

I would like to think I did this for the right reason, by ending the other relationships, but in truth the situation was clearly out of hand and besides, I couldn't keep up with the sexual demands of Sarah. I remember when we moved down to Weybridge to embark on what turned out to be a four-year relationship, she introduced me to her box of *friends*, which turned out to be an amazing treasure trove of sexual goodies. Rather than being surprised or upset that maybe my sexual appetite didn't match her own, I rejoiced in the fact that I might have a well-earned breather.

•

The next few years taught me many of life's lessons, that my own behaviour would come back to haunt me – 'what goes around comes around' was never more apt. Sarah had come from very humble beginnings. Her father was a likeable Yorkshireman; unfortunately, he had a roving eye and eventually separated from Sarah's mother – an equally likeable lady. Sarah's problem lay in the fact that her mother had remarried with a man who, although approaching sixty, acted like a child who was obviously used to getting his own way.

I vividly recall my first meeting with him in London; we all hopped into a taxi and the tension was clearly palpable. Worried that I had already made a bad impression on him, I was relieved that it had nothing to do with me but concerned the car auction about to take place at Sotheby's, which we were to attend. He stomped from the taxi and, as we hurried to keep up, I asked Sarah, 'What the hell is wrong with him?'

By this time, he had bypassed the long queues around the entrance and was being greeted like royalty.

'Don't worry about it, Ian's just worried that the auctioneer has set the reserve price on his Rolls-Royce too low,' responded Sarah. Apparently, there had only been two of these cars ever made and the second one had recently sold in New York for just over a million pounds. The problem was this *bloody* auctioneer had the audacity to value his at £900,000 – one was not amused.

I was introduced to a lifestyle that I could only deem as being more than agreeable. Although I was a lowly head waiter, I was now dining at a whole host of the finest restaurants in London. Ian's membership at the exclusive Royal Automobile Club in Pall Mall meant enticing breaks away, with me very much part of the cigar and brandy brigade I had only ever witnessed in films. What's more, I was now able to enjoy complimentary golf at their sister clubhouse, based in Epsom.

One day, as I surveyed all the names of chief executives on the club's membership waiting list, I couldn't help but find it amusing that this lowly waiter had joined the upper echelons of society. This was only the start and shortly after we were invited to join Sarah's parents at their retreat in Cape Town. This was a magical time. We enjoyed lunches at the Mount Nelson hotel, day trips to the vineyards, hikes up Table Mountain, seaplanes to look over Seal Island. I was entranced by the sheer beauty of the place and due to the generosity of Sarah's stepfather, I returned from the vacation with money still in my pocket. But like the seals that I had witnessed being circled by the great white sharks, I was soon to be swallowed up and spat out.

If I already knew that Ian was a little tricky to handle, my worst fears were soon to be realised when we were invited for shooting on their estate in Scotland. Expecting a little country pile, I was astounded to hear that, along with thousands of acres, the estate had its own hotel, a pub, several cottages and a recently built mansion. Although I was excited about the forthcoming trip, it soon became apparent that this really was a man who was used to getting his own way. Having only lived in Switzerland and London, at the age of twenty-four I had yet to learn to drive, a situation Ian thought was totally unacceptable. He thought of himself as the Jeremy Clarkson of the motor sport world and there was no way a potential son-in-law of his could possibly not know how to drive. Besides, he needed his Ferrari taken out as it couldn't possibly languish away in the garage!

Sarah received an agitated phone call from her mother, pleading with me to learn to drive. Not understanding the gravity of the situation and not wanting to be pushed around, I stated that once I had earned the money, I was more than happy to learn to drive. Having relayed this to the chief, Sarah's tearful mother had come back on the phone and declared that Ian would happily pay for my lessons. Not happy to be bought off, I only relented when he threatened to disinherit poor Sarah. If there was any justice, it took me four attempts to pass my test, so at least I got my money's worth.

The weekend in Scotland passed without a hitch. There were banquets that wouldn't have been out of place in the court of Henry VIII. I felt I had passed back through several decades as the men enjoyed port in the library while the ladies retired to the drawing room. It was something akin to a Jane Austen novel and I half expected Mr Darcy to jump out from behind the curtains. My last memory of that weekend was being greeted by an unusually happy Ian with, 'Come here, my boy, I need to show you how one gets their wealth out of South Africa.' I was staggered when he proceeded to snip the ends off toothpaste tubes, and diamonds scattered over the table!

•

I guess the warning signs were already there, but it soon became apparent that while our lifestyle was certainly fun, Sarah's recklessness with cash exceeded even my own. Although mine and Sarah's salaries were similar, eye-boggling amounts were being deposited into her account by her stepfather. Whereas I might think £100 was acceptable to pay for a meal, Sarah would find it normal to have one more drink, miss the train home and spend the same amount on a taxi back to Weybridge.

It wasn't as though I was jealous or even that I wasn't more than extravagant myself, but the amounts of money were out of my league. Also, two things happened. Firstly, Sarah was happy to spend as much time as possible with a coterie of Hooray Henrys, who I had no time for, as their sole purpose was to squander Mummy's and Daddy's money. Secondly, I was offered a job back in Switzerland – the kind that rarely comes along – but Sarah was unwilling to return and quite happily told me, 'We don't need that kind of salary, we have more than enough to survive.'

Stupidly, I turned the offer down, and when I announced that one day I would like my own business, Sarah scorned the idea with, 'Why on earth would you want to do that?'

You can imagine my reaction when, two months later, and spurred on by her stepfather, who declared that although I was an amiable kind of chap, I would always be a Fiat rather than a Ferrari, I was unceremoniously told that I had three days to leave the flat we now shared overlooking The Hurlingham Club, as I obviously couldn't afford it. The only upside was that I found a room in a houseshare with two Spanish girls. Every cloud and all that!

•

The relationship had been a whirlwind and there were many good times, but ultimately it taught me a lot of lessons and – having been given a taste of my own medicine – I certainly did my best to mend my ways. I would never say I was an angel, but by the time of my marriage to Ewa, I had certainly slowed down. This girl with the angelic smile but a fiery soul knew how to keep me in check and to be honest, she saved me from my own worst enemy – namely, myself. All joking aside, she tamed me in many ways. Perhaps if she hadn't, I wouldn't be here today, and for that I will be eternally grateful.

CHAPTER 22

1990–2005 – The many vices and pitfalls of catering – the demon drink

Over the years, I have seen how easy it is to let catering take you on a downward spiral of drink and drugs. I know because it almost happened to me. The problem is that the stress is constant and the hours are relentless. What you kid yourself into believing is just *high jinks* when you are in your early twenties soon becomes part of your everyday existence. Suddenly, you're older and you wonder how it all became *normal*.

I have seen chefs looking slightly dishevelled on TV, knowing they were *three sheets to the wind* just a couple of hours before the show. How do I know? Because I was with them on that *last one for the road* that never ends up being the last one. I have asked myself many times, why it is so easy for those in catering to take this road? For all of us, I would say, the hours are a common theme. In the case of chefs, it's the constant quest for perfection. In the case of front of house staff, it's trying to maintain perfection for an ever more demanding clientele. For all the shining examples of success that we are aware of on

TV, there are many more that I know have slipped down a path they can't recover from. Even some of those beacons of our industry only survive their diet of drink and drugs through tenacity of spirit.

Now aged fifty, I can understand the pitfalls and realise why friends of the same age have decided to take different career paths. It's only really those with office-based hospitality jobs or executive chefs with a brigade to delegate to who can sustain the hours. For the owner or manager trying to *do it all*, there comes a time where this becomes impossible.

I remember being at Swiss hotel school and wondering why the lecturers – obviously masters of their craft – weren't in some high-end hotel, showing off their undoubted skills. I mean, it made no sense to me at the time. They all had amazing CVs and were in most cases certainly under the age of fifty. But having gained parity in age, it is easy to see why. You just can't do it anymore, and perhaps those *shaky hands* weren't just a figment of my imagination and showed another reason why they had taken a different path.

Drugs are something I can't give an opinion on. I knew from my own somewhat addictive tendencies that this was an area I really didn't want to get into. In the case of alcohol, I always felt as if I had a semblance of control. But with drugs, I knew I would never have stood a chance. That would have been one of life's highs that would certainly have seen the end of me. This is not to say I haven't been surrounded by it from every angle, or that I haven't been tempted. But even from a young age, I knew it was a step too far.

If I ever want proof that I took at least one right course in my life, I need look no further than a chef who I helped with his business for a few months. This likeable Frenchman, although close to fifty, partied as though he were still in his early twenties. I must say that his considerable appetite for everything that should have been done in moderation was no mean feat of endurance. However, I would say his excesses probably overstepped the mark. His drug supplier, rather than collecting payment in cash, would instead be entitled to a free lunch with the compliments of the house. I guess it was something akin to a coupon, but unlike any I had seen before. I found it somewhat comical to be serving foie gras, washed down with rather a nice Sauternes, to someone with a dubious reputation for breaking your legs if you were unwise enough to miss payment. Luckily for us, he always seemed to enjoy his food.

Just before I stopped helping in this restaurant, the plot thickened when the said drugs dealer brought in his new *girlfriend* to join him for lunch. As I watched their love blossom over the table, I wasn't sure whether it would be wise to mention that I had encountered this rather charming young lady exiting one of my guest's bedrooms in the wee hours of the morning. Perhaps he knew that his new love was a high-class escort? But I thought it prudent not to mention it as they shared their crème brûlée.

If I was in any doubt as to the self-destructive nature of the French chef, these doubts were quickly put to bed when I discovered that the *friendship* between chef and dealer had hit a rocky spot, when the chef took it upon himself to sleep with the dealer's new girlfriend. To make matters worse, it transpired that he hadn't even been asked to pay! I'm not sure what happened after, but I'm guessing there were no more coupons on offer and precious little foie gras consumed.

As with most things, I think there's a fine line between being a heavy social drinker and becoming a total alcoholic, and just one seismic event can push anyone over this edge. We all love to be or be around the *life and soul of the party*, but we all look on aghast at some drunk, knocking back a Scotch first thing in the morning. Where is that limit? Where is that line you can't cross? I guess everyone is different and rather than quantities consumed, it's more about the person involved. I have known people who are *blotto* on a couple of drinks and friends who can down six pints as a warm-up without even breaking a sweat. I've known others with responsible jobs, who have loving partners and families, and are able to function despite consuming ten cans of super-strength lager on a nightly basis. These *functioning* alcoholics are aware of their problem but cannot see past the one extreme event that shaped not only their lives but also their addictions.

The fine line I alluded to first came to light in my twenties, at a time when I thought I was invincible. It was a wake-up call in the form of my stepfather, or 'The Boss' as he was affectionately known. When my parents divorced, The Boss and I became close, more in a friendship sort of way than a father/son scenario. That's not to say I didn't toe the line with him, but the occasion never seemed to present itself where we fell out. When my mother had run off with her hair-dresser, namely The Boss, it had seemed like a fairy-tale romance. I was always grateful that my mother had finally found love.

The Boss could only be described as a *man's man*. With his handsome looks and charming manner, he had countless women knocking his door down for their weekly cut and blow-dry. After my parents' somewhat acrimonious divorce and the subsequent fallout, I was happy to have The Boss in my corner and it was due to him, in no small way, that my teenage years turned out so happily.

I had known from an early age that we had similar traits, and I was aware during my late teens and early twenties that, like me, he could best be described as a heavy social drinker. To his friends of more than thirty years, he was of course the *life and soul* of the party. Yes, he did drink a bit too much, but it really wasn't a problem. By this stage, I couldn't really preach as I was now in Zurich, enjoying several pints in my split shift followed by several more after work. My mum had voiced her concerns about both of us but at that stage, and being young, I didn't see it as a problem. Mum had never really enjoyed drinking, so I thought perhaps she was trying to shackle The Boss a little – as partners can do – but not for one second did I think there was an issue. That said, I had on several occasions taken him to one side and told him he really should slow down; but by the wry little smile I received in return, I knew he wasn't taking me seriously and was probably thinking Mum had put me up to it.

While I worked in Switzerland, my visits to the UK usually ended up with The Boss and I sitting up until the small hours, discussing my outrageous exploits over several drinks, not to mention copious cigarettes. Most parents would have disapproved of my behaviour and rightly so, but The Boss seemed to revel in my stories. I don't think they were too dissimilar to his own. But as far as I was concerned, his and my mother's was a love story – one I would wish to emulate.

Having left their respective marriages with nothing, they had worked tirelessly to achieve their dream home and I can still remember when I returned home from school to find they had turned our two rooms into every boy's dream. This was made even more impressive by the fact that the rest of the house was a building site. For many years after, The Boss and my mother continued to sleep on a futon on a bare floor, while my brother and I slept in luxury.

When my weekends weren't taken up with studying, I spent the whole time toiling in the garden along with my mum and stepfather, but never once did I see this as a chore. From an early age, they instilled a work ethic that has stayed with me to this day. As they spent the following years building their dream home through pure sweat and tears, I spent less and less time there, and although my mother had been mentioning for a long time that The Boss's drinking was out of control, I really hadn't believed it to be a problem.

My wake-up call regarding my stepfather came some years later when I returned home and, as usual, we sat up late into the night, he with his customary Scotch and

I with my customary G&T. As usual, we had clambered into bed at around four o'clock, knowing all too well that we both needed to be up in only a couple of hours for work. The next morning, as I settled into a much-needed coffee, The Boss – much to my horror – offered me a brandy to go in it. 'Christ, Boss, we only went to bed a couple of hours ago and anyway, we both need to drive to get to work.' My pleas fell on deaf ears, and it was as the brandy went into his coffee that I finally witnessed what my mother had been telling me for years.

•

It wasn't long after, and as I approached my thirtieth birthday, that a turn of events led me to live at home for two months before I started a new job. As I was now home for longer than the customary couple of days, I became privy to how far The Boss had fallen. It was impossible for him to hide the facts in the way he had expertly done from all his friends. The man I had always looked up to was diminished before my eyes. His once outgoing demeanour was replaced by a sullen and ir-ritated version, one I had not encountered before. His handsome features were sunken, his nose bulbous and he had little pride in his appearance.

After seeing the evidence – the hidden bottles in the boot of the car, the sneaky Scotches before dinner and the blatant lies that occurred daily – even I pleaded with him to get help. But to my shock and dismay, rather than heed my pleas, he now branded me in the same camp as my mother – namely, the enemy. What amazed me more was that although he was openly hostile towards my mother and me in private, he still put on a semblance of charm with clients and friends.

I voiced these concerns with his friends, but it was just as I had once thought – they did not see his drinking as a problem. When you meet up once a week on a Friday night and consume multiple pints, you are just *one of the boys*. What they didn't realise was that his Friday nights were just the warm-up act.

Matters became so bad that on one excursion, and after several large Scotches, he managed to mount the car on the pavement. It was more luck than judgement that there were no pedestrians standing in his way. But as I hauled him from the driver's seat, still shaking from the ordeal, rather than feel remorse he berated me for '… becoming a killjoy, just like your mother'.

During those two months at home, I realised that my *hero* was starting down a more malevolent course and, knowing that he had refused help, perhaps it was best for my mum to run from this toxic environment. To my horror, my mother was by now consumed by self-doubt and self-recrimination. It was plain to see that he was not only embarking on an affair but, fuelled by alcohol, he was belittling the woman who plainly still loved him, despite his faults.

In the ensuing months, I left for a new job in the Cotswolds, my mother left for a new life in Switzerland, and The Boss moved a new woman in, only a week after my mother left. Not long after, I discovered he had not only lost his driving licence but was leaving his hair-dressing clients a little too long under the dryer for a natural perm. Even his friends started to worry when their annual golf tour turned into something of a farce as The Boss, rather than waiting for the *nineteenth hole*, became paralytic before even the front nine were completed. Once very much part of his darts team, he was now forced to join the spectators, as he was failing to hit the board, never mind treble twenty.

What I had always seen as the perfect partnership had disintegrated before my eyes. His new partner, having enjoyed the luxury holidays and the trappings of his former life, had deemed it prudent for him to sign over power of attorney to her. This in many ways was the final curtain call. A couple of years later, I visited him in his new home. Gone was the beautiful residence he and my mother had spent so many years creating. Now his lonely existence was in a council flat, surrounded by unpacked boxes and empty Scotch bottles. As Ewa and I sat down in his front room, which must have been reminiscent of his childhood, the irony struck home: he had always strived to be so much more than his working-class background.

There were so many emotions that almost became overwhelming during what was to be our final meeting. Pity, as I watched his shaking hands pour tea into his best china, horror as I noticed blood on the back of his trousers, clearly brought out for this *special occasion*, and anger that someone who had everything had thrown it all away. As my heart screamed in pain, I desperately wanted to shake him out of his deluded state. But all I could think about was how just a couple of hours ago I had sat next to my ninety-year-old grandmother, and how spritely she had looked in contrast to this former Adonis who appeared so much older than his fifty-seven years. His partner had left him to go cold turkey and, with no money to his name, he begged us for one small bottle before we left to go home. Little did I know at the time that those last pleas would be the final words I heard from him.

•

A couple of months later, he passed away, and although we were not invited to the funeral, Ewa and I attended. Listening to the eulogy from the back of the church, I realised that the man the rector was talking about was not the one I knew so well. It was hard to stem my anger as his new partner lorded it at the front of the congregation with mock tears – but at least she had secured a bulging bank account from other people's efforts.

To make matters worse, it wasn't long before I got wind of rumours circulating that my mum had run off with all his money and left him destitute and that he had only started drinking once she left. In hindsight, my anger was misdirected: only he could have originated these falsehoods. Rather than blame his mistress's greed, I really should have looked at his own recklessness.

With the passing of years, I try only to remember the man I loved, my friend, as well as my surrogate step-father. I had a wonderful childhood, due in no small part to him. I always wonder if we couldn't have done more to save him or what pushed a man who seemed to have everything over the top. Even from the start, in The

Boss's eyes, he had always been the one who worked the most and although he knew the trappings of his success would never have materialised without the ingenuity and sheer willpower of my mother, this fact did not sit well with my stepfather's macho side.

Over the years we had all pandered to his almost martyr-like behaviour and were constantly driven to massage his ego, but perhaps if we had set him straight years before, things might have turned out differently. As the dream ended, the house that had been the ultimate ambition became a competition between the two of them as to who could do the most. Ultimately, I believe it led to their downfall. In the end, The Boss wanted his cake and to eat it, but at the same time he forgot the one person who helped get him there. Blame is futile and no one can change someone who doesn't want to be changed. In terms of the perils of alcohol, he showed me that fine line that was perhaps a little too easy to cross and his example was certainly a contributing factor towards my own survival.

•

If my early years had always seemed to be full of youthful exuberance, by my late twenties, although not realising it at the time, I think my own demons were close to taking over. The antics that had always seemed fun were wearing thin. While I was warning my stepfather about the perils of drink, maybe I should have been looking closer to home. Although I never let it affect my work, during those heady days in London I sailed a little too close to the wind. I remember waking up in Green Park, having slept the night there – it always seemed more prudent to spend my last pennies on another round rather than take a taxi home. Or the time I insisted on hailing a cab, although I was precisely ten steps from my front door.

If these antics were amusing at the time, the same could not be said when one manager, who believed I did indeed have something special, had talked to his superiors to organise a meeting with one of the managing directors so that my career might be fast-tracked, only for me to overdo it the night before and miss the meeting.

Over the course of my career, I have worked while sick, volunteered to do extra hours, never been late and pushed myself in a desire to give the perfect service; but in this quest I have also put so much pressure on myself that on some occasions I have landed up in situations that were not far short of a sackable offence. I found that in London there was a multitude of temptations to lead me astray and although I had willing accomplices, they were astute enough to party once a week, not every night like I tended to do.

Even these friends were now questioning whether I was teetering on the edge, and I remember being shocked that they should have thought of me in that way. Of course, they were correct: who in their right mind would spend their month's wages on a single night out? The nights had become so farcical that on one occasion an Australian friend and I were hauled out of a strip club as, instead of watching the delights of the show, we had fallen asleep in the front row and were snoring rather loudly. Now, in his defence, he suffers from narcolepsy, but what excuse could I muster? Especially as the girl, irritated by our lack of appreciation, began kicking me from the front of the stage.

•

In my case, I guess I did heed the warnings, and as I ushered in the next era of management, I certainly became aware that it was impossible for me to function after alcohol. I also realised where that fine line was and, although I was by no means an angel, I have realised that drinking to fend off unhappiness or stress is not the answer. But to be honest, although those demons still hold temptation, it has been Ewa who ultimately saved me from myself. Have I reformed? Or do I just prefer not being nagged to death by a concerned partner? Well, a bit of both, I guess. But ultimately, I am grateful to still be here.

CHAPTER 23

Detoxing, Swiss-style

As many people do, in my latter years I have slowed down from my hedonistic earlier days. I am not sure whether this is through choice or necessity. Although I still enjoy the odd wilder night, my body certainly doesn't. But if I thought I might embrace a new yoga-loving, vegan-friendly lifestyle, one experience certainly curtailed that thought very quickly. After several years of stress in my B&B, my mother – not before finishing her fortieth fag of the day – decided that a health spa on the Swiss lakes might be the order of the day.

This in theory seemed a not altogether bad idea, but when we checked in to our spa, we discovered that our rooms were not dissimilar to prison ward isolation units. Oh well, I thought, go with the flow. We proceeded to go through a range of rigorous health tests, which unsurprisingly didn't have the best results. I might as well have had *Fat Bastard* tattooed onto my forehead as we were ushered in to the restaurant – or should I say canteen. On checking into the spa, I'd been momentarily delighted as the receptionist informed us that we would eat once an hour for eight hours, so I was understandably a little disappointed when this turned out to be one solitary biscuit, whose provenance remains a mystery. I was excited when one of the meals turned out to be a piece of fruit, such was the meagre diet on offer.

We were hooked up to any number of devices, enabling staff to monitor our progress, our diet and our daily exercise. When it came to the results, I was, for obvious reasons, losing weight, possibly because they were starving me to death, but that was nothing compared to the health experts' astonishment that my mother was top of the class in terms of how many kilometres she was walking each day. She was surpassing people half her age. I didn't want to burst anyone's bubble and mention that the reason we were walking so far was so we wouldn't bump into anyone we knew from the spa while my mother was smoking as many cigarettes as was humanly possible in an hour.

After one or two more pleasurable treatments, my mother decided, as only she could, that the only way to relieve my stress was through colonic irrigation. Not really knowing what this entailed, I happily stripped down and put on my robe, only to be greeted by a fairly buxom Hungarian nurse who looked like she might wrestle for her national team in her spare time. I was slightly anxious, but Martha, ever the professional and noticing my unease, did her upmost to allay any fears. As she explained the procedure, I actually felt sorry for the woman having to stick a tube up my hairy behind, but as she donned an outfit that looked like she was about to explore Chernobyl, I guessed she had seen it all before.

The procedure started, and it might have been my imagination, but I was sure I detected a gleam of pleasure behind Martha's goggles as she plunged the tube into my behind with a little too much relish. As my buttocks naturally constricted, much to Martha's disapproval, she decided that a little more force was required. As she started to pump water into my behind, poor old Martha now had to contend with her problematic client.

'How does it feel? Nice and warm?' she asked.

Pleasantly surprised and deeming it the right answer, I innocently replied that I couldn't feel a thing. This was obviously not the desired response, as Martha was now tapping the ends of the equipment and pumping like a woman possessed on the tube stuck into my arse.

'You must feel the water now?' she asked, clearly exasperated and definitely considering this to be beyond her job description.

'Not a thing,' I replied.

'But you must. I've used up all the water already!' Martha exclaimed. She then placed her hands on my belly and started massaging vigorously, causing a definite squelching sound from my stomach. Martha was clearly delighted at the turn of events, and the fact that not all the water had gone to waste.

'You are clearly stressed,' she observed.

My first thought was, *wouldn't you be, if some crazed Hungarian had stuck something up your arse and then proceeded to jump on your stomach*, and my second was that I was going to kill that bloody mother of mine, who I knew would be delighted by the turn of events.

Having done her best, Martha explained to me that in an hour's time I would start to feel the effects and need the toilet, so I should be close to one at all times. No problem, I thought; only my gut had other ideas. I smiled, cut the conversation short and made a mad dash to the nearest toilet. The noises that escaped, despite my best attempts to subdue them, were not dissimilar to the cows in the neighbouring field, and the emissions were certainly more toxic. Poor old Martha must have thought she had finished me off, because after about twenty minutes she tapped discreetly on the door to ask after my well-being. On vacating, I gave her my best apologetic smile and assured her that all was well. I will never forget the look of anguish on the faces of her next victims, in the by now full waiting room, obviously wondering what they had let themselves in for.

'How did it go?' Mum asked.

'Don't ask,' was my reply. 'You are one cruel woman.'

Undeterred, she happily informed me that she had booked me in for a nice relaxing massage. Thinking anything would be preferable to the torture I had just endured, I met another therapist, who at least looked a little safer than good old Martha.

Everything started out well and I was certainly feeling a little more relaxed. What they had failed to tell my mother (hadn't they?) was that this massage involved some form of nerve manipulation, which required some fairly vigorous pinching. Now, I have always considered myself quite tolerant of pain, but by the time she had worked her way from my nipples to the inside of my thighs, my tolerance was being severely tested. As she smiled down at me, I momentarily wondered what exactly my mother had booked for me and was half expecting her to tell me what a naughty boy I had been. But at least she had the grace not to follow me into the shower naked, as one male masseur had done while I was holidaying in Dubai. That would have been too much.

So, I guess you could say that's where my clean living started and ended. Although I had thought I might cut down on the cigars and booze, maybe I wasn't quite ready for this alternative lifestyle and, at a cost of 5,000 francs for the week, maybe I never would be.

CHAPTER 24

1997–2000 – The Bluebird Restaurant, King's Road, London

If Switzerland had taught me everything I knew, then the Bluebird was certainly the place where all those skills could be best utilised. Even during the interviews, I knew I was about to be involved in something special. The Bluebird Restaurant was based on the record-breaking car of the late Sir Donald Campbell. It was a vast *gastrodome*, housing a restaurant, café, food store, fine dining club and shop, all situated on the upmarket King's Road in Chelsea. When Sir Terence Conran opened this restaurant in 1997, it was at the cutting edge of both design and hospitality. You had to admire a man who was so ahead of the game and took such a bold step as to create these huge restaurants. Despite experiencing both success and failure with his furniture business, he was not afraid to take on these mammoth projects.

When we all assembled for training, you could sense the anticipation among the staff. I mean, we were having several days' training before we even opened. The cost must have been enormous, and it was certainly something I had never witnessed before. Many of my fellow head waiters had been managers before and we were enticed by the prospect of being part of something memorable and the fact that we were to have three days off a week, also unheard of in the industry.

Under the watchful eye of the *opening queen* Wendy Hendricks, an amenable Australian whose unflappable manner and eye for detail were legendary, we opened to a who's who of famous faces. Of all my bosses over the years, I guess Wendy was the one I respected the most. I could barely comprehend how she managed such an operation on a daily basis. I wouldn't say we were in any way close, but that was probably because my particular brand of blah de blah held little sway over her.

As we welcomed the great and good of sport, entertainment and showbiz, you really did have to pinch yourself. My colleagues included the chef John Torode and a young, French, fellow head waiter by the name of Fred Sirieix. Here, I made friendships that have lasted a lifetime.

It wasn't long before we were serving five hundred customers in a single sitting. The pace was relentless. I can remember questioning every single night how we would possibly get through this. When you look over at the bar and see the same number of eager faces awaiting a table as were already seated and you are nearing the edge of your capabilities, it certainly builds up the tension. The pressure was so intense, I remember certain waiters paying the busboys not to re-lay their tables too quickly, to give them a few precious minutes before their next arrival.

The *opening team* assembled by Wendy was probably something I will never witness again. Somehow, although it was stressful, we managed to make everything look pretty seamless. There were plenty of characters, both those working in the restaurant and those dining in the restaurant. There are certainly plenty of stories, too many to relate, but there are a couple that will forever be etched on my memory.

A couple of years in, it was getting towards the end of another busy lunch service when a rather ostentatious gentleman entered with a somewhat quieter man. Both had an aura that suggested it was perhaps not wise to get on the wrong side of them. It wasn't long before their cockney slang was in full swing and although the language was somewhat coarse, you couldn't help but be taken in by their charm.

It didn't take long for the more extrovert of the two to order a seafood platter, usually deemed sufficient for four people, which he would wash down with a bottle of Dom. To my surprise, his companion stuck to his mineral water and did not partake in the feast on offer. As I waited for the huge platter of goodies to be prepared, I was approached by one of the receptionists, who informed me that I had a telephone call. Somewhat perplexed, as it was forbidden to have personal calls during service, I took the phone from the receptionist, who shrugged her shoulders as if to say *I haven't got a clue either*. Not knowing what to expect, I heard a voice saying, 'Oi, Dave, where the fuck is my food?' A little surprised, I saw the cockney some thirty metres away, falling about laughing at his little prank.

As his platter arrived, he called me over again, pointed at one of my colleagues and said, roaring with laughter, 'Dave, go and ask that bird over there if she takes it up the ass.' Having never encountered such a situation, I was at a bit of a loss as to how to play my hand. In the end, I sauntered up to the girl in question, grinning inanely, and whispered, 'Don't ask me why, but please slap me in the face, not too hard. I'll tell you about it later.' A little bemused, she did as I requested, and I returned to the guest shaking my head. He was delighted by the short scene, and I had obviously passed some sort of initiation. That day, he left me a considerable tip.

In the months that followed, he dined several times at the Bluebird, sometimes with his colleague, sometimes with his wife, and with so many mistresses that it took all my powers of concentration just to remember their names. Trust me when I say I really didn't want to get them wrong, just in case I upset him. I also recall one morning coming into work and being told that my new *friend* had come into the restaurant with several of his *colleagues*, and on discovering I was not working he had promptly left the building, taking his entire entourage with him.

When it came to this gentleman, although he was always, shall we say, entertaining, I was somewhat on edge as I never really knew what to expect. Things came to a head, in more ways than one, when he came in with a rather attractive lady who was definitely not his wife. I should tell you at this point that the tables in the Blue-bird were so close together you needed to pull them out to let each guest in.

The guest, even by his own standards, was in an unusually buoyant mood, but looking at his rather alluring companion, I could kind of understand why. Taking me a little by surprise, as it was only the start of the evening, he said, smiling, 'Dave, mate, there will be no cash tip tonight.'

'No problem,' I replied to this clearly amused man, unsure why he had brought this up. Suddenly, he announced that he had dropped his napkin under the table, and would I mind grabbing it for him? I told him I could fetch him a fresh one, but he was adamant that the one on the floor was just fine. As I scrambled, undignified, under the tablecloth, I felt a hand on the back of my head and there before my eyes was the not altogether unpleasant sight of his dining companion's nether regions. She had obviously decided against wearing panties that evening. Before I knew what was happening, my head was unceremoniously thrust into the lady's crotch. After a few seconds, I was mercifully released. I came up for air, banging my head on the table, and made it back to freedom, albeit as red as a beetroot.

My *friend* roared with laughter, but the lady didn't blink an eye. I later found out that it was all in a day's work for her. Thankfully, our fellow diners were blissfully unaware, but the man, still beaming, declared, 'I told you, Dave – no cash tip today.'

The man in question always reminded me of someone out of *The Sopranos* and one day his quieter colleague took me to one side and told me he was, in fact, just that, and that he – the colleague – was actually his bodyguard. God, how was I supposed to tell my mother I was now chums with a bona fide East End gangster? I didn't tell poor Mum until many years later. I mean, I didn't want to upset her, but I shared the part about the delights I had witnessed with anyone who would listen.

Just before I left Bluebird, my *friend* invited me out to one or two of London's more infamous haunts with a few of his henchmen, as a Christmas present. As I sipped my old favourite, Cristal champagne, and experienced things an impressionable young man – recently single, I might add – really should not see, I did wonder if I was now officially a member of something akin to the Krays' gang. As I was unsteadily making my way from the club, the quiet bodyguard tapped me on the shoulder and said, 'Dave, look, he obviously likes your company but you're a nice guy, so if he ever asks you out for so much as a drink again, you decline graciously. This really isn't a world you want to be in.'

As I turned round to thank my host, I took in his ready smile, the two beautiful ladies, one on each knee, and the cigar in his mouth; and, waving goodbye, I knew that would be the last time I saw him. Oh, but what a memory.

•

As any waiter will tell you, tips can be quite substantial, and in the case of certain places they can easily exceed your salary. However, the concept of tipping highlights the problems within the industry. Take, for example, the dreaded 12.5 per cent service charge. Now, many hoteliers will argue that this is a good thing, as it guarantees the employees a fair wage. To my way of thinking it is plain wrong, both for the guest and the employee; the only winner is the owner of the hotel/restaurant.

I have many problems with the system. Firstly, it is seriously open to abuse. I know of many well-known brands who only pay out a fraction of the service charge to their staff, although they have already benefited by not paying VAT on this money. Secondly, why should the guest pay this *optional* charge? Surely it should be solely at their discretion? Thirdly, why should I receive the same service charge as a colleague who is clearly not interested in the job?

What about the chefs, you may ask? But in my opinion, chefs are usually paid far more than their front of house counterparts, so why should they profit from all sides? Let's face it, there are very few chefs who want to socialise with anything approaching a guest.

In the case of the Bluebird, there was a 12.5 per cent service charge. This meant it was highly unlikely that you would receive an additional tip, but it was by no means impossible, and when you did strike lucky on that front, the tip was often wildly extravagant. One such memory will stay with me forever. I had a family table of eight booked in for an early sitting. As the youngsters, all in their twenties, started to arrive, they informed me that their father was running late. The problem was that their booking was for seven o'clock and they needed to vacate the table by 8.30 p.m. As they waited, they indulged in a couple of bottles of champagne, priced at over £200 a bottle. When the dad did eventually arrive, it was closer to eight o'clock and time was running out. He called me over and asked if I could do anything about the time allocation and, although we were fully booked, the manager agreed to an extra hour on the table. Breathing a sigh of relief, I went back to the clearly delighted father and announced the good news.

The table then ordered another bottle of champagne and the father asked me to suggest dishes for all the family. He informed me that they would not have any starters, desserts or coffees, but wanted something nice for their main course. I naturally obliged and went around the table making recommendations. True to their word, they were in and out in no time, but not before I received my biggest surprise.

The father called me over and asked whether service was included on the bill, which exceeded £1,100. I told him it was and thought no more about it as he started to count out his cash. He handed it over and suggested with a trace of a smile that perhaps I should count it. I accepted the thanks he gave me for everything I had done for him but was perplexed as I counted the cash, as the amount was far more than the total on the bill. I looked over at him, and with a little smile he said, 'Just a little something for you.' With that, the family left the restaurant, with me looking down at the £2,000 he had left. Not bad for an hour and a half's work!

If one should underestimate the benefit of tips, I remember visiting a friend up in the Cotswolds. He and his wife had a successful B&B, along with a flourishing tearoom. While talking about business, he let it be known that he had been saving pound coins to buy his wife something nice, or so he led me to believe.

'The problem is, Dave, I don't know how to cash it all in. I can't exactly go into the bank with a wheelbarrow of coins. They might start asking questions and I haven't exactly declared them on my self-employment return,' he told me.

'Well, how many coins do you actually have?' I asked innocently.

With that, he took me to his room and started to pull crates out from under his bed. To my amazement, he declared, 'I really don't know what I can buy with twenty thousand pounds in pound coins.' A few months later, the new pound coins came in, and I never did remember to ask him if he managed to spend the old ones in time!

•

There are certain individuals who breeze through life and find the whole concept of stress rather absurd. One such person was my waiter, Will. Will had an easy charm, a wicked smile and didn't take himself too seriously. The fact that he had a gorgeous girlfriend and rode a motorbike made him the epitome of cool. Unfortunately, his laid-back attitude would on occasions bring me close to the brink of despair.

Each morning, the junior waiter – in this case, Will – would be responsible for stocking up the stations, including the napkins, cutlery and ashtrays. As is the case in most restaurants, staff weren't exactly careful when clearing off plates in the wash-up and, in their haste, items such as teaspoons were inadvertently thrown away, much to the annoyance of management. This led to there often being a shortage and a mad dash to make sure you weren't one of those who was short.

One morning, there seemed to be more than the usual panic in the air as none of the commis waiters could find any teaspoons. I was getting a little concerned that we wouldn't be ready for service. Looking at our near empty station, I became even more anxious. I looked over at Will, who was nonchalantly carrying on without a care in the world. When I berated him for not being ready, he merely smiled.

'Boss, you worry too much.'

He then shook his hips, causing his apron to rattle. Peering inside the front pocket, I was astounded to see what must have been over a hundred teaspoons. 'You see, boss, we are ready,' he said, sauntering off. The thing with Will was that it was impossible to scold him, because he just didn't care.

Another waiter who will forever live in my memory is Tony Botta. Botta was a lovable rogue who suffered from alopecia and, somewhat to his surprise, found himself the cover boy of the Bluebird restaurant. Botta loved clubbing and all that entails and, much in the mould of Will, he didn't take things too seriously. I remember working with him on one occasion and, to be honest, the end of the evening couldn't come quickly enough.

It started when an elderly lady sat down at a table for four, waiting for her group to join her. She was somewhat high and mighty and when Botta started laying out the menus, she haughtily reminded him that she was waiting for three other guests. Luckily for him, she was a little deaf, as he turned round and muttered, 'Oh, you think

I'm fucking blind or what?' As I chased him into the dispense bar, catching the back of his head, the somewhat perplexed guest was still trying to work out if she had really heard what she thought she had. But as I saw her shaking her head, I think she convinced herself that it was impossible that someone would have the audacity to speak to her in that manner.

If I thought we were over the worst, another guest then innocently asked if she could have the rest of her risotto bagged so she could take it home with her. Botta took her request a little too literally and, wreathed in smiles, he returned to the table and proceeded to scoop all the risotto from her plate into a plastic bag. Botta's saving grace was that he looked like an expectant puppy, and somehow you couldn't find it in your heart to scold him. So, off went the bemused guest without a word of rebuke, and with her risotto squelching in the bottom of her bag.

The problem with any new high-end venture is that not only are you going to be inundated with frequent food critics, but it seems the whole world knows far better than any restaurateur how an establishment should be run. We would all wait with bated breath at our staff meetings for the outcome of a Michelin review or a critique from A.A. Gill. Occasionally, though, the most unlikely sources can make or break a restaurant through the wonderful world of media. I remember the outcry when the restaurant had to have a delivery from McCain's frozen foods, as we had run out of our usual hand-cut triple-cooked chips. It wasn't long before the whole of London was aware of our faux pas, but I don't think for one moment anyone thought that maybe serving eight hundred hungry diners a day takes a fair amount of organisation. There was another occasion when one critic condemned our chicken Kiev as totally unacceptable. The next day, hundreds of diners flocking to the restaurant were quick to point out the review. However, to my amazement, everyone seemed to order chicken Kiev. As the saying goes, there is nothing stranger than folk!

I have learned that it is always wise to be prepared for just about anything. One evening, I had two gentlemen who were spending somewhat lavishly on their dinner. Towards the end of their meal, there seemed to be something of a commotion in our private dining room. This was a glass-fronted room that overlooked both the restaurant and the chef preparing seafood from our counter. On the night in question, the room was hosting a hen party and, although this was very refined at the beginning, events had taken a strange turn. Will, my waiter, had come over with a huge grin and pointed up to the private dining room. The girls had lost all their inhibitions and were now intent on engaging in a food fight. To add a bit of spice to the mix, they were also completely topless.

The commotion was over in a few minutes, as the manager raced up the stairs to pull the blinds and put an end to what I felt was a rather entertaining evening. Now, it must be said that nearly all the diners found the incident rather amusing; it was certainly a little different from their usual nights out on the King's Road. My two gentlemen were in particularly high spirits at the sight of so many scantily clad ladies.

However, events that I couldn't foresee were about to escalate rapidly. With a sudden change of expression, they called me over and told me that they were distinctly disappointed by what they had just witnessed. At first, I thought they were joking; I had seen their earlier laughter. That was certainly not the case now and they demanded to know what I was prepared to do about the situation. I chatted to the manager and told him the pair had enjoyed a rather expensive bottle of wine, so we decided to offer them desserts and an equally good bottle of dessert wine on the house, deeming this more than enough to appease them.

The two gents in question certainly had other ideas and called over the manager. He stood his ground; the situation that had so impacted their night had been over in a second, so he refused to offer further discount. Before we knew it, the pair had upped sticks, evaded security and were making their way briskly down the King's Road, having conveniently decided not to pay their bill.

Lo and behold, a couple of days later an article appeared in the *Evening Standard*, written by the two men and highlighting their depraved evening, which had cost the eye-watering amount of over a thousand pounds. Of course, this was front-page news for a couple of days, but in their arrogance the men had left their details with the paper. The restaurant informed the police and the pair were forced to pay their exorbitant bill. I guess what goes around does come around.

Although I will forever remember the opulence of the Bluebird, the excitement of the service and the huge demands of running such an establishment, it is the small details I will remember the most. One such fact is that probably one of the best-paid jobs in the entire place was that of cloakroom attendant. In winter, there was no salary, only tips for hanging up the coats. Now, with so many eager diners leaving their coats and nearly all leaving a pound tip for the privilege, this ended up being far more lucrative than the salary of a humble waiter.

Then there was the person whose job it was to offer the customer a shot of cologne after they had used the toilet and were busy washing their hands. I mean, who doesn't leave a tip after someone has seen you in all your glory as he indulges you in small talk. As he spritzes you with scent and wishes you a good night, all you can do is pray that you haven't dribbled all over your trousers. In those circumstances, of course, you hand over the cash as quick as a flash, as all you really want to do is get out of there as fast as possible.

There are so many things I take away from that time. The fact that Mark Knopfler, of Dire Straits fame, would use our basement as his car park; the nights after service where we drank jeroboams of champagne to relieve the pressure; the three courses for £10 over the road at the Stockpot, where my colleagues and I would enjoy a hearty late lunch of spaghetti Bolognese, having half an hour earlier fed diners lobster and caviar. I can still remember Kingue, one of the managers, who had worked his way up through the ranks and who, to me, epitomised what service was all about. Guests often brought in their babies and Kingue would wander around the restaurant with the child, both blissfully oblivious to the world around them. It turned out the man was god-father to half the babies in London! As I say, it's the small things you remember.

It was at the Bluebird that I met lifelong friends Greg Andrews and James Grant. The former later opened his own successful wine business and the latter became general manager of the prestigious Wiltons Restaurant in Jermyn Street.

At this point, it would be remiss of me not to mention my former colleague Fred Sirieix. I have watched Fred's meteoric rise over the years and two thoughts stand out in my mind. Firstly, he really hasn't changed from that charismatic Frenchman I remember meeting all those years ago, when we shared dinner at a colleague's house on our very first day at the Bluebird. Secondly, it is a pleasure to see someone front of house get the recognition they deserve and maybe make the public realise that it isn't just chefs who make the industry tick.

CHAPTER 25

2005–2020 – The essence of service

I guess to really enjoy catering, you have primarily to love people; that said, I have met many who couldn't stand going anywhere near a guest. Secondly, you must be a little crazy. With the relentless hours and constant stress, it is no wonder the industry attracts those with obsessive and addictive traits. Just like in the theatre, you must be a constant performer, only as good as your last curtain call. In catering, the same applies: you are only as good as your last guest.

The customer really doesn't give two hoots if the boiler has blown up, or the chef has decided to up sticks and take his whole brigade with him. Or even if the entire town has had a power cut – all of which has happened to me. I recently watched the film *Boiling Point*, which, to be honest, had me switching off, not because it wasn't excellent but because I felt so anxious watching it. You see, all the events in those episodes really do happen – thankfully, not all on one day! The point is, in the eyes of the guest, the show must go on. So those times when you have to improvise – serve by candlelight, cook on a two-ring burner or find a way to take payments without a card machine – are where a truly well-run place comes into its own.

I would describe myself as a swan on the surface, with the feet of a duck – frantically paddling to keep afloat. I have had many situations where I have felt physically sick with anxiety, but to the outside world, nothing would appear amiss. For those dismissive individuals who regard service as a menial job, I always remember my first maître d'hôtel, Herr Kuhl, telling me, 'David, anyone can be a waiter, but to be good at it is an art,' and those words have stuck with me throughout.

It's not just about putting a plate in front of a guest or giving them a comfy bed. It's about giving them a whole experience. To really excel at catering, you must be an accountant, marketeer, plumber, chef, host and even a social worker with some of the guests. I have been a shoulder to cry on, a go-between for a domestic dispute, a resuscitator for a heart attack victim... I have seen just about every situation.

I remember on one occasion delivering room service to an amorous couple who, quite oblivious to my presence, were happy to frolic on the sofa, stark naked and without a care in the world. Let's face it, even I found it a little close for comfort when I asked the gentleman to sign the chit and, lo and behold, I was confronted by his substantial piece of tackle, brandished in my direction. At least he had the good manners to tip me well!

In terms of the antics of some guests, I also fondly remember when we opened a deluxe B&B in the leafy suburbs of Bath, close to Royal Victoria Park. Despite being only six rooms, The Residence, a Georgian property overseen by its enigmatic owners, Cheryl and Mark Norman, radiated elegance. The house was a labyrinth of understated *cool*, with its secret doors, magnificent chandeliers, polished marble, underground sauna and open-plan kitchen. As a manager, it truly was a dream to run and even in the first year, word spread among the well-heeled patrons of Bath about this *private club*. It wasn't long before the likes of Nicolas Cage, Eddie Redmayne, then a young aspiring actor, the musician Jamie Cullum, rugby legend Jerry Guscott, and a host of other celebrities swept through our doors. We even won Best Place to Stay in the *Times* Travel Awards.

If our clientele could be described as glamorous, the same could also be said of our fledgling team. First, there was David Gledhill, former editor of the *Bath Chronicle*, who headed up the marketing and resembled an ageing rock star with flowing locks and a temperament to match. He was complemented by my assistant manager, Liz Lawler, now a successful author, who filled the house with her personality. The cast also included the late Richard Parmentier, our night porter, who had been a renowned actor and who appeared in episode IV of the *Star Wars* movies. He would regale customers with his screen stories over the odd drink or two. It was here that I also met the effervescent Eva Skornakevo, a Slovakian, whose loyalty led her to follow me through several establishments and who remains a lifelong friend.

This team was not what I would term a seasoned group of hoteliers, but what they did not know about the industry they certainly made up for in personality.

A prime example was Liz, who was always ready with a cheery smile and who exuded personality. I hope she will forgive me for writing this, but I remember on one occasion, when we were newly opened, I had a guest who had booked in a party of twelve. They pre-ordered their wine for the evening, and I duly wrote down their order next to their booking. When Liz walked in for work, the phone rang, and by the excited look on her face I could tell the caller was Mark, the owner, who asked whether we were busy that evening. Liz bounced over to the bookings book and proudly announced to Mark, 'Yes, we're extremely busy – can you believe we have a booking for six, under the name of Pinot Grigio, and another six under the name of Pinot Noir, and a further six guests under the name of Prosecco.' She was so delighted with our success; she went on to ask him if he knew any of them. As I said, what they lacked in knowledge they certainly made up for in personality.

Coming back to the make-up of the human mind, sometimes it really is difficult to predict the outcome. One such occasion occurred at The Residence when Mark came up with an ingenious idea. By this time, I was well rehearsed in indulging the whims of many an owner, but I have to say when I heard this idea, I was truly taken aback. When I noticed the broad grin on his face, I knew he had already made his mind up and any attempt at reasoning would fall on deaf ears.

'Why don't we put a selection of sex toys in each of the rooms, ones that can only be accessed by a key. It will all be very discreet, of course.'

You can imagine my first thought was how to drop

this fact into polite conversation while checking in the guest. 'Does madam feel like the rampant rabbit tonight, or maybe the anal beads are more to her liking?' Somehow, this didn't seem quite appropriate. Now, I am certainly no prude, but I have to say I had my reservations about this new and exciting enterprise. My fears seemed to be confirmed when I heard rumours abound in Bath that we were now actually running a brothel in our once leafy corner of Bath.

Matters were not made any easier when I received a phone call from a well-known rugby player, who asked if I minded if he brought along a few of his mates for an overnight party, along with a number of scantily clad escorts. Oh, he did of course have the grace to say I wouldn't hear a peep out of them. On this occasion, I did stand my ground and decline the booking, but I still smile to this day when I think of the following week when I just happened to see said rugby player in our local Waitrose, pushing along his trolley. I thought it would be remiss of me not to introduce myself and at least say hi to him and his wife!

Now, it must be said that our new *goodies drawer* was all very discreet, under lock and key, and the owner had done an admirable job in picking the packaging, but I was still expecting a deluge of complaints from our prim and proper clientele. However, although I thought by then that I was pretty adept at figuring out the human mind, I was in for quite a shock.

On the morning after our recently acquired goodies had made their way into their homes, it being 6 a.m. and breakfast needing to be prepared, I had in fact forgotten all about our top shelf offering. With it being so early, I was somewhat surprised to see my evergreen octogenarian guest shuffling down the stairs, still clad in his robe and slippers. The guest was well known to me and on principle was never down before 9 a.m., so I could only think that something was amiss.

Furtively checking if anyone else was around, the guest asked if he could settle up early before I got too busy and added, with the merest hint of a grin, that he had 'taken everything from the top shelf'.

Being distracted, and having totally forgotten about our new accessories, I listed down all the miniatures, naturally assuming he was talking about the minibar. Cutting in quickly, he whispered, 'No, young man, you've misunderstood. Not that top shelf, the other one.'

Finally cottoning on and rather taken aback, I blurted out, 'What, everything?'

'Yes, everything,' came the reply.

As I had seen the whole range and actually put them in the drawers, I wasn't sure whether to congratulate the old boy on an outstanding performance or call for an ambulance. Shortly afterwards he was joined by his somewhat invigorated wife, and it might have been my imagination, but I am certain I saw a glint in her eyes and a considerable spring in her step. Unlike her husband, she was totally unabashed as she asked him, 'George, have you settled all the extras with the nice young man?'

George, buoyed by his wife's enthusiasm, had regained his usual composure and was now pottering down the hallway to enjoy his usual fry-up. Well, I mused, if he hadn't earned it today, when would he?

If I thought my entertaining morning was over, there was one final twist in store for me. Bidding Mr and Mrs 'George' goodbye, I volunteered to take their luggage to the car. As if on cue, the luggage began to vibrate vigorously, and I realised the good old rampant rabbit had burst into life and was enjoying a solo performance. George again looked mortified, while Mrs George was obviously delighted by the turn of events. Trying to think of anything that might sound appropriate, and ever the professional, I came out with, 'I think you must have left your alarm clock on, sir.'

Clearly relieved, and depositing the case in the car as fast as possible, without examining the offending item, George made a hasty retreat, while I waved him and his wife a hearty goodbye.

Over the following months, the goodies drawer went down rather well, with not a complaint in sight, and to my surprise was enjoyed more by the silver surfers than the youngsters I had envisaged. But if poor old George and his wife were anything to go by, then perhaps they needed its help the most! The whole episode showed me that, despite everything, you never stop learning.

As always, there are always those who take things a little too far for comfort, and on one occasion a more amorous couple decided it would be appropriate to place all the used items back in the drawer for the next couple to stumble upon. I suppose they must have thought it was like handing over to a delighted recipient a parking ticket that hadn't run out.

Another aspect of looking into the human psyche and watching how people operate is through housekeeping. I think if you asked any housekeeper, they could recount a whole host of tales and I for one really can never tell what to expect when I delve into the inner sanctum of their room. Not only are requests bizarre, but so too are people's habits.

I have encountered outwardly elegant people who are coiffured to within an inch of their lives, resplendent in designer gear, and who would be the first to complain if there was a single element out of place in their rooms. Judging by their immaculate appearance, where not a hair is out of place, you would think that this obsession would follow to the bedroom, but instead you often find a trail of destruction that beggars belief. It is common to find foundation plastered on your carpets, talc on every surface, lipstick on all your towels, all with absolutely no regard for the person who is tidying up.

Any hotelier will tell you that it has become the norm to receive requests for soft pillows, hard pillows, a soft mattress, alongside requests for vegan biscuits, vegan milk, fresh milk, gluten-free bread. The list is endless. What really surprises me about all the requests is that what was once only encountered in a five-star hotel is now just as familiar in my £85-a-night B&B. It is commonplace to hear 'Can you book my train, a flight, a taxi, a ferry...' and yes, I am happy to oblige, but I do wonder how these people survive on a day-to-day basis. Do they all have butlers or maids to do their bidding?

Coming back to the bedrooms, I have had guests who have dismantled televisions from the walls and taken down all the pictures and rearranged the furniture, just because it's out of kilter with their feng shui. I have feared for my drains as people have deemed it acceptable to go through three toilet rolls a day. I had one regular guest who felt it entirely appropriate to wake me at 5 a.m. or to knock on the door at 11 p.m. to ask me to feed her dog because she might break a nail opening the can. Do I do it? I'm afraid to say, yes, I do. At times I feel like I'm a butler in some bygone age. Life can feel not dissimilar to being on the set of *Downton Abbey*.

It is common for guests to bring their own mugs from home, as they cannot possibly be parted from them. It has even been known for guests to bring their own duvets, pillows, sheets and even mattress protectors, for the simple reason that they think it will add to their comfort. Human nature never ceases to amaze. I had a lady who decided she couldn't possibly stay because she found the two-bedroom apartment, with its vaulted ceilings, private garden and lounge, too claustrophobic. Or the guest who broke down because she couldn't survive with only six coat hangers.

It also surprises me when a guest doesn't realise that the person who serves their breakfast in the morning might also be the person who cleans their room. I have one guest in particular who likes to wash her knickers in the sink – not totally uncommon, but she then likes to dry them on every ornament available. Housekeeping then tends to become a bit of an assault course. What is the etiquette for dealing with someone else's knickers? Hang them up somewhere more appropriate? Leave them there? I really don't know the answer. To make matters worse, the offending items were no bigger than dental floss; if I touched them, I worried that I would be branded a pervert. A life in hospitality leaves one with no end of daily dilemmas. To this day, I don't think for a moment that the lady in question wondered why I couldn't look her in the eye while sizzling up her breakfast sausage.

On the flip side, I have also been surprised in a good way. It might be a little strange, but any housekeeper will tell you that there are moments of pure joy when a guest doesn't use the shower or a towel: it's one less item to clean. I have also known guests who have left poems or artefacts that they've deemed appropriate for our historic building. I have had others who have planted flowers in my garden as a thank-you or left hanging baskets for the restaurant. I even had a lady whose room was left each day as tidy as she found it. It turned out that she was also a housekeeper, and when I pointed out that she was on holiday and really should be relaxing, she replied that she just couldn't help herself and she 'would be devastated if the nice young owner thought badly of her'.

In terms of human behaviour, it would be remiss not to mention two topics, those being children and dogs. Our B&B is both dog- and child-friendly and it is perhaps this element, more than any other, that has made the business so successful. To be honest, I have never had much of an issue with dogs; by and large, they are better judges of acceptable behaviour than their owners. However, the attitudes of grown-up people towards their pets and their offspring have often led me to question, 'Seriously, what the fuck is wrong with people?'

When I was growing up, it was still believed that children should be seen and not heard, something I always found a little archaic, but society now seems content to let the child rule the adult. All common sense seems to have gone out of the window. While we all have our moments, there are parents who have no problem with little four-year-old Timmy taking off his nappy and contentedly smearing its contents on my restaurant wall. You might think the parents would at least have the good grace to be mortified, but instead they proudly coo, 'Darling, you are *so* talented, I think you are going to be an artist.'

Over the last years, there seems to have been a discernible shift, and seemingly intelligent individuals give in to the ever more outrageous whims of a generation of children who, to my eyes, seem to be handed everything on a plate with little or no effort, or have resorted to some *bohemian-like* theory that children should be allowed to do exactly as they please.

In some cases, the parents don't appear at all perturbed if their little angels are screaming the place down, with scant regard for their fellow guests. Just to get some peace and quiet, children are now allowed to play on their iPads during mealtimes, while the parents are glued to their phones. The notion of a family meal, one where everyone chats, seems to have gone out of the window. It has got to such a stage that it is almost impossible to have a meaningful conversation with some of the surlier adolescents. A simple please or thank you is rare, and often, you are lucky to receive a grunt. There are parents who don't think this is a problem and put it down to them *just being teenagers*. The situation can be so ridiculous. I have even seen parents whose precious offspring have shouted threats of bringing in social services. No wonder teachers don't stand a chance against either the children or the parents.

I must clarify that not all children just grunt. One eloquent young lady, aged around five, chirped that she had been pleasantly surprised by my B&B and had found her stay '… far better than expected, as Mummy and Daddy usually only take me to five-star hotels'. Oh well, at least she was polite.

Maybe I'm just becoming a bit of a Victor Meldrew – one of the grumpy old men brigades – but I can't for the life of me see how parents who are an absolute delight put up with the behaviour of their offspring. On one occasion, I had a family stay with me for two whole weeks and the only time I saw their daughters was when they checked out. Each day I would converse with the parents, whose company I really enjoyed. When I asked every day whether the girls would be joining them for breakfast, I was met with the same response: 'Oh, you know what teenagers are like.' As they lazed in bed, I couldn't understand why this perfectly sane dad didn't put his foot down – after all, the breakfast was paid for. More astonishing was that at around 11 a.m., he would sheepishly walk to the café next door and hand-deliver bacon sandwiches in bed to his two princesses.

On another occasion, and with a different family, there had been a substantial downpour and the garden was pretty treacherous, so I explained to the parents that I was keeping the garden door locked because their small children might not be safe on the steps.

Some years previously, I had learned the hard way that *the guest is always right*. At the time, I was managing

The Close Hotel in Tetbury and there had been a severe frost, making the pavers akin to an ice-skating rink. I had closed the gate to the back of the restaurant and strategically placed multiple signs around the premises, informing guests not to use the garden.

However, this did not deter one elderly gentleman who, after one too many brandies, decided to navigate the *black run* and take a shortcut through the garden. Needless to say, he slipped and broke his hip. A lengthy legal battle with his family ensued and they eventually won the case because I hadn't locked the gate and had only put signs out. So once bitten, twice shy, as the saying goes.

Returning to the family in question, the parents had been totally understanding and even though the children were throwing me some disgruntled glances, I thought the parents had everything in hand. However, about an hour later I heard screams from the garden and realised my best-laid plans were not working out after all. It transpired that upon realising the door was locked, the children had instead clambered up to the window, destroying the wallpaper in the process and leaving behind a trail of destruction. The once understanding parents suddenly changed tack and saw nothing wrong with their actions.

It would undoubtedly be somewhat harsh of me to dismiss a whole generation of children, as I have encountered several delightful ones on my journey.

If some parenting could only be described as lax, this was not the case with one particular family, who took the whole idea of discipline to another extreme. One morning, the family in question came down for breakfast, but the younger members, rather than being their usual upbeat selves, seemed somewhat subdued and sleep deprived. It turned out that the previous evening, being in rather high spirits, they had inadvertently managed to lock themselves out of their room. Funnily enough, I had heard voices coming from the second floor as I nodded off but had thought no more about it. It transpired that the parents were none too pleased by their offspring's antics and decided to teach them a lesson. Rather than letting them come down to disturb me for the spare key, they allowed them to sleep on the hallway floor. On seeing their drained faces, this seemed a little harsh, but, credit where credit is due, the youngsters never once complained.

•

Moving on, we are often described as a nation of animal lovers. As an animal lover myself, I totally understand the adoration in which we hold our furry friends. What I find a little perplexing is that a dog is no longer treated as a canine member of the family but more like a human being. I am not naive enough to believe the shocked look on a guest's face or even to contemplate that this is the first time Bruce the bulldog has jumped on the bed, given that good old Brucie has – in the time it's taken for me to explain the amenities to the guest – managed to plump up the cushions for his ample behind and is now happily navigating with the remote to find his favourite Disney channels.

Even if the guest feigns mortification, the reality of the situation becomes apparent as good old Brucie clearly has no recollection of the instruction 'down' and is more likely to be rolling over for his belly to be scratched. Now, what I love about guests is that whenever I receive an email requesting a dog-friendly room, I always get firm assurances that their little pooch is a perfect angel, and they will go into such raptures about their little darlings that by the end you would be totally convinced they were describing a child.

If Horatio has indeed been described in such glowing terms, I know all too well that this will inevitably mean that by the end of check-in, my crotch will be a dripping pool of saliva, while their owners, without a care in the world, will be telling good old Horatio what a clever boy he is.

I can also recall one occasion when a certain couple checked in and found it totally acceptable to let their beloved go and explore its new home. This would have been fine, but the beloved dog in question happened to be an enormous Great Dane called Douglas. After brushing me aside, it wasn't long before I heard a resounding scream emanating from the kitchen. As I flew in, Ewa was a picture of terror, huddled in fear against the wall while the dog happily munched his way through that night's prep. Not content with demolishing our entire restaurant offering, he took it upon himself to explore our living quarters, where he soon picked up the scent of Cookie, our cat. By the time I arrived, our cat, who is partially sighted, was cowering in the corner, trying to put up some token resistance. The sight of Douglas licking his lips led me to believe that our prime fillet steak had perhaps not been enough sustenance. Trying to recall my more youthful days, I flew through the air with my best impression of a rugby tackle and landed on a clearly bemused Douglas. It was then that the guests joined us and saw me straddling their prize hound. They could only shake their heads, as though it had somehow all been my fault!

Talking of prime fillets, we come to the question of dogs in the restaurant – or perhaps it would be fairer to say dogs *dining* in the restaurant. Now, I have no issue with a dog being in the restaurant, so long as it's well behaved, kept on a lead and sits quietly under the table. Of course, the owners again always assure us of this. I'm always a little cautious as to what to expect when it comes to the dining habits of our four-legged friends, as there seems to be no end of undiscovered dining-room etiquette.

I have seen one guest, upon recognising an acquaintance from breakfast, go to his table to recount his day's activities. Oblivious of everything around him and happily detailing that day's events to his male counterpart, while his dog happily placed two large paws on the acquaintance's clearly terrified wife. To make matters worse, not only were the paws strategically placed on her breasts, but the dog was now trying to French kiss the woman. Her face reminded me of someone trying to avoid that first kiss at the school disco. If that wasn't bad enough, the dog had already devoured the wife's chicken supreme dinner before the owner even had the grace to turn round. The owner pulled a very contented dog from the woman's lap but did not for one minute register that there might be something amiss with the situation. In true British style, the couple didn't utter a single word of complaint.

Now, I'm all for providing our four-legged friends with dog bowls, dog beds, blankets, treats and even a sausage at breakfast, but it seems this isn't enough anymore. I have known guests request high chairs for their dogs, so they could feed them as though they were a child. I have even known a family turn up with their two boxer dogs and a case ready for the refrigerator. There was not a can of Chum in sight and, on unpacking the case, I was amazed to see only the finest cuts, which I would happily have put on my menu. Let's put it this way, it certainly put my beans on toast to shame.

Over the years, many people have been incredulous that I would allow dogs in my establishment, but in hindsight my experiences have only been positive. I have found our four-legged friends much easier to please than their two-legged counterparts. When I started out, I took on dogs firstly because my mum could never find suitable accommodation for her and her Westie, secondly because I love dogs, and finally, the business would never have got off the ground without them. In hindsight, would I accept dogs again? Absolutely. Their owners? Possibly!

As I have previously mentioned, service to me is an art. The key to any experience is in those first couple of minutes, whether someone is checking in at reception or merely waiting for a table. You see, in this window of opportunity, a hotelier can assess the needs of their guest and, in turn, the guest's whole experience will be determined by those first impressions.

For example, if you're waiting for a table and you are repeatedly ignored, your first instinct will likely be to walk away. However, even if the restaurant is full and you can see the waiter is extremely busy, a cheery hello, a bit of eye contact and a brief 'I'll be with you in a second' will make all the difference in the world.

A prime example of this was when I worked as a manager at the renowned Bettys and Taylors in Yorkshire. Such was the popularity of these tearooms that the queue would stretch down the high street. It was my job to go down the queue and reassure the guests on the waiting time, engage in a bit of banter and hand out samples of the goodies that awaited them. This philosophy proved spot-on, as often the guest would wait for up to an hour, merely for coffee and a scone.

Next, if you are seated at a table and again you are ignored, you will inevitably feel aggrieved and start becoming agitated. My attitude to this is that, however busy I am, I will drop everything and bring over bread and water, so that the guest knows I have acknowledged them. This also buys me a little time. Those two minutes are that crucial.

Of course, there are those guests who will never wait for anything. I remember on one particularly busy night at Paul Heathcote's in Preston, we had a table of eight businessmen. Although in high spirits and drinking copious amounts of wine, the table was for the most part very amiable, but as is often the case, there was one individual who took matters a little too far. Not prepared to wait for anything, he started clicking his fingers to gain attention. As any hotelier will tell you, this is certainly not the best way to ingratiate yourself with the staff.

At the time I had a Liverpudlian lass working for me, and to say she was a little rough around the edges was putting it mildly. She didn't take any *crap* from anybody, not the management, not the guests and certainly not from this man who was clicking his fingers at all and sundry. Watching her become more and more agitated, I went over to appeal to her better nature, but she was having none of it. She brushed me aside and I could only grimace at the events about to unfold.

As she tapped the man on the shoulder, she announced not just to the table but to anyone who was in earshot, 'Sir, I take a great dislike to anyone clicking their fingers at me and as I told my boyfriend last night, it takes more than two fingers to make me come!'

She strode off, with me cowering in the corner, his seven companions in stitches and said guest suitably mortified. Funnily enough, he didn't click his fingers again!

That aside, we come back to this issue of those first two minutes. With my B&B, the biggest issue has been that I have no parking and that the road opposite has double yellow lines. Not only that, but the nearest car park is a hundred metres away and is a pay and display. Now, most hoteliers might contend that having sent out a booking confirmation that highlights the lack of parking and points out where the nearest parking is, should surely be enough and the guest will have the common sense to figure it out.

In truth, reality is a totally different beast and rather than leave anything to the common sense of the guest, this an opportunity to make those first two minutes really count. The key is to realise that the parking is not only a problem to be resolved early, but also an opportunity to impress. You have to take into account any number of scenarios, which could include the ferry being delayed, that the guests don't have change for the meter, that the kids have been screaming on the back seat all the way from London, or maybe the guests are too elderly or too anxious to bring their cases one hundred metres from the car park before paying for parking, or they have come over from China and think nothing of stopping the car in the middle of the street to unload their bags.

All are a possibility and have the potential for disaster – or can be an opportunity to make those first few minutes count. In my case, I decided to meet the problem head on. Firstly, on booking, I include parking on the entire island in the price of the guest's room. I find out the time the guest's ferry arrives and enter their car registration at this time, so that they don't have to worry about finding change for the car park as soon as they arrive, and can even do a little hassle-free sightseeing before checking in.

Secondly, once I know when they are arriving, I make sure they know I'm there to help with their luggage. Again, it's those first two minutes. If the guest can't park or find the hotel or is hoofing luggage up the high street with screaming kids in tow, it might not necessarily have been your fault, but those first experiences will set the tone for their stay.

Of course, the guests can also set the tone themselves. I fondly remember checking in one family, who had organised their own parking and were waiting patiently in the hallway. Naturally, although you will have been waiting all day for your guests to check in, they will invariably all arrive at the same time. They're similar to buses. These guests were keen to make the most of their holiday and as I went back to help them with their luggage, we chatted amicably. After a while, the gently rotund dad waved away my attempts to help with his luggage and picked up two cases. He continued chatting without realising that his shorts had taken on a life of their own and were down by his ankles.

Before I could mention it, his aghast wife was trying to pull them back up. The husband didn't bat an eyelid and carried on chatting as though nothing had happened. His kids just rolled their eyes in a *we've seen this all before* way and we trooped up the stairs, with his poor wife apologising all the way to their room. As I said, those two minutes set the tone.

The next morning, I asked whether he would be suitably attired for breakfast and so the banter continued for the whole of the week. Knowing I could take the joke a little further, I thought I would surprise them on their final day. They were last down to breakfast, and when I took their order, they had no clue that anything was amiss. Normally I cook in shorts with an apron over the top; however, when I turned round, they saw that on this occasion, instead of my usual shorts, I was just in my underpants. I told him I thought it was only right to repay his first day's compliment. I never forgot them, and I hope they never forgot me!

I have to say that even after thirty years in the industry, I still have the odd butterfly as that door opens; you never know who is going to be on the other side. All I can say is, be prepared for anything. One memorable moment was when two lovely Australian ladies descended on my doorstep at Keats Cottage. As they chatted away, they mentioned they had brought along their mum, Barbara.

My initial reaction was one of worry – they had only booked a twin room and I thought, *where the hell am I going to put her?* While I was expecting Mum to come along at any moment, the two sisters proceeded to produce her from their hand luggage – in the form of an urn. Rather than being taken aback, all I could think was, *thank God I don't need to find another bed.* As they delighted in telling me about their plans to scatter Mum into the Solent, my mind drifted and, being ever the professional, I started to think of any problems that scattering Mum could create. It was then that I thought of Angie, our housekeeper, and her rather overzealous attitude to cleaning. I could just imagine poor old Mum disappearing into the hoover bag and how that might take some explaining, so I quickly made a note to myself for the next morning.

Aside from those first impressions, my next core belief is that it's the small details that people remember. This could be the complimentary drink on arrival, the home-made jams, or simply the biscuits in the room. Many of my management colleagues are driven purely by the bottom line and wouldn't dream of emulating my overtly generous nature and giving so many little things for free. But my thinking is twofold: firstly, they remember the small acts of generosity and will tell their friends about the experience they have had; secondly, if there is a small fault with their stay – say the television goes on the blink or the Wi-Fi fails – these small grievances will be overlooked. I am also a firm believer that, as the saying goes, what goes around comes around. So, if you are penny-pinching, then so will your guests be!

Okay, all guests want a comfy bed, a powerful shower, a good night's sleep and a decent breakfast, but it's what sets you apart that makes you truly special. I remember years back, staying at the Chewton Glen in Hampshire. The stay was exceptional, but what I remember most was that they had their own postcards with a postage stamp on, ready to send. Not only was this a perceived freebie, but an ingenious way to advertise, so I took the idea away with me. Over the years, I have seen this idea in other places, but interestingly, where a stamp is not included, the postcard is never taken away.

On another occasion, I stayed in rather a nice hotel in Lisbon. Now, I have to smile at the hotels that ask their guests to reuse their towels and save the environment. What they are really saying is that they might well be thinking of the planet, but it also represents a nice increase to their bottom line. This particular hotel showed that they really were environmentally friendly by stating that for each day the guest reused their towels, their minibar would be restocked free of charge. Win-win for everyone, including the planet.

As Ewa always pointed out, my philosophy will never make me rich, but it will make me memorable. How often have you come out of an establishment and shaken your head in amazement at how you have been charged for every little extra and suddenly you have an astronomical bill? This might make a hotel a short-term gain but would certainly dissuade me from going back.

Now, you can take the attitude that greedy little James has devoured all the home-made biscuits that you left in the room in one go so there is no way he is getting any more, or that you are going to hide the marmalade from Frank because he polishes off a jar on a daily basis. Again, to me, this is a chance to shine and yes, sometimes you lose, but if you have the right attitude, you will eventually win. I would rather bid James farewell with a gift of more biscuits wrapped for the journey and give Frank a complimentary jar of marmalade to enjoy when he gets home.

I can imagine many colleagues deriding my stupidity. It was my hope that the parents would remember this small gesture and book for next year as soon as they got home. This ended up being the case. As for Frank, he was so touched by the gesture that he decided to buy my entire stock of sixteen jars. You see, it's all about the small details.

There are many occasions when generosity goes unnoticed and there are other times that will surprise. One family that did make me smile was a Chinese couple who booked my last twin room at the very last minute during a bank holiday. When the lady checked in, she told me that her husband was parking and was there any chance that the twin room could be made into a double? Unfortunately, this was not possible because of the configuration of the room, and the lady merely shrugged the problem off. As her husband had taken rather a long time to park, I asked if I could go and help him. At this point, I noticed that the lady had become somewhat anxious. With limited English, she told me that she had her *baby* in tow, and although the room wasn't the biggest, I told her I would happily make up a bed for the *baby*.

'No, no, the baby can share with us,' she replied. Now it dawned on me why she wanted a double bed. Or so I thought.

When Dad finally made it, I realised why he had taken so long, as their *baby* happened to be a seventeen-year-old, built like a sumo wrestler. Now I had two dilemmas. One was whether to kick them out, as it clearly stated that the room was only suitable for two – but I knew that on a bank holiday they had little to no chance of finding accommodation elsewhere. The other was: how the hell did the mother expect this giant of a baby to share her bed?

In the end, I squeezed a futon in between the beds and, as it quickly became apparent that the baby wasn't going to have a comfortable night, I told the parents there would only be a supplementary charge for breakfast. The next morning, the clearly delighted mum tipped me far more than the cost of another adult. Yet again, what goes around comes around.

Another aspect of good service that I have learned over the years is never to judge a book by its cover. You never can tell anything by appearance alone. In my view, it is also important to treat everyone the same. This notion of a VIP is utter nonsense – surely you should aim for the same high standard with every customer you serve? I can already see many of my colleagues shaking their heads at my naivety but say, for example, I have a food critic in, do I really want to know who they are? The answer is no, because if I fawn over one individual and don't act the same way to all my other guests, then surely, I'm not worthy of any accolade that may be bestowed upon me. At the end of the day, people are just people, and it doesn't matter if it's David Beckham in front of you or the tea lady from his old club (and yes, I've served both).

We have all become a little star-struck by celebrity, and I do admit that occasionally I have to pinch myself because many situations are so surreal. But I think it's just as important to give someone who has saved up a hundred pounds for a rare treat the same experience as someone who doesn't think twice at dropping several thousand. It isn't just that it's my duty to make someone feel special; in truth you never know how this attitude will influence your own life.

If the scene in *Pretty Woman* where Julia Roberts goes clothes shopping, somewhat underdressed, and gets kicked out – only to return elegantly attired, having spent thousands elsewhere – may seem a little clichéd and old hat, I have found similar situations pop up surprisingly frequently.

My first experience came during my time at the Brasserie Lipp. This majestic restaurant was something of an institution in Zurich, showcasing an amazing array of seafood flown in fresh daily from France. Although the menu hasn't changed in the past thirty years, the restaurant still boasts over five hundred guests on a typical evening. The glittering chandeliers, multitude of mirrors and quintessential Paris vibe have ensured this restaurant has welcomed a discerning clientele for decades.

The pace of this restaurant was so frantic that it was daunting serving seventy guests by yourself. It was pretty much a given that by the end of any evening you could barely put one foot in front of the other. However, during my probation period I was assigned the least desirable station, at the back of the restaurant. This station was tucked away and guests who enjoyed being seen in such an establishment would shy away from this part of the restaurant. Whereas the other stations were full all night, this station was full just once, the benefit being that you did at least finish early.

On one evening, I was just about finished and saying goodbye to my colleagues when I noticed a young couple approach one of our supervisors and a hostess at the reception desk. The hostess in question was always somewhat aloof and the supervisor was, to put it mildly, a little blasé about his role as a service provider. So, it came as no surprise when they paid little heed to the rather dishevelled couple in front of them. When they enquired whether we had a table, they were dismissed rather curtly, with the hostess stating that we were 'far too full'.

I later found out that the couple had in fact run from the train station to try and get a table, hence their appearance. However, at the time I noticed their disappointment and went over to tell them that if they didn't mind eating on their own, then I was happy to open the back room. This received a sneer from the hostess, which

I ignored, and I led them through the masses to the now deserted room.

The couple were full of gratitude and told me they wouldn't stay long so as not to keep me late, but I assured them that I was only too happy to stay and proceeded to recommend some dishes. On ordering their food, they asked to see the wine list and astounded me by ordering a Lafite Rothschild, priced at over 400 francs. Now, you will remember that I was on commission and 12 per cent of that wine cost alone had just gone into my pocket, so perhaps my gesture had been well worth it.

This couple turned out to be an utter delight and we chatted away while they set about their dinner. As they finished the last morsels from their plates, the young man asked if I minded terribly if they had another drink. Enjoying their company, I happily agreed, and to my amazement they ordered another bottle of the wine. All in all, they were in and out in an hour and a half and at the end it became apparent that this was just a normal night for the rather dishevelled young man. However, as they strode off, arm in arm, I didn't think much about it when he turned around and his parting words were 'I will make sure to put in a good word for you'.

Several weeks later, the incident was already a distant memory and there was a particularly busy lunch service. I had the station 'Rive Gauche', which happened to be the most popular with the guests; that meant the most lucrative earnings to whoever was serving on it. One policy of the restaurant was that it didn't matter who you were, you could not reserve specific tables, so it came as a bit of a surprise when a supervisor came over, rather flustered, to ask when one of my tables was likely to be free. I said to the clearly unimpressed Marco that it was unlikely to be any earlier than another hour. What I couldn't understand was what all the fuss was about; there were still plenty of tables free.

Out of the corner of my eye, and to my utter amazement, I noticed that Herr Maenl, our general manager, had entered the fray and was serving the customary Swiss Stange beer to six rather well-heeled gentlemen. This was particularly notable for two reasons: firstly, I had never seen Herr Maenl serve anyone, and secondly, these gentlemen were stuck on the tiniest table, next to the dispense bar, so they could not have been more uncomfortable.

After serving the beers, Herr Maenl came over to me and, although pretending to smile, he was not his usual epitome of Swiss cool. When he asked if I knew the gentleman standing by the dispense who was now manfully trying to dodge the equally perplexed waiters, I honestly thought I must have done something wrong.

'I don't know what you have done, Herr Woodward,' the ever formal Herr Maenl began, 'but that man refuses to be served by anyone except you and doesn't mind waiting as long as it takes for one of your tables to become free. He also happens to own the brewery that supplies our restaurant and is by far our biggest client.'

None the wiser, I furtively looked over at the man, but still couldn't place him.

Eventually, a table became free and Herr Maenl, who now looked as if he was about to have a coronary, came over with the man and introduced me to him.

'Hello, David,' he said, smiling. 'You don't know me, but my son told me you give excellent service.'

It was only then that the penny finally dropped. I never worked the back room again, but I did always serve the gentleman in question and was delighted to receive my customary two-hundred-franc tip. You see, you really shouldn't judge a book by its cover.

When it comes to money, you will see many scenarios play out. You have those who are ostentatious and love to flaunt it and those who are so mean with it that you realise just why they are so damn wealthy. As is my philosophy with most things, sometimes you win, sometimes you lose, but if you treat people well, you are more likely to win. We have all heard of the fabulously wealthy who take delight in packing their bags with half the contents of their hotel. As they are paying an exorbitant price for their room, the management will overlook it – because they *are* paying a ridiculous amount.

It's not only the rich who will try to get one over on you. I have had many guests who go through twenty teabags in a day and then claim they were never replenished. Or you have the guest who orders three breakfasts and inevitably leaves one unfinished, just to get his money's worth, but do these things bother me? The answer is, not at all.

I remember working at the Bluebird restaurant, where we had ashtrays with the Bluebird car engraved on the side. We were losing, and I use the term loosely, around thirty of these a week. Often you could hear them rattling in Gucci handbags as immaculately dressed ladies, with legs that went on forever, exited the restaurant, a knowing smile suggesting they had got one over on us.

They could be bought for the paltry sum of £8, so did we run over and call security? Of course we didn't.

Why? Because we knew the ashtray would be adorning some pied-à-terre on the King's Road and would make a lovely story for the hostess during one of her soirees. In turn, the restaurant would invariably be the topic of conversation for the evening. The ashtrays were relatively inexpensive to make, so of course the management turned a blind eye!

This is not to say that I have the word 'mug' etched on my forehead. Believe me, two can play at that game. The secret is to make sure the guest believes he has won.

I had one wealthy client in Bath, who, to put it in the mildest terms, was very brash and arrogant. He also thought of every transaction as though it were a business deal, and that included a restaurant bill. It was as though he constantly had to think he had got one over on you.

It was my job and my aim to make him feel like the most special person in the world. We were only just starting to establish the Bath restaurant and it was going to be our first Christmas open to the public, so it was essential that it was a success. The man in question came over to the bar and demanded to know the price of the Christmas lunch, as he was thinking of bringing a party of ten along. At £70 a head, I didn't think we were overly expensive, but he scoffed at the price and said he was only willing to pay £45 tops. He also said that as he was a regular guest, he wanted a substantial reduction on the price of the champagne he liked.

He knew I needed the business, so was naturally trying to pull a fast one. Most of my colleagues would now be advising me to tell him, in the nicest possible way, to go and take a jump. I told him I would have to think it over and get back to him. When I told the chef, he nearly had a nervous breakdown and my owner, knowing the man in question, told me to 'tell him to piss off'.

I guess that's what you can say when you are extremely wealthy, but I begged the indulgence of both the owner and the chef and assured them they wouldn't lose a penny. It would also bring a huge amount of word of mouth to our fledgling business.

The next day, I went back to the delighted guest and agreed to his demands. You see, I had a plan. I knew this guest and his gang of cronies loved to drink and their usual sessions started at lunchtime and rarely finished before closing time. I also knew they loved to show off and this guest liked nothing more than to impress his friends.

So, on Christmas Day, my animated guest started off by regaling his fellow revellers with the story of how he had managed to get this super lunch at the bargain price of £45 a head, much to their delight. As they whiled away the hours, consuming copious bottles, the guest, as I had predicted, was keen to move on to a little port with his cheese. By this stage, the guests, while not legless, were certainly in high spirits, and it was with something of a flushed face that my guest asked if we had a rather nice port that would go well with the cheese, but which of course wouldn't break the bank.

I then made a big show of bringing out a decanter of port and as he sipped it, I said, 'I'm sure you'll agree it's a bargain at just twelve pounds a shot.'

'Absolutely,' said the clearly delighted guest, 'and make sure you keep it coming.'

'I'd be delighted to,' I replied. With the cheese course finished and with several bottles of port decanted and consumed, I happily made my way back to the kitchen. The chef was eyeing up the label on the port and looking at me rather curiously.

'Is this your special bottle of port?' he asked in a hushed tone.

'I think you'll agree that Tesco's do a remarkable own brand and with their Christmas offer of eight pounds a bottle, it's remarkable value for money,' came my reply. Looking at the number of empty bottles, he suddenly twigged what I had been doing. Smiling at him, I said, 'I told you you wouldn't be losing any money.'

As the guests departed, content to spread the word around the great and good of Bath, I reminded myself of the importance of the guest believing they are always right.

Having been lucky enough to stay in some of the finest hotels in the UK, usually owing to some kind colleague giving me a complimentary stay, I thought I had seen the pinnacle of truly great service, but a trip to Dubai put everything I had previously seen into the shade. I was staying at a rather expensive hotel called the Al Maha (my mother still berates me for my earlier hedonistic lifestyle!) and I have to say it was beyond anything I had ever encountered.

The hotel is situated in the desert and was an oasis of tranquillity and calm, with a price tag to match. I even took out a loan to pay for the holiday to impress my previous missus, a fact my mother still reminds me of seventeen years later.

'Oh well, at least I have the memories,' I always say, only to infuriate my mother further. In turn, she will always remind me of how she had to scrimp and save, barely able to afford a new pair of knickers, but to be honest I don't have any regrets. The problem is, I've always been good at making money but pretty much a disaster at keeping any of it.

As for the hotel, the rooms were lavish, with their own butlers and their own pools. We could dine on whatever took our fancy and even had our own chef to cook for us and waiter to serve us. We enjoyed trips on camels where we were entertained with champagne and canapés under the stars. We flew peregrine falcons and even rode Arabian stallions in the dunes.

It was a magical experience and even beat our one night at the seven-star Burj Al Arab, with its underwater restaurant, white Rolls-Royce to the airport and a room big enough to have housed an entire rugby team. Well, at £1,000 a night, it should have! Mum, if you are reading, look away now.

However, my overriding memory of the stay was that during our first night, the barman and the staff paid special attention to all our likes and dislikes. At the time I didn't think much of it, but the next day the housekeeper stocked the bar with all the drinks we had mentioned, and the butler would tempt us every hour with yet more of the delicacies we had enthused about to the staff. Now, that's what I call service!

The trip to Dubai was an experience I will never forget. Hotels were springing up everywhere, each more opulent than the next, while the other side of the road would resemble a building site. I would look on in astonishment at the shopping malls lined with gold, the golf courses that were like playing off carpets, state-of-the-art racecourses that seemed to appear as if by magic out of the desert. It was truly mind-blowing.

You couldn't help but admire the feats of engineering and the sheer imagination of the place. But what stuck out was the utter arrogance of the wealthy, who seemed to look down on the very people who made their lives so seamless.

In terms of service, it wasn't the hotels that left the lasting impression but a much more humbling experience. My then partner and I had booked several excursions through our hotel. On one particularly hot day, I had booked for a 6 a.m. round of golf at the renowned Dubai Creek golf course. I pitched up with my golf clubs – they had definitely seen better days – and I can vividly remember someone taking them away to be cleaned. That was to be their first and last clean ever! Anyway, I digress.

The day had started at 5.30 a.m., when I was picked up by my endearing Indian driver, Vic, whose infectious charm made the journey to the golf course even more enjoyable. Later that day, we had booked to go into town at around 10 p.m. to have a look at the malls, as again it was much cooler. To my amazement, Vic picked us up again with his ever-ready smile and regaled us with his many stories on the way to the mall.

When I mentioned how long a day he'd had, I was dismissed with a cheery wave and a genuine 'Take as long as you like'. The next day I was booked into another golf club, called the Emirates, so was yet again up early and eager for the day to start, knowing that after the golf I could enjoy the World Cup rugby in their rather opulent bar. I mean, I was watching England versus Wales, so it really didn't get much better than that. As I headed out alone, I should add that my partner was an understanding type, happy to accommodate my rather laddish days out. Or perhaps she relished the peace and quiet? I was never quite sure.

But as I went to the car, Vic – who had dropped me off at around midnight the previous night – was there again, with that genuine smile of his still in tow. This time, we chatted about life and family. To my amazement, I discovered that Vic worked from 5 a.m. until midnight. Coming from a catering background, I was accustomed to crazy hours, so this wasn't so surprising. But when he told me he worked seven days a week, never took holidays and lived an hour's drive away and was living on three hours' sleep, I was truly astounded. He even offered to show me his home. When I told him of my sincere admiration, he shrugged it off and told me he was happy. His work meant that he could provide for his whole family in India and that he had a far better life than he could have dreamed of back home.

As we made our way in our air-conditioned car, happily chatting, I could make out the construction workers on cranes hundreds of feet up and with barely any safety measures, toiling in temperatures of over forty degrees. Vic turned to me, smiling: 'Now that's what I call a hard life.'

It's this service and humility that will forever stay with me, and the extremes of the place. Don't get me wrong; I love some of the nicer things in life, but the experience really did put my own problems into perspective. If my training in Switzerland showed how hospitality should be done, Dubai took it to another level. That said, the hotel's head chef told me over several pints of beer that in Europe, most five-star hotels have an average of one member of staff to each guest, whereas in Dubai, due to the lower salaries, there were five staff to each guest!

•

At this point I am going to go on a little Ronnie Corbett 'aside', as it would be remiss of me not to mention the strange game of golf and a story that recently made me smile. I have been told that I have the worst swing and stance, and even a pro told me it probably wasn't worth the money to get a lesson, but as any golfer will tell you, that one good shot will always bring you back for more.

However, one of my guests showed me just how ridiculous the game of golf really is through the following story. He was playing a round with someone who was known around the club for having something of a fiery temper. This man had recently kitted himself out with a brand-new set of clubs, but it obviously hadn't improved his golf as he was *shanking* the ball all over the place. As he hit one shot after another into the water, he became angry and declared to my guest that he'd had enough of this bloody game and then proceeded to hurl his clubs into the water after the offending ball.

He then stormed back to the clubhouse and left my friend to continue his round on his own. When my friend returned to the clubhouse, he noticed the man was soaked from head to toe and asked, 'I thought you had given up golf for good?'

'I have,' came the reply. 'But I left my fucking car keys in the bag.'

So, anyone out there mad enough to play golf as badly as I do, be warned.

CHAPTER 26

The rich and famous

I think when it comes to the rich and famous, the thing to remember is that they are just people like you and me. Sure, there are situations when the whole scene seems rather surreal, but even the famous have their problems, and it's usually the smallest detail or the tiniest moment that will define them in your mind – and in the minds of others too, when you relate the story of meeting them.

You see, for the most part, they are not superhuman, even if the public does seem transfixed with putting them on pedestals, as if they were higher beings.

I have carried celebrities out of toilets, had food fights with a famous footballer, watched as household names have slipped across the corridors of my hotel into the embrace of their mistresses. All while their wives sleep on, blissfully unaware, in the room opposite.

Back in 1999, I was working at Heathcotes in Manchester and Manchester United had just won the 'treble', three of the major footballing competitions. The players were welcomed back through the city's streets in their open-top bus as though they were conquering heroes, which in some ways they were. But as they waved up to me and my fellow waiters, watching from the first floor of the restaurant, I could only think of them as the young lads who had sat in the very seats in front of me eating their dinner, a couple of weeks previously, under the watchful gaze of Sir Alex Ferguson. Of course, while they were in front of Sir Alex their behaviour was impeccable, but it was not quite the same once he departed. It was then that you realised that these heroes were young adults with the same flaws as you and me, albeit with a considerably larger bank account.

It was around this time that David Beckham celebrated his birthday in the restaurant, with his wife and some of his teammates. At the beginning of the night, several guests had clamoured for autographs, which of course I had not allowed. But as the night wore on, although some members of the *gang* were polite and respectful, this couldn't be said of all of them, and I remember seeing the looks of disapproval from those same guests, who realised these heroes were really no different from us all.

Judgement of your idol is often based on a brief encounter, a snatched meal or, at most, a few days, but that snapshot will stay with you forever. You will undoubtedly pass this on to anyone who will listen. It could be argued that any insight is grossly unfair, as it is no more than a short acquaintance and it is only natural for someone to have an off day. But to be honest, I am only as good as my last guest and if my smile is not permanently fixed, my guests would be the first to notice. These celebrities are probably on downtime, so should we really judge them for one *poor* performance? The answer is no, we shouldn't; but naturally, those tiny glimpses into their world will be forever remembered, whether they have had a bad day or not, and rumours will undoubtedly follow. There have been so many of these occasions over the years where I have peeked into the goldfish bowl that is a celebrity's life, and it really is the small details that come to mind.

I remember being bleary-eyed at around 6 a.m., getting hampers and breakfast ready for the day's pheasant shoot. It was one of my first days working at Hartham Park, which was situated in a delightful setting just outside the picturesque town of Corsham. As I set out flasks of steaming coffee and got ready to welcome my first guests, you can imagine my surprise when there was a knock on the door and those guests were Nick Mason from Pink Floyd and Roger Taylor from Queen. There I was, serving bacon sarnies and enjoying idle chit-chat with two of the creators of the first albums I had enjoyed as a kid.

Other moments that spring to mind are the time Sir Jackie Stewart brought along a rather large bottle of champagne to The Close Hotel in Tetbury, which I was managing at the time. As anyone who works in catering will testify, or anyone who enjoys ridiculously large bottles of champagne knows, they really aren't that easy to open. As I struggled behind the scenes, Sir Jackie joined me, and we ended up with Jackie pulling on one end of the bottle and me hanging on for dear life to the other. So, it's safe to say it isn't all refined elegance. To make the situation even more comical, our audience at the time was none other than Princess Anne and the opera singer Dame Kiri Te Kanawa.

There are celebrities who really do make you feel as though we are all no different, whatever our backgrounds. I have been invited to join Lisa Riley of *Emmerdale* fame for coffee after she had enjoyed her lunch at Heathcotes, I have sipped cognac with Mikhail Gorbachev and watched on in horror as Sir Rocco Forte grabbed a handful of pistachio nuts and placed the whole lot in his mouth without looking, or realising the shells were still on. All I could think was, I hope he's got bloody strong teeth, or those dentures are going to cost a fortune.

On one occasion, I didn't know whether to laugh or cry when I caught Alice, the then wife of Nicolas Cage, just before she fell over on our bar's marble floor. Luckily for me, in true movie style, good old Nic turned around to his clearly displeased wife with the classic put-down, 'You shouldn't have worn such bloody stupid shoes.' I just breathed a sigh of relief as a potential lawsuit was averted. The rest of the night proceeded with Nic picking my brains on potential schools for his kid. At the time, he was intent on buying up half of Bath and the surrounding castles. Later, I was dismayed to read in the newspapers that perhaps he wouldn't be coming back anytime soon as he had fallen foul of the taxman. I have to say that I had enjoyed his company and was happy that Johnny Depp managed to avert a crisis by bailing him out of his taxation problems.

Then there are celebrities whose behaviour is most definitely just as you imagine and those who are really nothing at all like their personas. Yes, I can confirm that

Nigel Havers really is that charming, Joanna Lumley is absolutely fabulous, Jane McDonald does make time for everyone, and Ulrika Jonsson is really that flirty. Three husbands, I'm surprised it's so few! Even I, a humble waiter at the time, thought I *had a chance*, but perhaps she thought I'd said I was half Swedish rather than half Swiss? But she certainly made me blush and dream in equal measure.

When the Bluebird restaurant first opened, it was probably on most celebrities' bucket list. Such was its appeal that it became commonplace to see Michael Douglas eating with Martine McCutcheon (I can't remember if this was before or after his therapy for sexual addiction!). Then there was Kevin Keegan joining his old mate, John Toshack. It was hard not to be a little star-struck as I served Dustin Hoffman, for his birthday, on one table, while Terry Wogan was on another. Then there was Jeremy Clarkson with the late A.A. Gill, and acting giants such as Willem Dafoe or Guy Pearce. Not to mention music legends such as Mark Knopfler, Bryan Adams and Eric Clapton. After a while, their presence became almost routine.

Then of course there was Arnie (Schwarzenegger), who one day joined us at the end of lunch service when the place was pretty much deserted and there was barely a handful of diners left in this immense gastrodome. I can't remember whether the chairs weren't good enough for his finely toned buttocks, but good old Arnie spent twenty minutes going from table to table, trying to decide which chair was worthy.

Finally seated, and with most of the chefs already

on their way home, Arnie decided that the seventy-odd dishes on the menu weren't to his liking and '. . surely, we could rustle up something else?' Unable to satisfy his demands, I sought out the manager on duty, who was normally adept in these situations, but he too was clearly not winning this battle. Arnie, a wee bit disgruntled and certainly puffing out his considerable chest a little, fixed me with his movie stare and although I was expecting the words 'I'll be back', he instead warned me of his credentials as a restaurateur. Racking my brains, I remembered his Planet Hollywood opening and without really thinking came out with, 'Of course, sir, you own the burger joint down the road.' Luckily for me, I'm still here to tell the tale, but I don't think dear old Arnie was too impressed.

If Arnie wasn't quite what I had hoped, there are those who really do revel in their own self-importance. One such person was the late Michael Winner. On joining the queue, he proceeded to demand not only a particular table, but one that already had people eating at it. To make matters worse, out he came with that classic line, 'Do you know who I am?' Thankfully, common sense prevailed, and he was politely ejected.

There are always surprises – take, for example, the snooker legend Jimmy White. Following a lifetime of rooting for Jimmy, I can safely say that after one particular lunch, he was sullen enough for me to change camps and root for Stephen Hendry the following year. If one Jimmy came as a disappointment, then another Jimmy, Mr Carr, came as a surprise. So incredibly quick-witted on stage, I found him reserved and keen to avoid being noticed. Perhaps, after so much time in the public eye, he wanted some peace and quiet, or maybe the receipt for his dinner troubled him, as it included tax! I really don't know. That said, he was courteous enough to give me free tickets to his show, which could only be described as highly entertaining.

If celebrities are guilty of the odd faux pas, then it's only natural that we are entitled to our own slip-ups. I remember being excited to meet Tony Adams, the ex-Arsenal football captain, whose battles at the time with alcohol had been well documented. Talk about putting my foot in it – my opening gambit came out like a kamikaze pilot as I stupidly asked if he fancied a glass of beer or wine before his meal. I don't know who was more mortified!

One world I have been privy to is that of the celebrity chef. It seems now that every other channel has a programme dedicated to cooking. Although I delight in how far English cuisine has come over the past thirty years, what rankles is that, while there are countless celebrity chefs on our screens, there is still little recognition for those front of house managers who not only create the whole ambience of a restaurant but in many cases keep in check the inflated egos of the chefs.

The problem for me is that chefs are seen as the *gods* who make a restaurant, and, in many ways, they are perceived as the indispensable part of the operation. I have worked with many owners who would quite happily dispense with the services of a very talented front of house employee but will tiptoe on eggshells to pander to the ego of a chef. The chefs I truly admire are perhaps not the ones with names in headlights but those who really understand the importance of the back and front of house relationship. A server might go into a kitchen and request that a guest be served first, only to be rebuked by a chef who believes their food is the most important element of the whole experience. If the trust is there, then the chef will realise that the front of house isn't being difficult: there really is a valid reason for a request. This quality in a chef, as much as any ability to cook, is the one I most admire.

I have been lucky enough to work in the same restaurant as John Torode and watch him masterfully control a kitchen where hundreds of dishes are prepared. Conversely, having seen two other household names in action on the television, and although theirs are two of the finest restaurants I have ever eaten in, I am ultimately glad that while I was offered positions with both, I never worked with either. This is not because I don't think I could have handled their demanding standards or even their fiery temperaments, but rather that they would never hold someone who is master of their own front of house craft in the same esteem as someone who works in the kitchen. It took me two minutes in their company to realise this.

This mention of a chef's elevated position might seem exaggerated or even smack of jealousy to the reader, but I can assure you it's true. Many of my guests will happily tell me that I only have to look pretty and come out with the chat while my chef does all the hard graft, and they forget who makes all those magical moments happen for them. Namely, the waiter.

For this reason, I admire the likes of Raymond Blanc, who I've met and served on several occasions. Not only does he have the passion of all these great chefs, but he takes the time with every mortal who passes through his door. In this respect, it would be remiss of me not to mention my friend Marc Hardiman, who funnily enough is head chef at Fred Sirieix's old haunt, Galvin at Windows fine-dining restaurant in London. To me, he is the epitome of a great chef. With a Michelin star in tow, he realised from a very young age the dynamics between back and front of house that make a great restaurant tick.

It's easy for us all to sit in judgement. Has Marco Pierre White, a three-Michelin-starred chef, sold his soul to make a quick buck? Is Jamie Oliver a proper chef or just a personality who's made it big? Is Gordon Ramsay a tyrant or a legend? We all have an opinion and that's the world we live in; and I guess there is always an element of truth in every and any statement. Yes, I admire Ramsay more than any other chef, but could I work for him? Debatable. When I have watched Fred in service with Gordon, even in jest, I think it is clear to see that Gordon believes the skills of a chef outweigh those of the manager and that is why I don't think I would last.

As for Jamie Oliver, I admire him more for his training restaurant and his attempts at making kids healthy than for any of his restaurants or his cooking ability. There is one instance that I carry with me when it comes to Jamie. When I was heading up Greene King's flagship hotel, The Close in Tetbury, the managers and head chefs participated in a company version of *Ready Steady Cook*. It was decided that a celebrity chef would host the day and I remember happily enjoying my lunch next to the amiable Irishman Mr Paul Rankin. I later discovered from one of the bosses of the company that they had approached Jamie Oliver for a few hours of his time, but after going through all the red tape, they decided to plump for Paul with his modest £5k day rate rather than Jamie's £50k. Nice work if you can get it. As I said, it's the small things you remember.

From a young age, the world of celebrity has fascinated me. It is not so much that I am star-struck but has more to do with the way in which we, the public, deal with them. I can remember back in 1991 when I first started out in Switzerland, my friend and I had switched on the TV only to see the final moments of a little-known Welshman by the name of Ian Woosnam winning the US Masters golf tournament. None of my co-workers were remotely interested but I remember being transfixed, praying that he would sink that final putt. But in that sporting cauldron where only legends have won, I found it strange to think of this *family friend* who hailed from my hometown of Oswestry as anything other than the amiable chap who liked a beer or two, who always stopped and threw us youngsters a couple of balls back at our own club. You see, I found it hard to imagine these superstars as anything other than normal people that I just happened to have met. This is not to say that their lives are in any way normal. I remember being at the Ryder Cup later, watching the scenes unfold and thinking the golfers were like gladiators in a coliseum, such was the roar and intensity of the spectators. My overriding thought was that I wouldn't have been able to hold the club, never mind hit the ball, in that atmosphere.

There have been many interesting moments over the years, and occasionally I was a little in awe of the person sitting opposite me. I'd be lying if I said I wasn't. But as my mum always said, 'Treat everyone the same and you can't go far wrong', and that is what I have tried to do. That said, owing to the generosity of friends, I have been lucky enough to eat in some fairly amazing restaurants and it's fair to say that even I had a wry smile as waiters hovered around me and my partner as we tucked into complimentary champagne and lobster, with the diners at the tables next to us wondering who these two VIPs were. On one of the tables in question were football manager Martin O'Neill and his wife, and on the other was Nigella Lawson and her later ex. Just for a moment, I thought maybe I had arrived!

On another occasion, I was managing at the Kings Arms in the beautiful Cotswold setting of Chipping Campden when a gentleman entered the restaurant before service, in a rather buoyant fashion. Now, it must be said that this gentleman was certainly no celebrity, but still to this day the events that followed were rather surreal. Firstly, he asked me if he could have the table in the window, and before I could reply he was placing a £50 note into my hand. I tried to give it back, telling him that the restaurant wasn't too busy that lunchtime and I would happily reserve the table for him, but he insisted anyway.

When he appeared shortly afterwards with two friends in tow, they could only be described as amiable northerners who were certainly very down to earth, which made the whole £50-note episode feel out of character. It wasn't long before three fish and chips were ordered, as I had anticipated, but to my surprise the dishes were accompanied with bottles of Laurent-Perrier Rosé. Being used in Chipping Campden to the racegoers who attended Cheltenham races, this wasn't unusual either, but I still couldn't quite grasp what was happening. As the gent who had booked the table pottered off to the toilet, his high-spirited friends told me that their mate had just won the lottery. Of course, I thought they were pulling my leg, but on returning the guest took me and my assistant manager to one side and said, 'Boys, go and take my new car for a spin.' Somewhat aghast and not knowing what to expect, we followed the gent outside and, beaming from ear to ear, he handed us the keys to his brand-new Aston Martin. Luckily for him Richard drove, but it will always be one of those occasions that will go down in memory. He really had won the lottery!

But if in most cases celebrities can be thought of as mere mortals, then there are times when it does seem as though certain individuals come from an altogether different planet. The story told by a friend of mine confirms this. A couple had booked into a hotel where he worked in Cheshire for a wedding. Everything was organised, the invites had gone out and the wedding dress had been made. Shortly before the big day, the couple received a call from the hotel manager, asking them if they would consider changing their dates. Of course, they declined. The manager then said that if they reconsidered, the cost of their wedding would be picked up by the hotel. Knowing the inconvenience this would cause, they again declined. The hotel rang back and said they would pick up all associated costs, even the honeymoon. Realising something was afoot, again they declined. Then came the final offer. They were asked how much was owing on their mortgage; £250k was their reply. To their amazement, the manager said that if they changed their dates, the mortgage would be paid off. They accepted. When they arrived at their complimentary Caribbean destination, there was a bouquet of flowers and a note: 'Thank you for accommodating us. Best wishes, David and Victoria.'

Obviously, this is a great story, but at the time, all I could think was that on David's birthday – while I was managing at Heathcotes restaurant in Manchester – Victoria had picked up the bill and hadn't left a penny tip! You see, it is always the little things you remember!

Friendships, owners and those who left an impression

I have been lucky enough to have met so many characters over the years, many of whom I seldom see but who I still count as friends. Our meetings always feel as though time has stood still and the joy of our earlier years is still there. At every meeting, our dubious encounters are endlessly retold, with perhaps the enormity of the tales expanding. I am fortunate to have become acquainted with countless nationalities from varying backgrounds and met so many who could never be deemed as boring. With the nature of the industry, those with whom I have spent every day for years suddenly vanish and turn up twenty years later. Guests have become lifelong friends; peers are now household names.

In all this time, I have always tried to treat everyone the same. Race, sexual orientation, wealth, I can honestly say it really has never mattered. Regrets? Yes, the nature of the business means I regret not always being there for special occasions or missing the fact that certain friends were crying out for help. We become so immersed in our own worlds and our own problems, it's easy to forget the sufferings of others. I think on top of it all, we are all guilty of standing in judgement. Why is someone an alcoholic? Surely, they can stop. Why is such and such going bankrupt? They must have been careless. That person can't be depressed; they have the perfect lifestyle. People constantly surround them, so they can't be lonely. I know, because I have felt all these things, and in so many of these situations, I could have been describing myself. So now, as I get older, I try to have more empathy with those around me or those in need of help. I mean, this life of ours has never been easy.

Despite the countless magical moments I have shared with numerous people, the adage that true friends can be counted on one hand is oh so true. There have certainly been moments when I have hit rock bottom and, trying to drag myself from the edge of the abyss, I have wondered where my family and friends were to help me.

A few years ago, I tried an enterprise that I hoped would allow me to have a work–life balance. Unfortunately, it was 2008, and little did I know we were just about to hit a major recession. What started out so optimistically soon turned into a nightmare and everything I touched seemed to result in ever increasing problems. As the income slowed, the debt rose, and there came a time where I worried whether we would have a roof over our heads.

Just as I thought matters couldn't get worse, a cheque was paid late to me and my lenders, who were themselves in dire straits, called in the whole loan. In the short term, I knew it would be impossible to pay, and many around me urged me to declare bankruptcy. Pride wouldn't allow this, and I was determined to find a solution. I took on two extra jobs, but this still didn't solve the problem of the immediate loan. Reasoning with the company proved fruitless, so I went with my tail between my legs to family and friends. From the conversations I had, I could see that the initial reaction was one of scorn. *How on earth could he have got himself in such a predicament?* was written on all their faces. I guess if it had been me, I would have felt the same, but now when I hear that you are only a bit of bad luck and a couple of pay cheques away from being homeless, I know it's true. Dejected, I turned to my estranged father, and, against my better judgement, I asked for help. Although this would be a drop in the ocean as far as he was concerned, he magnanimously declared that although he wasn't prepared to help me financially, he would graciously represent me in court for my bankruptcy hearing. At that moment, words failed me.

With the deadline fast approaching and on the cusp of giving up, suddenly a ray of hope appeared. Our next-door neighbours, Peter, a retired artist, and his wife, Pauline, had become friends, to the extent that we invited each other over for dinner. It was on one such evening that I recounted our tale of woe, including the meeting with my father. To my shock, and without being asked, they agreed to loan me the money and bail me out. It took me twelve months to pay them back, but that generosity has stuck with me over the years and in turn I have tried to help others in need. As a wise friend told me, 'Only lend what you can afford to lose', and this has proved too true.

Friendships, I have realised, like relationships, can come in many forms and in many cases are not really that dissimilar to having a platonic other half. In catering, you are more likely to spend time with a friend or colleague than you ever are to spend time with your partner.

With this in mind, I would like to introduce you to Pascal. Pascal and I met back in 2002, when I was made restaurant manager and he assistant manager at the beautiful Manor House Hotel at Castle Combe in the Cotswolds. I can safely say that when I was interviewed, I felt this was to be my dream job. With its Michelin-starred restaurant, magnificent setting and a building steeped in history, this small slice of heaven would come to feature in many of my life-affirming events; but when I took up my appointment, my first impressions were not so favourable.

If on the face of it the Manor was the epitome of glamour, the same could not be said of the working conditions, a problem that unfortunately is widespread within the industry and has ultimately resulted in it being impossible to find staff. The hotel, despite its accolades, still thought it was totally acceptable for staff to work sixteen-hour days on £9,000 a year, living in accommodation not fit for purpose. It wasn't long before Pascal and I discovered we were doing the jobs of the four managers who, after many years of service, had decided to walk out en masse, so dismayed were they by the antics of the senior management.

To their credit, senior management had set up an amazing property, but having paid their dues, they thought it acceptable to sit on their laurels and let the minions get on with it. To compound matters, the highly acclaimed food and beverage manager had a serious drink problem and spent the whole time standing at reception, so that he could pocket the not inconsiderable tips.

Matters came to a head one Saturday when Pascal – who I picked up for work each day, so he didn't have to cycle in – and I started breakfast at 6 a.m. Having served near on a hundred for breakfast, we then turned round the restaurant to accommodate a wedding party, while at the same time serving countless afternoon teas.

With the wedding guests departing at 4 p.m., we sent our staff off for a short break and re-laid the restaurant alone, for another hundred eager mouths. As we carved duck and flambéed crêpes in front of our adoring guests, we received no help with our endeavours. Collapsing into chairs at the end of service, we were just delighted that we had made it through the day. However, two events of that day led to both Pascal and I resigning from the hotel.

Firstly, the food and beverage manager had appeared during the wedding and ordered me to tell the host that they had run out of champagne after twenty-four bottles, although they had ordered and paid for thirty-six. The guests were paying £75 a bottle, so I naturally refused, which led to a heated debate. In retaliation, the food and beverage manager approached us at the end of the evening and told us that the stocktake needed to be done that night. With several thousand bottles, the job was not complete until 4 a.m. and we were both back on duty two hours later.

Although the general manager tried to appease me, I was so alarmed that I asked for a meeting with the owner. Unfortunately, I didn't get the reception I was looking for and was shot down in flames. Should I have hung on? Probably. Just a couple of years later, the management team who had made the hotel so great no longer had jobs! So, I guess the owner had seen sense after all.

The pair of us took part-time jobs at The Close Hotel, rated in the top 200 in the country. Our luck changed shortly after. The couple who had managed the hotel so successfully decided to move on soon after we arrived and recommended that I become general manager. In the summer of 2003, I made Pascal my restaurant manager. Our comical friendship has endured to this day and Pascal and his partner are now godparents to my son, Jack. Pascal was best man at my wedding, or should I say, second wedding.

Now, in what way is a friendship comical, you might ask? Well, firstly, when we met back at the Manor House, Pascal was living with a young lady, and I naturally thought they were together. In my naivety, for a couple of years I had no inkling that he was gay, and Pascal – who, unlike me, is very discreet – never let on either. Although it would never have been a problem for me, the possibility hadn't dawned on me.

For someone who believes he can read people so well, I am able to look back at the farcical nature of the situation with some hilarity. Firstly, I spent the first few months trying to set him up with our head housekeeper and was surprised when this was met with little enthusiasm. Secondly, after about a year, when I received my work bonus, I invited Pascal to London as a thank-you. We stayed in the Goring Hotel and enjoyed a raucous night out. At the end of the night we, or should I say I, decided we should head over to Stringfellows. As I enjoyed the entertainment, I thought Pascal's lack of enthusiasm was because he was tired.

My immense naivety came to a head when I invited him on holiday to stay with my mother in Switzerland. As she only had one spare bed, I said it wouldn't be a problem and of course we could share. I still had no idea, although apparently all my colleagues had known from the start. But as I have mentioned before, Pascal has always been very private, and I must have been completely blind. Just to compound matters, several years later, Mum and I were discussing the holiday and I mentioned that I had had no idea that Pascal was gay. I then asked my mum if she had known.

'Of course, it was blatantly obvious,' came the reply.

'Well, why didn't you say anything? I mean, I was sharing my bed and everything.'

'I thought you knew. And anyway, I presumed you were going through some experimental phase in your life and didn't want to get in the way of your fun.'

Typical Mum!

The thing that makes Pascal special is, one, he is very loyal and, two, he has a work ethic second to none. After he left The Close, he went back to Paris and worked for Guy Savoy for over ten years. Now, this institution, which holds three Michelin stars and can boast of having trained Gordon Ramsay, is always busy. Anyone in catering would know that to maintain this standard for so many years requires a very dedicated team of employees, and in Pascal they certainly had one of the best.

In the early days, our friendship quickly turned into something akin to a marriage. We worked extremely hard, and we partied just about as hard. The team included another lifelong friend, Marc Hardiman, who was my very talented twenty-one-year-old sous chef. I knew from the start this young man was going places. This team, although small, was brimming with talent. Along with Marc and Pascal, there was my young trainee James Wiseman, who would go on to be a general manager at Hand Picked Hotels, Marie, my ex-wife, who would manage the hospitality at Ascot races, Rachel, who became one of the country's best pastry chefs, and a crazy half-Italian who I honestly thought wouldn't amount to much and who went on to own a chain of boutique cafés in Australia. Little did I know!

As Pascal and I looked after numerous wedding parties, functions that had Princess Anne dining with us, and all the pressures that came with running a Red Star, 3 Rosette property, our working relationship went from strength to strength and Pascal was unflagging in his constant support. After a hard week, and with the Sunday lunch service finished, our routine kicked off with my supportive wife, Marie, cooking us Sunday lunch. Soon after we were in our local, The Ormond Head, where we would consume copious amounts of beer, chased down with a bottle of sambuca.

The pattern of conversation remained pretty much constant, with Pascal telling me during lunch what a great boss I was and how I worked too much and then, by the end of the evening, my loyal friend berating me for working him like a bitch, not paying him enough and me being full of blah de blah. I guess he was right on both the good and the bad points. By Monday morning, he was telling me to have a lie-in and forget doing breakfast, as he had it all covered.

I will never forget one morning after a raucous night out, Pascal and I were in full swing at breakfast, a little the worse for wear. Well, that's not really accurate – we were pissed. The buffet had run out of yoghurt and the only tub available was a large catering pack on the top shelf in our storeroom, located directly by the restaurant. I climbed on a chair to reach it, not realising that the lid on this enormous tub hadn't been secured properly, and as I brought it down, it unloaded its contents onto my head, my suit and my shoes.

There was no other means of escape; I had to make an undignified exit through the middle of the restaurant, dripping with yoghurt, past a collection of startled guests and a clearly horrified Pascal, who realised he would be doing breakfast on his own for the next half hour. I can only imagine what I must have looked like, racing down Tetbury High Street to my nearby apartment with yoghurt flying everywhere.

Looking back on my management days at The Close Hotel will always remind me of a great young team who strived for excellence and were duly awarded a number of accolades. However, this harmony was somewhat shattered when we were acquired by Greene King, the brewers. They were happy to have a flagship hotel – the only one to have been awarded rosettes and to include royalty among its clientele – but in the end their only real motivation was the bottom line. This wasn't to say we didn't make money, we certainly did. But somehow it was never enough.

I moved on and the team disbanded. On leaving, I warned management that putting pub managers in a property like The Close was a recipe for disaster, and lo and behold four sets of pub managers came and went in the space of two years. Profits dwindled, and the property sold for next to nothing.

If The Close taught me anything, it was that you must always be prepared for the worst and never rest on your laurels. One incident highlighted this. We had in a family of regulars who were celebrating their daughter's wedding with a group of around fifty friends. I had always got on well with this family and this proved to be about the only saving grace in what could have been a potentially disastrous outcome.

The family had enjoyed their wedding and when they departed, I had no idea what was to ensue. On our menu was a starter of home-made chicken parfait. Unfortunately, the commis chef in charge of this dish had failed to check its temperature. The next day, the mother of the bride, although perfectly pleasant, informed me that thirty-two of their guests had come down with food poisoning. Naturally panicking, I immediately rang the environmental health department and, although it could not be proved, it was obvious to me what had caused the outbreak.

After ringing the bigwigs of Greene King, I attended a meeting, and a strategy was put in place. If the media got involved, the repercussions could have been disastrous, not only for the hotel but also for the company. Luckily for me, the family were understanding and happy to accept back the money they had paid for the wedding. It was another lesson well learned!

•

Later in life, while working as the restaurant manager at Hartham Park, I met Andy, the then properties manager of the estate. We didn't really see that much of each other while working, mostly as Andy was inevitably playing darts in his office while I was actually working! Joking aside, our friendship blossomed over our mutual love of playing golf, or should I say our attempts at playing golf. Now, the fact you must remember is that we live in two totally different worlds, which always makes for an excellent catch-up.

Andy has always been in awe of my achievements, or more likely surprised that I have managed to come through my usually chaotic episodes relatively unscathed, whereas the appreciation really should be the other way round. Here is a man who, despite not having it easy, has juggled a large family, with two jobs, run the New York marathon in full firefighter kit, been entered in a national competition by his daughter for best Dad – and actually won! – not to mention having attended Buckingham Palace on several occasions, as his lovely wife, Nicky, is PA to the explorer Sir David Hempleman-Adams. And he says my life is interesting.

But as he so eloquently puts it, 'We don't want anything from each other, other than friendship.'

•

In terms of owners, I have pretty much seen it all, the good and the bad, but through all my ups and downs I've realised that I haven't really been good at playing *the game* and perhaps if I had, my career would have gone further. I have had owners who love to play Lord of the Manor while they haemorrhaged money at such an alarming rate they were constantly in debt, but still put on a facade to their friends. I had another owner who as a young millionaire had reminded me of Gordon Gekko from the film *Wall Street*. His attitude was certainly one of 'sleep is for wimps' and don't even contemplate a day off, let alone a holiday. He did reward hard work, but ultimately you really weren't allowed any sort of life of your own.

However, there was only one owner, still with a rather prestigious property up in Cheshire, who could really rile me. His arrogance was legendary, and he was almost universally disliked except by the staff in the kitchen, who he held in high esteem. He expected the front of house staff to drop everything and, rather than serve the guests, to traipse over to serve his young children as though they were royalty. God knows how those two turned out. The man was so dire, staff would up and leave in the middle of the night (even though pay cheques were withheld on employees who had the audacity to leave) and one disgruntled chef even had the temerity to firebomb his car. At least he did it in style: it was a Ferrari.

But there were two instances that stuck out during my short time there. Firstly, I was employed by the restaurant manager as his assistant. Now, from the start this Frenchman was far too arrogant for his own good. Nonetheless, he worked extremely hard and had accrued a monumental amount of annual leave that the owner had promised to pay out for but which, for the time being, was not forthcoming.

After around a month, I realised that although this Frenchman's reluctant wife was pulled in to work and his poor baby slept in the wine cellar during service, he thought himself a bit of a Casanova, and we were all aware that he was carrying on with a young waitress. She was certainly a willing companion, so it was something of a surprise when all the staff were hauled into the owner's office, one by one, to sign a declaration that the restaurant manager was sexually harassing the girl. I had seen with my own eyes that this was clearly untrue. But, for whatever reason, others signed, and the man who had given so many years' service was dismissed. I always knew that it had more to do with the £10,000 the owner owed him in backdated holiday pay.

A couple of months later, I saw the Frenchman walking down a street in Manchester. A shadow of his former self, he told me he was now working as a porter, as the owner had let him go with no reference. I always wondered what happened to him and I'm as sure as hell he never received that back pay.

The second experience that made me decide enough was enough was shortly after the restaurant manager was dismissed. As I was now mostly alone, I carried out an extremely busy breakfast and lunch service with just one waitress. As I hurried around with the hoover to prepare for dinner, I was called into the owner's office. I honestly thought he was going to congratulate me for managing the whole thing on my own, so as you can imagine I was a little dismayed when he instead had the audacity to question my personal hygiene.

After the initial shock, I suggested none too politely that perhaps he should finish off the hoovering himself, and with that I stormed out of the office. I have to say in my defence that I am not prone to outbursts. The head chef, with whom I had a good relationship, was sent to cajole me back for the evening service. A couple of weeks later, I went to work for the amiable Paul Heathcote. At least the chef made me laugh as he told me that the owner, who was strictly vegetarian, was being served his daily soup not with what he thought was deep-fried tofu but rather with deep-fried foie gras.

'Well, at least that will teach the bastard,' he said, as he left, smiling.

Two owners, not caterers but who made me realise the true meaning of life – namely, that friends, family and loyalty to your staff are just as important as the bottom line – are Mark Norman, who owned The Residence in Bath, and Peter Sherwin, an antiques expert who owned Henrietta House in Bath. It would also be remiss of me not to mention hotelier Ian Taylor, who I had met in Chipping Campden and whose expertise helped me secure my mortgage on Keats Cottage.

•

In life, you occasionally meet people who to all intents and purposes embody everything that you believe life should be about. For me, this came about while I was managing The Residence. It was there that I met an un-assuming gentleman by the name of Dick. The Residence attracted the great and good of Bath and due to its pri-vate location, select membership and not overwhelming size, it was a perfect place for a rendezvous. Although many of the guests were ostentatious with their perceived wealth, Dick and his wife were utterly charming, with-out an air or grace between them. I thoroughly enjoyed their visits and discovered they were widely travelled, so I looked forward to their tales.

Some months later, Dick approached me and asked if I would be interested in supplying the catering for his wife's birthday party. He informed me that there would be around thirty people for the dinner, and could we pro-vide breakfast the following day for those staying over? I promised to organise the food and drink at cost, and they would pay the staff a decent rate for their time, thus benefiting all parties. The only real downside was that we would need to provide all the chairs, tables and crockery, but after some wheeling and dealing, I managed to organ-ise this and only had to pay for a van to deliver.

For the event, I dragged along my chef and his commis, my wife, Ewa, and Jackie, my blonde dynamo of a friend who owned a local wine shop, radiated charm and had an encyclopaedic knowledge of wine.

We had been given the address on the day before the party and we rattled along in the old van, with the commis, Dan, squashed into the back and holding on for dear life to the crockery. We made our way into the affluent area of Batheaston, a couple of miles out of Bath. I don't know what I had really been expecting, but as Dick greeted us enthusiastically at the door, I could only marvel at this magnificent building.

The Georgian property oozed character and wealth, but if the house was impressive, the garden took your breath away and wouldn't have been out of place in any country magazine. I was later told by one of Dick's guests that it was one of the most photographed houses in the whole of Somerset. I could see why, with its beautifully manicured lawns, a lake big enough for its own boat with mooring next to the canal, a swimming pool, tennis courts... the list was endless. The place radiated unassuming opulence and was to me a little slice of heaven that I could only dream of.

As Dick animatedly showed me around, I could only speculate on how he had come to make his fortune. But what I truly admired was that not for a single minute in his presence did I ever feel like anything other than a friend doing him a favour. There was never an ounce of arrogance, just a bubbly enthusiasm from a gentle man who knew how lucky he was.

As Jamie, my chef, was shown the kitchen by Dick's wife, Ewa and I set up the tables in the grand lounge, ready for that evening's activities. As we went about our task, Dick was happily dad-dancing to a tune I recognised but couldn't quite place. 'Dick, remind me, who is that singing?' I asked.

'Oh, it's my wife's favourite band, Ray Lewis and The Drifters,' came the reply and then, with the biggest schoolboy grin, he continued, 'Actually, I'm flying Ray Lewis in from the USA, to play tomorrow night at the party.' As Dick continued his moves around the room, all I could think was that I had agreed to everything at cost price – but as I've always said, what goes around comes around.

The following night was a roaring success. Jamie and Dan had managed to pull off a magnificent buffet, serving everything from lobster to beef fillet. Jackie had managed to sell some unusual vintages and secured several new accounts, while Ewa and I had even been asked to join the party at the end of the evening and in turn, I could show off my own dad moves. A successful night was had by one and all.

That night, as I had been serving up the buffet, I happened to strike up a conversation with Basil, one of Dick's guests and one of my regulars at The Residence. Basil was well known around Bath and had set up a successful business selling toys to generations of the city's youngsters. As I mentioned what a beautiful house Dick had, Basil smiled and said, 'Not bad, considering he only spends three weeks of the year here.'

It later transpired that Dick had been the highly successful CEO of a multinational company that everyone had heard of and in fact they owned properties in New York and on Sydney Harbour, with a couple of yachts in Tuscany thrown in.

As we were returning to cook breakfast for a few of the guests in the morning, Dick and his wife even came to help with the washing up, after which he produced a cheque that paid me more for my thirty-six hours than

I earned in a month, plus a not unsubstantial tip for the rest of the team. After that, the team and I went on to do two more events for Dick, which left me with memories that would last a lifetime. You see, you never know who you will meet in life!

To me, it was Dick, more than any other person I have met or, for that matter, more than any celebrity I have met, who showed me the true essence of life. To appreciate everything you have, retain your humility, enjoy the family and friends you have, and truly embrace life.

Part Five

CHAPTER 28

2022 – The finale – what will life have in store?

As I marvelled at the view over our new paradise in the Algarve, I couldn't quite believe that Keats was finally sold, and we were actually here. The water from the pool glistened in the glow of the setting sun and the birds chirped in the palm trees overhead. The garden was an abundance of scents and colour that were an assault on the senses. Huge cactus plants towered throughout the garden, bougainvillea trailed all over the balconies and the scent of oranges, lemons, grapefruit and apricots pervaded the air. Mum reclined on her lounger, thumbing through her phone and gratefully taking in the last of the sun. Even Zeus, our ever-faithful Westie, seemed delighted with his new surroundings and had rediscovered some of his youthful exuberance, contentedly chasing the local cats away from his new *estate*.

What a difference a few months had made as we averted yet another disaster by the skin of our teeth. In truth, we'd had just five days to go before our lives would have taken a huge turn for the worse. The stress and strain all seemed worth it now we had secured our new home in this little corner of heaven.

I had even launched into a detox campaign, which, although in its infancy, was progressing nicely. Copious amounts of alcohol had been replaced by a daily ritual of lemon juice, and pasta was now banished – my new diet revolved around fruit freshly plucked from our own trees. I spent hours swimming up and down the pool, where just a couple of months previously it was a challenge to get into a pair of trousers without falling arse over tit.

Mum, who only a few weeks earlier had seemed to be at her wits' end, was more relaxed and contented. No, I hadn't managed to get her to lie in past 6 a.m., but at least she had a more laissez-faire approach to life.

Jack dangled his legs in the water and surveyed all around him, taking in every detail. I mean, what little boy could help but be impressed by his own swimming pool, a fish pond, and Astroturf that had been converted into his own football pitch, even if Zeus had other ideas for this hallowed patch. Beneath these outward signs of happiness, I knew this sensitive young man was still reeling at the fact that his parents seemed unable to coexist; but that was a problem for another day.

As we settled into my son's week-long vacation, we took it upon ourselves to enjoy every second as though it were our last. Our mornings were taken up with me showing him countless photos of myself in my more youthful days. Expecting him to be quickly bored, I was surprised when he absorbed himself in every photo with a never-ending flurry of questions. There even seemed to be a semblance of pride in his old dad.

But if I was on a high, this was to be momentary. The fact dawned on my pensive son that if he did look like me when I was younger, then the same could also be said about when he got older. Looking a little dejected, he glanced at my now bald head, stroked my somewhat portly belly and stated, 'So, this is what I have to look forward to in the future.'

I wasn't sure whether to laugh or cry.

As I smiled down at my still absorbed son, I couldn't help but think how matters could have been vastly different.

•

My mother had moved in with me at Keats a few months earlier and we were going through our daily routine. This entailed me berating her for smoking outside the guests' windows or scolding her for traipsing through the B&B at 5 a.m., Westie in tow, waking my once peaceful guests, while she in turn had reverted to a period long gone in my eyes, where I was again seventeen years of age and needed to be reminded of my constant failings.

It was a strange coexistence that friends found comical. In truth, we were both used to being kings in our own domains. When my mum was living down the road in the sleepy village of Niton, it was easier to separate our two worlds, with all that involved. When she helped me with anything that resembled interior design or even DIY, I would bow to her superior knowledge and let her laughingly call me Dick Strawbridge, from *Escape to the Chateau*, as yet another of my efforts to hang a gate or even work a fairly basic tool failed miserably.

In return, she never questioned my knowledge in running the B&B and she put up with my assorted demands, from not waking the guests at 5.30 a.m. to stopping the dog from slobbering over every new arrival. However, the enforced limbo land of lockdown meant a new defining of our roles. By that, I mean I was seventeen again and living at home with the parents. After thirty-three years of freedom, this took some getting my head around.

Unlike most normal people, my mother thought that getting up at 5.30 a.m. was perfectly normal. Even her Westie, Zeus, knew what was coming and rather than getting up to be walked at such an ungodly hour would pretend to be deaf and escape to the comfort of my bed. But even after suffering a life-and-death scare and being told by her doctor to start taking it easy, she couldn't be tethered as much as I might want her to be.

I was now accustomed to the daily routine of 'I didn't wake you, did I?' as cigarette smoke poured through the open window below me and her forgotten alarm clock bleeped relentlessly in the background. As I staggered down the stairs, I would be greeted with, 'Did you enjoy your lie-in?'

Pointing out that 6.30 a.m. was hardly a lie-in was fruitless, so I didn't even bother trying. By then, a fruit smoothie would be ready, complete with chia seeds. 'We need to keep healthy, you know,' she would observe as she extinguished her fifth cigarette of the morning.

That said, used to being the one who waited on others, it was rather nice to have my clothes ironed, dinner waiting on the table, and all those niceties I scoffed about when I heard of thirty-year-old children still living at home with their parents. Although there is always a catch, and if I mentioned 'I am more than happy to do it myself', she would never listen but would happily spend the rest of the day reminding me.

'Isn't it nice to have your mother waiting on you hand and foot.'

I knew this was an argument I could never win, but if I felt I would receive any commiseration from my son, I would soon be put right with, 'It sounds like living with you, Dad.'

So, I guess it's true – we do all end up being like our parents.

Our daily lives had descended into a farce. After thirty years of inactivity, I was attempting to regain some of my youthful fitness. Previous efforts had seen me play the occasional games of squash and tennis where my opponents would limber up with a few stretches, while I would warm up with one last cigar. Now, though, the dog plonked himself down in the middle of my training run and my mother egged me on with yet another cigarette in hand. If I thought for one moment there would be any recognition as I broke the forty-minute barrier for three miles, it was obvious that my success had not at all impressed my mother, who would show me one of her catalogues with the latest spandex on offer.

I did at least receive a more positive response from my son, who informed me, 'You're not as fat as you were, but you've still got a bit of a doughnut.'

So even if my Seb Coe days were long behind me, perhaps there was some hope.

The rest of our day seemed to be spent with me wondering where I had left all manner of items, from car keys to gloves. Basically, anything that couldn't be stuck down. I had always been good at organising my work life but now, at the age of fifty, it seemed that although I could remember exact details from thirty years ago, I was totally incapable of remembering what I had done just five minutes ago. I also spent much of my time trying to turn down the heating. My idea of warm was not the same as my mother's, so in that regard it was very similar to being married. But joking aside, there was endless laughter through what was a very happy time.

That said, for some time my mother had been getting itchy feet and we had bandied about the idea of relocating to sunny Portugal. After three years of near misses, Keats finally looked like it was about to be sold, so my mum took it upon herself to travel to Portugal to investigate the area. Or so I thought.

I sent my mum on her way, with a guidebook and several properties to have a look at. I thought that should keep her occupied for a month or so, and when she returned, we could explore our options. But things don't usually happen as you plan, especially when it comes to my mother!

The peace wasn't to last. My mother rang me on day two of her *vacation* to exclaim, 'Darling, I have found our dream home.'

At the time my mother broke this startling news, I was in the process of delivering one of my guest's breakfast requests. Trying to make light of the situation, I did my best Peter Kay impression to show my guest that it was Mum on the phone, so I wasn't really taking in what was being said.

'That's nice, dear, and what are the locals like? What's the area like?' I asked with eyebrows raised to my guests, who were now glued to my conversation.

'You're not listening to me, are you?' she retorted. 'I don't know anything about the area or the locals, but the house is a dream. That's why I decided to put in my offer.'

Nearly spilling my coffee, and now definitely not in Peter Kay mode, I tried to reason with her. 'But Mum, I've lined up fifteen properties for you to look at. Surely you can't just jump into it,' I pleaded, thinking of all those wasted hours of research.

'No, the owner needed an answer as someone else wanted the house. So the nice estate agent took me down to the lawyer and I have paid the ten per cent deposit.'

I almost choked on my coffee as realisation struck. She had just parted with £50,000 on a whim. For those of you who are unfamiliar with the Portuguese process, you pay the 10 per cent and have a certain time to complete – in our case, three months – otherwise you forfeit the deposit. The problem being the purchase was partially dependent on the sale of Keats.

'But Mum, we haven't sold Keats yet. Don't you think we should have waited?' I beseeched.

Refusing to countenance any negativity, her logic went clean out of the window, and I could only sit back and shake my head as she replied, 'I've read my horoscope and it assured me nothing could go wrong.'

Several months later, I could have wrung that bloody astrologer's neck.

What was first perceived as a straightforward acquisition proved anything but. Our buyer's solicitor was next to useless and there was plenty of stalling on their own sale as we waited in trepidation for yet another amendment. In her own true style, Mum had decamped to a self-catering apartment next to the castle in Silves, but not before she had cajoled the owner of the property we were attempting to buy into letting her store her belongings there. The fact that we did not own it yet never occurred to her. In her usual understated fashion, she told the poor man it was just a couple of boxes, so you can imagine his delight when the removal lorry turned up and, after several attempts at finding a way in, deposited one hundred and twenty boxes, which filled the entire house.

If that wasn't farcical enough, the only way to transport both my mum and her beloved Westie to the sunny climes of the Algarve had been to take the ferry from Portsmouth to Santander and then to drive the rest of the way down. Of course, Mum, using all her powers of persuasion, had managed to charm her poor friend Frank into making the journey with her. This was not uncommon; I remembered one occasion in my childhood when my mum returned to our home in the middle of nowhere in a limousine, having just arrived back from Manchester airport. She jumped from the back and introduced me to some affluent gentleman who she had befriended on the plane and who insisted on making a two-hour detour to drop my poor mother off at her front door. I mean, she couldn't possibly carry those heavy bags on the train. That, I'm afraid, is the effect my mother has, whether you like it or not.

The problem with her now impending journey was that poor Frank had first to make it over from Ireland. Also, he was a notoriously bad driver, who almost had a seizure if his van went over twenty, including on the motorway. It would probably have been quicker on a horse and cart, I thought. So what could possibly go wrong?

On the day of her departure, I had arranged to take my mum over to Portsmouth, where we would meet Frank at the Holiday Inn. As expected, Frank rang to tell us that he was having a bit of trouble finding the place, although according to his satnav he was only five minutes away. We waited patiently at the gates for an hour, and still no Frank. Then a van passed us with no back windows and cardboard flapping in the breeze.

'That wasn't Frank, was it?' I exclaimed. Of course it was.

Getting out of his Del-Boy-inspired contraption, it transpired that he had managed to reverse into two poles, which had taken out his back windows. Alarm bells started ringing. At this stage, they hadn't even made it out of Portsmouth.

•

The next day, I waved goodbye to them both, along with a very bemused Westie who couldn't understand why he was unable to see out of the windows. I could only pray they made it in one piece and that I wouldn't pass them on the road when I went over the following month to join her.

At the end of another busy season, when I did eventually make it over, not only was the sale of Keats still ongoing but I discovered that, without residency, Mum had to leave Portugal within ninety days. With this realisation, even I was starting to panic. Firstly, all Mum's belongings were in the house; secondly, because of Covid there was no way of getting the Westie back; and thirdly, Mum was only one month away from losing her dream home and £50,000.

For the next month, we tried to enjoy our surroundings, but our nerves were frayed by the endless Portuguese bureaucracy, which even gave the Isle of Wight a run for its money. Our situation seemed almost hopeless. For one thing, since Brexit, the Portuguese had deemed the Brits persona non grata, making residency almost impossible; then we heard that our buyer's sale had fallen through.

Far from *living the dream*, we had resorted to drowning our sorrows on our balcony on a nightly basis.

•

Christmas passed with little festivity in our household. Even I was starting to lose some of my usual optimism and was wondering, if the worst happened, how the hell were we even going to get home? Fortunately for us, our luck changed in the New Year and the owner of the property gave us an additional three months to complete. We also had the good fortune to meet a nice young lady at the council who informed us that with a Swiss passport, residency was a pretty simple process. After thinking we would have to wait at least eighteen months to gain residency, four offices later, a couple of stamps and hey-ho, in five days we were officially residents of Portugal. *Thank God for a Swiss passport* was all I could think.

At the same time, our buyer informed us that they had another buyer, but of course the whole process went down to the wire, and we completed five days before our deadline. With the two of us, I wouldn't have expected it any other way!

Yet if this period could only be described as extremely stressful, then at least I learned some very good lessons. Firstly, perseverance pays off in the end; secondly, don't give up on your dreams; and thirdly, recriminations are pointless. It would be easy to say we were stupid and yes, in many ways we were, but we followed our dreams and here we are now. But in all that time, my mother and I still laughed and didn't have a cross word. Even though many others were happy to point out our stupidity, to give Mum her credit, the house was a dream.

My mother embarked on her latest adventure with all the vigour of her twenty-year-old self, even if her powers were slightly diminished. If Portugal didn't yet know much about the diminutive figure, it wasn't long before the cobbled streets of Silves became accustomed to the sight of the white-haired tidal wave, bobbing along with her white-haired Westie companion.

Although some habits never die and she was still the first at the bakery, waiting on her fresh croissants, long before the doors had even opened, then at least she was starting to warm to the idea of basking in the winter sun and taking the odd afternoon siesta. That said, she would never admit that she was sleeping, even though the gentle snores radiating from the sofa proved otherwise. Even her irrepressible spirit could not help but be seduced by the warmth of the locals, the constant scent of orange blossom and the languid evenings, enjoying a glass of wine or two.

During our extended stay in our self-catering apartment, she would still find time to murmur her disapproval of the builders working in front of the apartment at a snail's pace. But whereas previously she would have marched down to get them to speed up, now she was happy to view the proceedings with a wry smile. So perhaps the sun was doing her some good after all.

If this relaxed air was bringing back some of her old sparkle, the same could not be said for the endless bureaucracy. Whether it concerned residency, driving licences or social security, we seemed to spend whole days waiting in queues, only to be told we needed yet more paperwork. Eventually, even we, who wanted everything done yesterday, had no option but to adopt the more laissez-faire attitude of the Portuguese and if it didn't happen that instant, there was always tomorrow.

The farcical nature of the bureaucracy came to a head when we decided to change over our British driving licences for Portuguese ones. We were told in no uncertain terms that a *thorough medical examination* was required and off we sauntered to find our nearest medical expert.

We entered the sparse surgery and were informed by the receptionist that Herr Doctor would be back shortly and could see us straight away. Delighted by this small success, we sat back and tried in vain to fathom out a single word on the Portuguese TV. The waiting room quickly filled, and it wasn't long before the surgery resembled more of a jolly boys' outing: all the patients seemed to know each other. We took in the scene before us as the gestures became more and more animated.

Eventually, an elderly gentleman entered the building and I instantly presumed from his stooped gait that he was in fact a patient. On his arrival, a hush descended on the previously animated congregation, and almost in tandem they greeted Herr Doctor with 'Bom dia'.

We were ushered in by the receptionist, and I watched in amazement as my mother put on yet another of her command performances. You have to remember that only two years previously, my mother had suffered a double aneurysm, but of course to her this was of no consequence.

'Are you generally fit?' asked the doctor.

Suddenly, my mother resembled a mixture of angelic schoolgirl and Mother Teresa. Of course, knowing her as I do, I saw where this was heading, while the poor doctor had no idea what he was letting himself in for.

'Oh yes, I am as fit as a fiddle,' she assured him, and I wouldn't have put it past her to start doing a jig, there and then.

'Are you on any medication?'

'Only vitamin supplements,' came my mother's demure reply, mumbled through her Covid mask.

This was actually true. What she failed to mention was that she had refused all medication after her aneurysm. But in technical terms, I guess she wasn't lying.

After she had shed multiple layers, despite it being well over twenty degrees, the doctor proceeded to take her blood pressure.

'Excellent,' he declared, much to the delight of my mother. I decided it was probably advisable not to put a dent in the obvious camaraderie forming between the ageing doctor and my mother and mention the fact that maybe the pressure might be best taken on her actual arm, rather than close to her wrist. But then, who am I to argue with Portugal's finest medical practitioner?

Perhaps it was my imagination but suddenly there seemed to be a discernible rise in the temperature in the room as my mother shed yet more layers and eagerly awaited the stethoscope to measure her heart rate. With her breasts now proudly displayed, I averted my eyes, but not before I noticed the once aged doctor seem to spring to life with far more enthusiasm than he had previously shown. I wasn't sure if he was actually listening to his own accelerating heart rate rather than my mother's, but apparently all was well on that front too.

By this time, I thought it was probably better to keep shtum and not mention that perhaps my mother rather than the doctor should be paid the 50 euros she was about to hand over for her Oscar-worthy performance. After what I was witnessing, I had serious reservations about whether the poor old boy had the stamina to see the rest of his adoring congregation.

It wasn't long before Mum had flown through the final eye examination and hearing test, once the doctor had remembered to remove the stethoscope from his ears. But I suppose the odd mistake could happen to anyone!

Outside, I smiled to myself as I helped my mother into her jacket, as her arm had been plaguing her for months – also conveniently not mentioned to the doctor. As she lit her cigarette with her one working hand, I thought it best not to burst her bubble. Proudly, she looked at her passed medical certificate as though she had won first prize in a school contest.

Over the years, I had realised that very little defeated my mum. As I scrolled down my messages, I noticed a Facebook quote from a friend who was the same age as me: 'I have heard of people my age whizzing down on zip wires, but I find it a success to put my leg through my knickers without falling over.'

I smiled over at my mother, who you could tell was already imagining herself on a Harley-Davidson, probably with a toy boy in tow, and realised she would always be the one on the zip wire, while I would always be the one trying not to fall over with one leg stuck in my pants.

If I was coming to terms with much of my life and was ready to embrace the future with a new sense of calm, the same didn't seem true of the rest of the world. Never had I seen people so polarised in their opinions, whether it was about the ongoing feud between Harry and Meghan and the royals or the roll-out of Covid vaccines. Social media, as well as the news, seemed to be awash with negativity. Countless examples of extremism and all and sundry jumping on some bandwagon or other. I am all for people airing their views, but the vitriol being spewed out on every topic, from Black rights to Piers Morgan to the handling of demonstrations by the police, sexism, racism or even Donald Trump, had left me concerned for the world we live in. And, of course, now there is Putin to contend with.

But at least my eight-year-old son had the answer to the world's problems. I had laughingly mentioned an article I had read to Ewa, asserting that global warming could be reversed if everyone stopped flushing the toilet and peed in the shower. The next day, my son hollered to me from his daily scrub and, not sure what to expect, I saw his little face beaming at me through the shower curtain as he proudly exclaimed, 'I'm helping global warming, Dad.'

His mum might have been less than amused and chided me with 'Now look what you've started'. But perhaps the world did have a chance after all.

•

If the past year had taught me anything, it was that little was to be gained from harbouring resentment or bearing animosity. You couldn't change a person or a situation and the only person you hurt in the long run was yourself. So, my newfound optimism seemed to be bearing fruit. I had recently been recommended the book *The Secret*, and to be honest was totally sceptical of the whole concept, but to my surprise I did find that I started to think about life in a totally different light. Instead of believing that everything was only achieved through struggle, I started to let things take their natural course with the new belief that whatever I touched would start to come out right. The premise of the book argues that a person struggling with poverty can suddenly become wealthy, merely by visualising that they have money. I can totally understand the scepticism, but thinking I was about to read some psychological mumbo jumbo, I realised it really did change my way of thinking.

After two years of toiling with trying to sell my business, suddenly I had multiple offers. Having had my ups and downs with money, I suddenly seemed to be gifted with it from all angles. Rather than thinking every illness was the dreaded *Big C* or an impending heart attack, my health, which had been a constant source of worry, had suddenly improved and I had more energy than I'd had in years. Small inconveniences that usually took weeks to resolve suddenly miraculously disappeared. Even my relationship with Ewa, which might not have been all moonlight and roses and had been on a downward spiral for as long as I could remember, became a friendship rediscovered with a path for the future. Was this all a coincidence? Possibly, but whatever the reason, my new frame of mind was certainly helping me.

My friend Andy, who has had his own fair share of ups and downs, once told me, 'It's pointless to think you can change anyone else, you just have to be happy in yourself.'

I hope that over the years, I have managed to light up some people's lives. I also know that I have let people down. In most cases, probably without even realising it. I am also aware that when we think of our friends and their lives, we often dwell on their failings rather than the positives, as I'm sure they do with me. Isn't it always a case of, 'Oh, I like him, but he's got a dreadful gambling habit' or 'Isn't she great, but why is she married to such a dick' or 'Why didn't such and such turn up to my wedding, I bet they weren't busy' or 'Surely they could have lent me that money, they're loaded'. But my mindset has changed, and I have forgotten all the negatives and now try to focus on the good.

Why not invite someone to your B&B for free, rather than thinking that there's no such thing as friends and family in business. As I have put this new philosophy into practice, I have been invited for dinner at a friend's restaurant, been invited to countries I've never visited and have heard from almost forgotten friends who have turned up out of the blue and skyped me from some remote corner of Australia or America. Coincidence? Maybe. Lockdown syndrome? Quite possibly. But if it helps, why not?

What is more, who am I to judge if a family member has kept their mistress two streets down from their wife for fifty years? Or if a relative has taken back a husband who left her for another woman? It's not my place to tell my friend he's mad for staying with his wife just so that he doesn't lose half their money. I have seen my mother struggle with never feeling loved by her own mother and I have let my resentment of my stepmother fester over many years. But all those people who you have vented your frustrations against will never change, so why hurt yourself?

•

As for my own legacy, I guess most parents would agree that the most pleasure they derive is from their children, and for me that would certainly be the case. Of course, life has its twists and turns and although there are many joyous moments, there is the added hardship that the relationship I have with my beloved son, Jack, is often long distance through the medium of video calls. If our meetings might be full of adventure and fun, the same cannot always be said of our calls.

'What are you up to today, Jack?' I will innocently ask.

'Well, I'm talking to you, aren't I, Dad.'

If not the answer I was looking for, I suppose my boy had a point.

'And how many friends have you made, Jack?'

'Can I include you, Dad? Then I guess I have one true friend.'

Not sure whether to laugh or cry on this one.

Always one to tease, I ask, 'What about the girls, Jack? Any trying to kiss you?'

'I've seen the problems you have, Dad, so I'm sticking to Mum for the time being.'

Wise beyond his years.

·

Do I have regrets? I do regret some of the antics of my youth, or maybe not my antics but the hurt I caused to several girlfriends during my early years. But as we know, what goes around comes around and I certainly had my own comeuppance on that front a couple of times over. They also say that women tend to like the naughty boy, and in those early years I did get away with murder. But after spending sixteen years of marriage trying to be the perfect husband and never really succeeding, I'm not sure I believe there is a right or wrong way.

As for my career in catering, I have reached many forks in my path and often because of my stubbornness or my inability to play politics, as well as some pretty stupid behaviour. I have taken many wrong directions. But in all this time I have met a whole host of remarkable people, seen many incredible things and had days that others would never see in a lifetime. I have never been wealthy. I have missed out on so many things, partied too much, ruined relationships, but major regrets? No, I don't think so.

Catering is an amazing industry, even if most of my joints wouldn't agree, and if you are a little crazy, have an engaging personality and the stamina of an ox, give it a go.

After such a life, do I think I'll go to heaven? Of this I can't be sure, but I would like to think so. I do know that when I reach the pearly gates, God will read my CV and have a chuckle. And if I do get sent downstairs, at least I will see my mother again. She never did like to be in the cold!

Thank you for taking the time to read my memoir.

If you enjoyed this book, please take a few
moments to write a review of it. Thank you!

ACKNOWLEDGEMENTS

I would like to thank the whitefox publishing team for all their valuable assistance in helping me achieve my dream of publishing my memoir. I would also like to give special thanks to Lesley Hart, editor from Author'sPen (www.authorspen.co.uk), who not only helped me edit the book, but whose advice throughout this journey has gone above and beyond the call of duty. Thank you also to Ted Gooda for her support with my marketing and to Liz Lawler, who not only inspired me to write but whose knowledge has guided me along the way. Last but not least, special thanks to all those people I have met along the way and without whom this book would never have happened.

Over the years, there have been several extraordinary people I have met, celebrities I have served and friendships I have cherished. There have also been a number of establishments that I have been lucky enough to work at or have visited that have had a large bearing on my life.

I would like firstly to thank the following friends who have stuck by me over the years and have contributed to many of my life's stories, as well as the colleagues who have made such an impact:

Herr Ziegler, my first boss and director of the five-star Kulm Hotel, Arosa.

Don Mcdiarmid, lifelong friend from my days at Brasserie Lipp, Zurich.

Pascal Bensse, godfather to Jack and star of The Close Hotel, Tetbury.

Marc Hardiman, friend and chef at the London Hilton's Galvin at Windows.

Kingue Nkembe, friend and inspirational restaurant manager at the Bluebird.

Eva Skornakevo, star employee, who followed me to The Residence, Bath and Hartham Park, Corsham.

Andrew Webster, friend, manager at Lacock Abbey, golfer?

Paul and Karen Owens, owners of Badgers Hall bed and breakfast, Chipping Campden.

Mario Cuccuru, talented chef, amazing human being, not forgetting his dear wife, Vivienne.

Greg Andrews, former colleague at the Bluebird, owner of D Vine Cellars.

James Grant, former colleague at the Bluebird, owner of No2 Pound Street.

James Wiseman, general manager of Hand Picked Hotels and previous downtrodden trainee.

Tina and Keith, friends from my Hartham Park days.

Kate Wilson, friend and so much more, colleague at Henrietta House.

Anjay Talwar, friend, hotel school room-mate, and general manager, Holiday Inn.

Panos and Cathy, Chris and Maria (guests and friends from the Isle of Wight).

My old school friends from Oswestry (Toddy, Markie E, Howie Jones, Freddie F, Duncan, Des M, Chris R, Neil, James Woody).

Former colleagues: chefs Paul Heathcote, Jamie Holland and Matt Nugent (Heathcotes), John Torode, Wolfgang Spenke, Fred Sirieix, Wendy Hendricks, Chris Galvin (Bluebird), Tom Morrell (River Café and MasterChef finalist), Jamie Hirst (The Residence and Hartham).

Owners/bosses: Mark and Cheryl Norman (The Residence), Janet Todd (Bettys and Taylors), Peter Sherwin, Hanni and Juergen (Henrietta House), Ian Taylor (Kaleidoscope), Joe Marshall (Café Rouge, Esher).

Liz Lawler (author and former colleague at The Residence, who gave me the desire for this project).

My exes, Marie, and Ewa. Sorry! To my family, in particular Mel, my cousin, and Zoe, my aunt.

Lastly, I would like to thank my mum, whose belief in me has never wavered throughout all the ups and downs. Her work ethic and zest for life have been my constant inspiration, and thanks, Mum, for giving me so much of my material!

ACKNOWLEDGEMENTS

Some of the people I have served:

ACTORS/TV Dustin Hoffman, Michael Douglas, Nicolas Cage, Lenny Henry, Joanna Lumley, Zoe Ball, Lisa Riley, Martine McCutcheon, Guy Pearce, Eddie Redmayne, Jim Sturgess, Nigel Havers, Paul Martin, Raymond Blanc, Marco Pierre White, Michael Winner, Arnold Schwarzenegger, Jeremy Clarkson, Ulrika Jonsson, Terry Wogan, Willem Dafoe, Jeremy Paxman, Jane McDonald, Jimmy Carr, Patricia Routledge.

SPORT Sir Jackie Stewart, David Beckham, Neville brothers (Gary and Phil), Paul Scholes, Ryan Giggs, Nicky Butt, Kevin Keegan, John Toshack, Dennis Wise, Ian Woosnam, Graeme le Saux, Tony Adams, Jimmy White, Dennis Taylor, Vinnie Jones, Nigel Mansell, Willie Thorne, Jeremy Guscott and the Bath rugby team.

MUSIC Nic Mason, Mark Knopfler, Alannah Myles, Roger Taylor, Ronan Keating, Jamie Cullum, Fatboy Slim, Dame Kiri Te Kanawa.

OTHERS Princess Anne and Timothy Laurence, Peter Phillips, Mikhail Gorbachev, A.A. Gill, Sir David Hempleman-Adams, Sir Rocco Forte, Victoria Beckham.

Ab Fab (TV sitcom) **181**
Abbey Hotel, Bath **36**
Adams, Bryan **310**
Adams, Tony **312**
Al Kadri (Lebanese waiter) **136–7**
Al Maha, Dubai **300–1**
alcohol **235**, **236–8**
  DW and **25–6**, **61**, **123**, **137**,
    236, **239**, **245–7**, **326**
  functioning alcoholics **238**
  stepfather and **166**, **239**, **240–3**
Amsterdam red-light district **196**,
  197
anal sex **145–6**
Andreas (Italian waiter) **112**,
  116–17
Andrews, Greg **267**
Andy (university friend) **66**, **67**,
  68, **69**, **78–9**, **80**, **81**, **86**, **87**,
  88–9, **90–1**, **97**, **98**, **101**, **106**,
  107, **108–10**
Anne, Princess **309**, **326**
The Apprentice (TV reality show)
  211
Arosa **78**, **104**, **111**
  see also Kulm Hotel
Attenborough, David **5**
Automobile Association (AA) **34**,
  212

B&B (bed and breakfast) *see* Keats
  Cottage, Isle of Wight
Babs (mother-in-law) **33–4**, **35**
Badrutt's Palace, St Moritz **129**
banter **223**, **285**, **288**
Bath **34–6**
  The Residence **35**, **270–4**, **298–
    300**, **332**, **333**
Beckham, David **293**, **307**, **318**
Beckham, Victoria **318**
Bell's palsy **157**
Bensse, Pascal **39**, **322–3**, **324–7**
bereavement and loss **155–7**
Bettys and Taylors, Yorkshire **285**
Big Fish (film) **39**
Bill (DW's uncle) **27**
Blanc, Raymond **313–14**
Bluche, Switzerland **148**
Bluebird Restaurant, London **131**,
  253–67, **297–8**
  celebrity clientele **310–11**
  cloakroom attendants **266**
  food critics **263**, **264**
  opening team **254**, **255**
Boiling Point (film) **268**
Booking.com **203**
The Boss (stepfather) **72**, **166**,
  194–5, **228**, **238–45**
  death of **244**
  DW's relationship with **238–9**,
    240

hairdressing business 72, 242
heavy drinker 166, 239, 240–3
lifestyle deterioration 241–4
looks and charm 239
new partner 242, 243, 244
Botta, Tony 262–3
Brasserie Lipp, Zurich 129–37,
    150, 293–7
Bratschi, Herr 130
breakfast and lunch buffets 80,
    84–5
brother, DW's 71, 73, 74, 183
Bryan (American friend) 149
Bryan (handyman) 43
bungee jumping 125–6
Burj Al Arab, Dubai 301

Cage, Nicolas 270, 309
Campbell, Sir Donald 253
Candy (girlfriend) 199–200
Cape Town 231
car seats 160–1
Carr, Jimmy 47, 311–12
celebrity clientele 293, 310–11,
    364
  see also the rich and famous
Charlie (Dutch waiter) 122–6
chefs 312–15
  arrogance 314
  celebrity chefs 206, 312, 314–15
  constant quest for perfection 235
  drink and drugs 235, 236,
    237–8
  old-style cheffing 206–7
  stress 207, 235
  young chefs 207–8
chefs de rang (head waiters) 83,
    93, 94
Chewton Glen, Hampshire 290

children in hotels and restaurants
    277–9, 280–1
Chloe and Lesley (Four in a Bed
    contestants) 213, 219
cinema, erotic 141–4
Clapton, Eric 310
Clarkson, Jeremy 310
'clicking fingers' 286
cloakroom attendants 266
The Close Hotel, Tetbury 31, 280,
    308, 314, 324, 326–9
colonic irrigation 249–51
commis waiters 82, 86
Conran, Sir Terence 253
Cotswold House, Chipping
    Campden 30, 31
Covid 19 pandemic 5–6, 8–9,
    16–19
  end of lockdown 11–15
  reset button 5, 9, 16
Crans-Montana 138, 148
Crieff Hotel, Gleneagles 24–7
Crowe, Russell 6
Cullum, Jamie 270
cutlery, cleaning and polishing 88
Cyder House Inn, Godalming 68

Dafoe, Willem 310
Daniela (Swiss girlfriend) 118–19,
    121, 122, 138–9, 229
Depp, Johnny 309
dogs 277, 281–4
  hotel guests 281–3
  in restaurants 283–4
  special requirements 284
  see also Zeus (Westie)
Dolder Grand, Zurich 129
Donna (Four in a Bed contestant)
    213, 216, 217, 219, 220
Douglas, Michael 310

Downside School 23
drugs 18, 137, 236–8
Dubai 300–4
  service workers 302–4

East End gangsters 255–8
Egli, Herr 85, 97–8, 120
Elleray (chef) 30–1
Eric (Australian waiter) 98, 99,
  126–7, 128
Ermitage Hotel, Küsnacht 111–16
Ewa (ex-wife) 6, 9, 10, 31, 37,
  169–70, 187, 247, 282, 290,
  333, 335, 355
  character 32, 37, 234
  deteriorating relationship with
  DW 48
  family 33–4
  Four in a Bed 212, 213, 214, 215,
  219–20
  and Keats Cottage 40, 44, 46,
  48–9, 57
  meets DW 29, 137
  restaurant chef 48–9, 57
  returns to live and work in Bath
  6, 10, 39, 62, 90

father, DW's 23, 72, 74–5, 321
  DW's relationship with 23, 321
  legal career 20, 321
feng shui 275
Ferguson, Sir Alex 307
food critics 263, 264, 293
food leftovers 86, 263
food poisoning 328–9
Forte, Sir Rocco 309
Four in a Bed (TV reality show)
  209, 210–21
front of house managers 267, 312,
  313, 314

Fuchs, Herr 112

Galvin at Windows, London 314
gambling 109, 149
gay men 116–17, 324–5
Gill, A.A. 209, 263, 310
Gledhill, David 270
golf 302–3, 304–5, 315, 329
Gorbachev, Mikhail 309
Goring Hotel, London 325
Graham (Scottish friend) 149–50
grandfathers, DW's 71, 73–4,
  105, 196
Grandjean, Herr 100, 102,
  123–4, 126, 128
grandmother, Swiss 71, 72–4,
  243–4
Grant, James 267
Grant (TV producer) 211, 212,
  215
Great Ormond Street Hospital
  156
Greene King 314, 327–8
guests and the guest experience
  269, 284–5, 286, 289–90
  accidents 280
  anticipating needs of 95, 223
  appreciative guests 15–16, 96–7,
  277
  bullies 222, 224–7
  champagne lifestyle 82, 221
  demanding guests 205–6,
  221–2, 275–6
  extra touches, importance of 14,
  289–91, 291, 301
  first two minutes 284–5, 286,
  287, 289
  friendships 319
  'guest is always right' 279, 300
  meanness 297–9

snobbery 222
theft of items 297–8
treating everyone the same
    292–3, 316
Guscott, Jerry 270

Hans, Great-Uncle 75–6
Hardiman, Marc 48, 205, 206,
    314, 326
Hartham Park, Corsham 308,
    329
Havers, Nigel 310
Heathcote, Paul 209, 210, 285,
    306, 318, 332
Hedy, Great-Aunt 74, 75
Hempleman-Adams, Sir David
    329
Hendricks, Wendy 254, 255
Hendry, Stephen 311
Henrietta House, Bath 332
Hoffman, Dustin 310
housekeeping 274–7

Imogen (girlfriend) 27, 28
Isle of Wight 36, 55–6
    see also Keats Cottage, Isle of
    Wight

Jackie (friend) 333, 335
John (friend) 133, 135, 136
Jonsson, Ulrika 310
Jurg, Uncle 70, 105

Katja (German girlfriend) 138,
    139, 229
The Kaufleuten club 113
Keats Cottage, Isle of Wight 5–11,
    40–59, 61–2, 166, 277–93
    Covid 19 pandemic and 5–17
    Four in a Bed and 209, 210–21

garden and outdoor dining space
    14
ghostly happenings 56–7
marketing 47–8
mortgage 332
online reviews 204–6
opening for business 45
parking arrangements 286–7
Red Funnel best B&B award 221
renovation 40–2, 43
restaurant 46–8
sale of 5, 6, 7, 339, 347–8
staffing problems 12–13, 208
Keats, John 55, 57
Keegan, Kevin 310
Kim, Alice 309
Kings Hotel, Chipping Campden
    29–31, 316–17
Knopfler, Mark 266, 310
Kuhl, Herr 82, 83, 86, 87–8, 89,
    90, 93, 101, 102, 103, 104,
    112, 120, 121–2, 126, 127–8,
    269
Kulm Hotel, Arosa 78, 79–81,
    82–109, 112, 119–28

Lawler, Liz 270, 271
Lawson, Freddie 110
Lawson, Nigella 316
Les Roches hotel management
    school 111, 138, 148–50
Lewis, Ray 334–5
Lion Pub, Zurich 130, 133–4
Loiseau, Bernard 50
lottery winners 317
Lumley, Joanna 310

McCutcheon, Martine 310
Mcdiarmid, Don 135, 136, 168
McDonald, Jane 47, 310

Maenl, Herr 296

Manchester United football club 306–7

Manor House Hotel, Castle Combe 322–4

Marco (German chef) 115

Margot (sister-in-law) 33

Mariacher, Herr 100, 102, 126–7

Marie (ex-wife) 31–2, 326

Martin and Sara (*Four in a Bed* contestants) 213, 215, 218–19, 221

Mason, Nick 308

massage 251–2

melon balls 25

Mercury, Freddie 61

Mike (German chef) 115, 118

Mike (hotel owner) 29–30, 31

mother, DW's 28, 51, 139, 144–5, 162, 163–90, 195, 210, 248–9, 301, 316, 325

  attractiveness 167–8

  bleed on the brain and hospitalisation 17, 163–90

  cataracts 165

  character 71, 73, 167–8

  dog *see* Zeus (Westie)

  family background 71–2

  first marriage 72

  at Keats Cottage 7, 10, 11, 42, 43, 166, 341–4

  leaves DW's father 23

  moves to the Isle of Wight 36–7

  moves to Portugal 339, 340, 344–5, 346, 347, 348, 349–53

  second partner 72, 239, 240, 241, 242, 244

  sells house 18–19

  smoking 7, 8, 249, 342

  Swiss background 7

  work ethic 42–3, 73, 89, 166, 240, 342

New Inn, Shalfleet 43

Nic (B&B guest) 224–7

Nkembe, Kingue 266–7

Noel Arms, Chipping Campden 30

Norman, Cheryl and Mark 270, 271, 332

Nuts nightclub 106, 119, 123

Oliver, Jamie 206, 314, 315

Oliver Twist pub, Zurich 136, 138, 140

Ollie (Australian friend) 149

O'Neill, Martin 316

Osborne House, Isle of Wight 51

owners, hotel 330–2

Palace Hotel, Lucerne 129

Panos (barber) 47

Park Hotel, Arosa 119

Parmentier, Richard 270

Paul (restaurant manager) 83, 86–7, 93, 94, 95, 96–7, 100–1, 119, 120, 127

Pearce, Guy 310

Pease-Watkin (headmaster) 21–2, 193–4

picnics 104

Planet Hollywood 311

Portugal

  David moves to 339–53

  Portuguese bureaucracy 350

Pretty Woman (film) 293

private catering 333–6

public schools 20–3

punctuality 83

Rachel (stepmother) 23, 31, 356
Ramsay, Gordon 206, 314, 325
Rankin, Paul 314–15
Ready Steady Cook (TV game
    show) 314–15
Rebecca, Aunt 70, 174–5, 181,
    182, 183, 184–6
recession (2008) 320–1
Redmayne, Eddie 270
The Residence, Bath 35, 270–4,
    298–300, 332, 333
  celebrity clientele 270
  sex toys 271–4
  team 270–1
  Times Travel Award 270
restaurant failure rate 49
reviews
  constructive criticism 204
  Keats Cottage 204–6
  negative or false 203–4, 223,
    226–7
  rankings 204–5
  restaurant reviews 205–6
  TripAdvisor 203–4, 221, 226–7
the rich and famous 306–18,
    333–6
  celebrity chefs 206, 312, 314–15
  lottery winners 317
  self-importance 311
Riley, Lisa 309
room service 114, 269
Royal Automobile Club 230

salaries and commission 131–2
Salvatore (chef) 120
Sarah (girlfriend) 228–33
Savoy, Guy 325
Schwarzenegger, Arnie 310–11
The Secret (Rhonda Byrne) 354
sex toys 271–4

Sherwin, Peter 332
Sibi (waiter) 112, 115
silver burnishing machines 88
Sirieix, Fred 206, 254, 267, 314
Skornakevo, Eva 270
social media 202–3
  negativity and vitriol 202–3,
    218, 353
  see also reviews
Soho 144–5
spa, Swiss 248–52
staff
  diversity 115
  hierarchy 84, 92, 93, 94, 112,
    128
  politics, playing 82, 128
  salaries and commission 131–2
  see also tips/tipping
Steephill Cove, Isle of Wight 51–2
Stewart, Sir Jackie 308
Strawbridge, Dick 341
stressed lifestyle 13, 137, 156, 235,
    268–9
  catering couples 48, 49
Sven (university friend) 68, 69,
    109
Switzerland 65–7, 70–109, 111–
    44, 144–50
  Brasserie Lipp, Zurich 129–33,
    150, 293–7
  citizenship 105
  conservatism 105–6
  Ermitage Hotel, Küsnacht
    111–16
  Kulm Hotel, Arosa 78, 79–81,
    82–109, 112, 119–28
  military service 105
  Swiss drinking habits 133
  Swiss orderliness and efficiency
    17, 65, 79, 105

traffic violations **105**
Syed (waiter) **211**

Talwar, Anjay **149**
tasting menus **101**
Taylor, Ian **30, 36, 332**
Taylor, Roger **308**
Te Kanawa, Dame Kiri **309**
Thai chefs **89**
Times Travel Awards **270**
tips/tipping **93–4, 96–7, 112, 113, 114–15, 121, 131, 258–9**
  generosity **96–7, 114–15, 260, 316**
  service charge **258–9**
  splitting **94**
Torode, John **254, 313**
Toshack, John **310**
towels, reusing **290**
TripAdvisor **203–4, 221**
  false reviews **203, 226–7**
  negative reviews **203–4, 226–7**

Urs (Swiss friend) **133, 135, 136**

Voyo (Yugoslavian waiter) **92–3, 94, 95, 97**

Webster, Andy **329**
White, Jimmy **311**
White, Marco Pierre **314**
Will (waiter) **261–2, 264**
Wiltons Restaurant, London **267**
wine
  expensive **99, 100, 101**
  leftover **99**
  opening and decanting **99–100**
Winner, Michael **311**
Wiseman, James **326**
Wogan, Terry **310**

Woodward, David
  AA hotel inspector **34, 212**
  alcohol use **25–6, 61, 123, 137, 236, 239, 245–7, 326**
  apprenticeships **24–7, 78–109, 150**
  attitude to money **301**
  B&B business *see* Keats Cottage, Isle of Wight
  Bell's palsy **157**
  charm **81, 102, 103, 121**
  chooses career in catering and hospitality **20, 23–4**
  deteriorating relationship with Ewa **48, 49, 50, 60–2**
  detoxing **340**
  drugs and **137, 236**
  dysfunctional upbringing **31**
  ear trouble **17–18**
  emotional lows **7, 58–60, 320–1**
  family background **71–7**
  financial difficulties **320–1**
  Four in a Bed **209, 210–21**
  friendships, importance of **319–27, 329, 332**
  gambling **109**
  golf **302–3, 304, 329**
  high society experience **230–3**
  at hotel management school **125, 138, 148–50**
  hotel and restaurant career *see* Bluebird Restaurant; Brasserie Lipp, Zurich; The Close Hotel, Tetbury; Ermitage Hotel, Küsnacht; Hartham Park, Corsham; Kings Hotel, Chipping Campden; Kulm Hotel, Arosa; The Residence, Bath
  inquisitiveness **139, 141–4**

limelight moments **209–10**
love affair with Switzerland 78,
  109, 151
marriages *see* Ewa; Marie
meets and marries Ewa 29, 31,
  32, 35
mindset, change of 354–6
moves to Portugal 339–53
naivety 139–41, 198, 201, 324
relationship with father 23, 321
relationship with mother 42–3,
  166
romantic entanglements 27–8,
  108–9, 118–19, 138–9, 146–7,
  199–201, 228–34
schooldays 20–3, **193–8**
sexual education 193–9
spa experience 248–52
storyteller 39
university student 67–70
work ethic 42–3, 89–90, 240

Woodward, Jack (son) v, **6, 8,**
  9, 10, 35, 48, 50–1, 52–4,
  157–60, 161–3, 187, 190, 209,
  340–1, 343, 353–4, 356–7
Woosnam, Ian 315
work ethic 42–3, 73, 89–90, 166,
  240, 342
Wynnstay, Oswestry 27–8, 58

Yugoslav Wars 98

Zeus (Westie), 36–7, 39, 40, 164,
  165, 169–70, 284, 339, 342,
  346, 347
Ziegler, Herr 90, 103–4, 107–8,
  119, 122, 128
Zurich 116
  Brasserie Lipp 129–33, 150,
  293–7